METATHEORIZING

KEY ISSUES IN SOCIOLOGICAL THEORY

Series Editors
JEFFREY C. ALEXANDER, *University of California, Los Angeles*
& JONATHAN H. TURNER, *University of California, Riverside*

This series of annual publications is designed to crystallize key issues in contemporary theoretical debate. Each year, the chair of the Theory Section of the American Sociological Association has the authority to organize a "conference within a conference" at the annual meeting. The intention is to provide a forum for intensive public discussion of an issue that has assumed overriding theoretical importance. After the miniconference, the chair assumes the role of volume editor and, subject to final approval by the series editors, prepares a volume based on the reworked conference papers.

We hope that this periodic focusing of theoretical energy will strengthen the "disciplinary matrix" upon which theoretical progress in every science depends. Theoretical consensus may be impossible, but disciplinary integration is not. Only if a solid infrastructure is provided can communication among different orientations be carried out in the kind of ongoing, continuous way that is so necessary for mutual understanding and scientifically constructive criticism.

Volumes in this series:

1. **Neofunctionalism**
   edited by *Jeffrey C. Alexander*

2. **The Marx-Weber Debate**
   edited by *Norbert Wiley*

3. **Theory Building in Sociology:**
   Assessing Theoretical Cumulation
   edited by *Jonathan H. Turner*

4. **Feminism and Sociological Theory**
   edited by *Ruth A. Wallace*

5. **Intellectuals and Politics:**
   Social Theory in a Changing World
   edited by *Charles C. Lemert*

6. **Metatheorizing**
   edited by *George Ritzer*

METATHEORIZING

Edited by
GEORGE RITZER

6

KEY ISSUES IN
SOCIOLOGICAL THEORY

 SAGE Publications
International Educational and Professional Publisher
Newbury Park London New Delhi

For information address:

SAGE Publications, Inc.
2455 Teller Road
Newbury Park, California 91320

SAGE Publications Ltd.
6 Bonhill Street
London EC2A 4PU
United Kingdom

SAGE Publications India Pvt. Ltd.
M-32 Market
Greater Kailash I
New Delhi 1 10 048 India

Printed in the United States of America

Library of Contress Cataloging-in-Publication Data

Main entry under title:

Metatheorizing / edited by George Ritzer.
        p.   cm.—(Key issues in sociological theory : 6)
    Includes bibliographical references and index.
    ISBN 0-8039-3990-6 (cloth). — ISBN 0-8039-3991-4 (pbk.)
        1. Sociology—Methodology. 2. Metatheory. I. Ritzer, George.
II. Series.
HM24.M4722   1992
301'.072—dc20   91-44206

92   93   94   95   10   9   8   7   6   5   4   3   2   1

Sage Production Editor: Diane S. Foster

CONTENTS

Chapter 1

METATHEORIZING IN SOCIOLOGY
Explaining the Coming of Age

GEORGE RITZER
University of Maryland

THE GOAL OF THIS CHAPTER is to explain the recent coming of age of metatheorizing in sociology. Metatheorizing is defined, most broadly, as the systematic study of the underlying structure of sociological theory.[1,2] Evidence will be marshalled in support of the contention that there has, in recent years, been an explosion of interest in sociological metatheorizing.[3] The bulk of the chapter will be devoted to an analysis of why it is that metatheorizing, after a number of promising but false starts in the earlier history of sociology, has suddenly achieved such prominence. This is, in effect, a meta-analytic effort to explain the rise of metatheorizing in sociology. It simultaneously deals with the rise of metatheorizing and demonstrates the utility of metatheoretical analysis.[4] Finally, we will offer some thoughts on the near-term prospects for metatheorizing in sociology.

THE CURRENT EXPLOSION
OF INTEREST IN METATHEORIZING

Before getting to the reasons for the coming of age of metatheorizing, it needs to be demonstrated that in fact there is at least some evidence (albeit largely subjective) to support the idea of a boom in interest in metatheorizing. By this I simply mean that there is a great increase in the quantity of work that is explicitly and self-consciously metatheoretical.[5] The most objective evidence comes from a study by Fuhrman and Snizek (1990) of publications over the last decade, which indicates strong and growing interest in metatheorizing in sociology. A very large proportion of the references in their article are to recently or soon-to-be published works. Many other metatheoretical works have appeared in the brief time since that study was completed (e.g., Berger, Wagner, and Zelditch 1989; Turner 1989a). This growth is notable in the journal *Sociological Theory*, which has devoted increasing space to essays that are explicitly metatheoretical (for example, Ritzer 1988; Levine 1989; Fararo 1989). In addition, a number of recent and forthcoming books have also been overtly metatheoretical (Fiske and Shweder 1986; Osterberg 1988; Turner 1989b; Ritzer 1991) and many, perhaps even most, other books in sociological theory are implicitly metatheoretical. In March, 1990, *Sociological Forum* devoted a special mini-issue to metatheorizing in sociology (Ritzer 1990c). Beyond this is a whole, and seemingly expanding, range of works that have dealt with more specific metatheoretical issues, such as the micro-macro linkage (Alexander, Giesen, Münch, and Smelser 1987; Collins 1981a, 1981b, 1988; Ritzer 1990d), the relationship between agency and structure (Archer 1982, 1988; Bernstein 1971; Giddens 1984), and levels of social analysis (Wiley 1988, 1989; Ritzer 1989b). Although it is possible that all of this represents a peak in metatheorizing in sociology, there are many reasons to believe that it is more likely that it represents the take-off point for a wide variety and an increasing number of explicitly metatheoretical works in sociology.

FACTORS INVOLVED
IN THE MATURATION OF METATHEORIZING

Assuming that the reader accepts the premise of the boom in interest in sociological metatheorizing, and that premise is based on a largely subjective assessment, the issue, and indeed the focal concern of this chapter, is an explanation of this dramatic increase in interest. In the following pages three broad sets of factors will be explored that help explain the rise of sociological metatheorizing. Some of the factors discussed below are proximate causes of the rise of metatheorizing; others are more remote and distant. It is the cumulative effect of these proximate and remote factors that helps us understand what is currently transpiring in metatheory.

Factors Internal to Sociological Theory

The Increasingly Overwhelming Body of Classical and Contemporary Theory. The simple fact is that with each passing year the cumulative body of sociological theory continues to grow, perhaps exponentially. Practicing theorists, let alone other kinds of sociologists, are hard-pressed to keep up with and make some sense of this growing and increasingly esoteric literature. To the daunting need to know the intricacies of the ideas of such classical theorists as Marx, Durkheim, Weber, Parsons, and Schutz is added the burden of keeping up with the most recent works of Habermas, Giddens, Bourdieu, Alexander, Collins, Coleman, and many others. Each day it grows increasingly difficult to be a casual student of sociological theory. What is required are more and more careful studies of sociological theory; in other words more metatheoretical work.

The Work of Many Theorists Is Implicitly Metatheoretical. Most important classic and contemporary theorists developed their theories, at least in part, on the basis of a careful (metatheoretical) study of, and reaction to, the work of other theorists. Among the most important examples are Marx's theory of capitalism developed out of a systematic engagement with the work of Hegel and Hegelian philosophy (e.g., Bauer, Feuerbach), political economy (e.g., Smith, Say, Ricardo, Mill), and utopian socialism (e.g., Cabet, Owen, Fourier, Proudhon); Parsons's action theory based on a serious study of the work of Marshall, Pareto, Weber, and Durkheim; Schutz's phenomenology, which relied heavily on a study of the work of Weber, Husserl, and Bergson; Alexander's multidimensional, neofunctional theory based on a detailed analysis of the work of Marx, Weber, Durkheim, and Parsons; and Habermas's communication theory rooted in his examination of the ideas of various critical theorists, as well as of the work of Marx, Weber, Parsons, Mead, and Durkheim.

Although Marx, Parsons, Schutz, Alexander, and Habermas are all known primarily as theorists, it is becoming increasingly clear that they developed their theories largely through metatheoretical analyses. Such a realization is leading to the understanding that a large body of (implicitly) metatheoretical work is already in existence, as well as to the appreciation that there are a number of exemplary pieces of metatheory that can serve as models to contemporary metatheorists.

The Sense of Crisis in Sociological Theory. Turning to more proximate and direct causes of the rise in metatheorizing, a key factor was the feeling of "crisis" in sociological theory (and sociology in general) in the 1980s. The problem with thinking in terms of a crisis in contemporary sociological theory is that it is hard to think of a time when theory has not been in crisis. After all, did not Gouldner (1970) forecast an imminent crisis in 1970? Assuming Gouldner was right, have we been in a state of perpetual crisis for the past 2 decades?

Whatever the liabilities of describing the current situation as a crisis, the fact is that many sociological theorists are deeply worried about the state of theory. This worry takes many forms. There are those who are concerned, for example, about a lack of theoretical progress, the endless proliferation of theories, the (mis)fortunes of specific theories, and the growing gap between theory and research.

In the past, most of this worry has translated into position statements by one side or the other along with vitriolic attacks on each other. Metatheorists adopt an agnostic position toward these position statements and debates and they are not willing, at least until they have had a chance to study the various positions in such disputes (Fuhrman and Snizek 1990), to be drawn in on one side or the other. Metatheorizing promises a methodology, studies, and data that will allow sociologists to come to more reasoned conclusions on the various issues raised by these debates. This is not meant to imply that metatheorists will not come down on one side or another in a theoretical dispute. They may well take a stance or articulate a new, synthetic position, but it will be on the basis of their studies of theory rather than as a result of allegiance to a given theoretical orientation.

Postmodernism. Another proximate, and much more specific, source of the increase in interest in metatheorizing is the rise in fascination with postmodernism (Brown 1987, 1990; Kellner 1988, 1990; Lemert 1990). Because this issue has been dealt with by Weinstein and Weinstein in this volume (Chapter 8) and I draw heavily on their work, I will briefly mention a few key points. Metatheorizing has a number of things in common with postmodernism and, to some extent, can be seen as a postmodernist development within sociological theory. The basic works in postmodernism (e.g., Foucault 1966, 1969; Jameson 1984; Lyotard 1984) predate the recent surge of interest in metatheorizing and thus it would appear that they played a role in that development. However, overt references to postmodernism and its linkage to metatheorizing are of fairly recent vintage. Thus it seems more likely that the same conditions that made postmodernism attractive to sociological theorists has also helped lead to the growth of metatheorizing.

Although metatheorizing, like postmodernism, tends to find much irrationality and indeterminacy in sociology, one of the ways in which it is distinguished from postmodernism is by the fact that it does not reject anything; everything in sociology becomes an object of study and analysis. Of course, in operating in this way, metatheorizing relativizes all sociological approaches. Metatheorizing is not focally concerned with what sociological theory ought to be, but rather with studying and gaining a deeper understanding of what it is in all its branches, varieties, and manifestations. To some metatheorists such increased understanding is an end in itself; to others it is a means to creating new theory or an overarching theoretical perspective.

A good portion of what metatheorizing is about is caught by the postmodernist term *deconstruction*. As deconstructionists, metatheorists often reread and reanalyze theorists, sociological theories, paradigms, and so on. These are all treated as "texts" that need to be reinterpreted using contemporary perspectives and tools. The object of such deconstruction is often a better understanding of the entity being reanalyzed. Deconstruction can also be undertaken for the ultimately more constructive purpose of putting together diverse sets of ideas drawn from various perspectives in order to form a new theory or a new overarching theoretical perspective.

Another orientation shared by metatheorists and postmodernists is a critical attitude toward grand narratives, metanarratives, or totalizations.[6] It has become clear that none of these perspectives is adequate in itself, let alone fully adequate to analyze society as a whole. Rather than being caught in the battle among faulty grand narratives, metatheorists have turned their attention to a study of the narratives, the reasons for their faults, and the ways in which the faults can be overcome in new, more delimited synthetic efforts (Antonio 1990; Antonio and Kellner Chapter 5).

These new synthetic efforts are also in line with, although not explicitly derived from, the postmodern notion that the boundaries between extant theories need to be subverted or exploded (Kellner 1990, p. 277). Contemporary theoretical syntheses (e.g., Alexander and Colomy 1990; Cook, O'Brien, and Kollock 1990; Fine 1990), most derived from careful metatheoretical analyses of one or more extant theories, are not oriented to the production of new grand narratives that encompass all of sociology and explain all of the social world.

Rather they can be thought of as a set of new theoretical syntheses, rather than a new theoretical synthesis (Ritzer 1990a).

A New Generation of Sociological Theorists. The 1980s witnessed a change in generations of sociological theorists. The giants of sociological theory for over a half century—Parsons, Gouldner, Merton, Homans, Blumer, Coser, and others—had either retired or died by the close of the decade. The younger generation of theorists was less committed to traditional theoretical perspectives. This is clear, for example, in the way in which Alexander and Colomy (1990) deal with structural functionalism, Fine (1990) uses symbolic interaction, and Cook et al. (1990) work with exchange theory. One need only contrast their eclecticism with the more parochial orientations of their predecessors—Parsons in structural functionalism, Blumer in symbolic interactionism, and Homans in exchange theory—to see the dramatic generational change. Among other things, the new generation of theorists is open to critical analyses of their own theories, to open-minded studies of competing theories, and to efforts to synthesize a range of different theories. In other words, they are open to meta-theoretical analyses.

Factors Internal to Metatheory

Fatal Flaws in Earlier Explicitly Metatheoretical Works. Clearly, explicitly metatheoretical works preceded the boom in interest in the subject in the 1980s. The issue is why these earlier works did not ignite widespread interest in this topic. One general answer is that they tended to be widely spaced and very different works that failed to connect with one another and to form a base for more general and widespread interest in metatheorizing. The best examples of this early work are Parsons's ([1937] 1949) *Structure of Social Action* in the 1930s, Furfey's ([1953] 1965) *The Scope and Method of Sociology: A Metasociological Treatise* in the 1950s, and Gouldner's (1965, 1970) *Enter Plato* and *The Coming Crisis of Western Sociology,* which were products of the 1960s. A few major works[7] over a period of 4 decades hardly constitutes a critical mass on which to build.

Furthermore, these works, although expressing interest and often engaging in metatheorizing, are very different from and often at odds with one another. For example, Parsons sees metatheorizing as the empirical study of theoretical predecessors, Furfey conceives of it mainly as a distinct positivistic undertaking, and Gouldner views it as a reflexive specialty. Both Parsons and Gouldner would have rejected Furfey's positivistic orientation, but Parsons and Gouldner would have been uncomfortable with each other's approach (to say nothing of the fact that a major portion of Gouldner's *Coming Crisis* is devoted to a far-reaching attack on Parsonsian theory). For example, Parsons would have had difficulty with the degree to which Gouldner focuses on biographical factors in the development of theory, whereas Gouldner explicitly disagreed with many of the theoretical conclusions Parsons derived from his metatheoretical studies. Thus the basic problems in the major early works in metatheory were that they were too dispersed and too much at odds with one another to form a base for the broader development of this area.

In addition to this shared problem, each of these promising early works had fatal flaws that prevented them from acquiring a paradigmatic role in sociological metatheorizing. For example, Parsons was really far more interested in the development of theory, especially structural functionalism, than he was in the legitimation and development of metatheorizing. More important, as has been amply demonstrated by a variety of critics (e.g., Pope, Cohen, and Hazelrigg 1975; Cohen, Hazelrigg, and Pope 1975), Parsons was prone to distort his metatheoretical findings in order to fit his theoretical objectives. For example, Parsons tended to find the voluntaristic theory of action in places where it did not exist. In his propensity to distort his metatheoretical findings, Parsons, then, represented a poor example for later metatheorists.

Furfey's metasociology does not, in fact, involve the study of sociology but is instead a set of principles that is prior to, and presupposed by, sociology. Furfey's ([1953] 1965) work is dominated by his view that sociology is a science and metasociology is "an auxiliary science which furnishes the methodological principles presupposed by sociology" (p. 17). Turner (1986) argues, and quite rightly in my opinion, that "such meta-theorizing has put the cart before the horse" (p. 9). I think Furfey is here mistaken in his priorities. Metasociology should not provide a service to scientific sociology (or, for that matter, antiscientific sociology) but rather should take sociology as a subject of study. Another problem with Furfey's approach is his idea that metasociology (and implicitly, metatheorizing) is a field distinct from sociology. Metasociology in general, and metatheorizing in particular, are part of sociology; they are subareas within the larger field.

Although Gouldner's *Enter Plato* was, in many ways, exemplary metatheory, it did not attract a lot of attention because its focus on Plato seemed too far removed from the concerns of most sociologists. This difficulty was overcome in Gouldner's *The Coming Crisis of Western Sociology* and its "reflexive sociology," which concerned itself with a "crisis" of concern to many sociologists and, more specifically, with a theorist of great reknown at the time—Talcott Parsons.

However, *The Coming Crisis of Western Sociology* was limited by the fact that it reflected, and was a product of, the radical rhetoric of the late 1960s. Thus Gouldner tends to take positions that sound naive and antiquated today. Also limiting this work was its association, despite Gouldner's explicit warnings against it, with the highly limited "navel gazing" that appeared under the guise of the "sociology of sociology" in the pages, primarily, of the *American Sociologist.*[8] A barrage of criticisms helped lead to the cessation of publication of the *American Sociologist* under the sponsorship of the American Sociological Association, although it has since reappeared under private sponsorship. The minutia of concern to many sociologists of sociology helped to give it a poor reputation. The use of the term *metatheorizing* here constitutes an effort to distance the more recent developments from the sociology of sociology. Metatheorists have learned from the failings of the sociology of sociology and seek to grapple with issues that go to the essence of sociological theory.

Work on the Paradigmatic Status of Sociology. One important but highly specific impetus to the development of metatheorizing in sociology came from Thomas Kuhn's (1962, 1970) *The Structure of Scientific Revolutions* (and from the philosophy of science [e.g., Laudan 1977] in general and the philosophy of social science [see A. Rosenberg 1988] in particular). Informed by Kuhn's views on the nature of a paradigm and scientific revolutions, a large number of works appeared (e.g., Friedrichs 1970; Effrat 1972; Mullins 1973, 1983; Ritzer 1975a, 1975b) that examined the paradigmatic status of sociology, particularly sociological theory. The paradigm concept remains useful, and we continue to see works that analyze the paradigmatic structure of sociology (e.g., Falk and Zhao 1989, 1990; Bealer 1990; Gottdiener and Feagin 1988; M. Rosenberg 1989).

Examinations of sociological paradigms are clearly metatheoretical because they almost always involve a study of sociological theories. However, these works have a comparatively narrow focus, generally focusing on gaining an understanding of theories within their broader paradigmatic context. The significance of the body of work on paradigm analysis is that it played a major role in leading the way for, and opening the door to, a much broader range of metatheoretical analyses.

Micro-Macro and Agency-Structure Linkage. Concern for micro-macro and agency-structure linkage constitutes a second set of specific metatheoretical concerns that emerged in the 1980s and contributed to the development of a broader interest in metatheoretical issues.

Micro-macro linkage emerged as the central problematic in American sociological theory in the 1980s (Ritzer 1990d). Collins (1986) argues that work on this topic "promises to be a significant area of theoretical advance for some time to come" (p. 1350). Eisenstadt and Helle (1985) conclude that "the confrontation between micro- and macro-theory belong[s] to the past" (p. 3). Similarly, Münch and Smelser (1987) assert that "those who have argued polemically that one level is more fundamental than the other . . . must be regarded as in error. Virtually every contributor to this volume has correctly insisted on the mutual *interrelations* between micro and macro levels" (p. 385, italics added).[9]

Paralleling the emergence of interest in the United States in the micro-macro linkage is the development of a metatheoretical concern in Europe for the relationship between agency and structure. Margaret Archer (1988) has contended that "the problem of structure and agency has rightly come to be seen as the basic issue in modern social theory" (p. ix). In fact, she argues that dealing with this linkage (as well as a series of other linkages implied by it) has become the "acid test" of a general social theory and the "central problem" in theory (p. x).

The Positivist-Antipositivist Debate. A third specific source for contemporary metatheorizing has been the long-running and seemingly irresolvable debate over whether sociology is, or can be, like the natural sciences. In this debate the naturalists (or positivists) have been arrayed against the interpretationalists (antinaturalists or antipositivists; Overington 1979, as well as the ensuing debate; A. Rosenberg 1988). In addition, a number of new, postpositivist positions have been articulated (Shweder and Fiske 1986; Alexander and Colomy Chapter 2, 1990). This debate continues, and additional positions are being articulated (e.g., Collins 1989; Fuhrman and Snizek 1990); it is certainly a metatheoretical issue; and it is unlikely to be resolved anytime soon. But like the literature on paradigms and micro-macro and agency-structure linkage, the debate over positivism-antipositivism is rather specific; it occupies only a small space in the broader arena of metatheorizing in sociology.

The Reaction to the Mid-1980s Critiques of Metatheory. Several important works appeared in the mid-1980s (Collins 1986; Turner 1985, 1986; Skocpol 1986) that in part or whole were devoted to an attack on metatheorizing in sociology. What is difficult to understand about these critiques is that sociological metatheory in the mid-1980s was unfocused and lacking in coherence and unity.

The coming of age of metatheorizing in the late 1980s can be traced virtually directly to this set of critiques. The critics were so hostile, and at the same time their sense of metatheorizing was so limited and ill-defined, that their work galvanized metatheorists into offering defenses of metatheorizing as well as into efforts to better define the field and to demonstrate its utility (Fuhrman and Snizek 1990; Lemert Chapter 7; Ritzer 1988, 1989a, 1990b; Wallace Chapter 3; Weinstein and Weinstein Chapter 8).

Factors External to Sociological Theory and Metatheory

The Impact of Work in Other Fields. There are still other sets of developments, both in and out of sociology, that are related to the growth of sociological metatheorizing, although metatheorists are only beginning to integrate ideas from them into their work. Included here are works in the history of sociology (Jones 1977, 1983a, 1983b, 1985; Seidman 1985), the sociology of knowledge (Mannheim 1936), the history of ideas (Lovejoy 1948; Skinner 1969), the history of science (Crombie 1986), the primarily French history of mentalities (Burke 1986), and the German "Geistesgeschichte" (Schulin 1981).

To this point, metatheoretical works have only been modestly affected by ideas derived from these other fields. Examples include Nisbet's (1967; also see Mathews 1989) use of Lovejoy's perspective on the history of ideas to develop a sense of sociology's "unit ideas," the influence of Skinner's revisionist history of ideas on Jones's work, and the fact that the sociology of knowledge has had a direct or indirect impact on a number of studies of sociological theory (e.g., Tiryakian 1988; Vidich and Lyman 1985). The future expansion of such work promises to significantly enrich sociological metatheorizing in the next few years.

The Parallel Growth of Meta-Data-Analysis and Metamethods. Although we have focused on metatheoretical efforts in this chapter, there is a parallel growth in interest in metamethods and meta-data-analysis. Metamethods involves the study of sociological methods and meta-data-analysis is the study of the results of a range of research studies, often with the objective of synthesizing them.

Among these works are attempts to synthesize an array of methods (fieldwork, surveys, experiments, nonreactive studies; Brewer and Hunter 1989), to synthesize qualitative studies (Noblit and Hare 1988), to develop quantitative foundations for qualitative research (Gephart 1988), to analyze the relationship of research methods to the micro-macro problem (Fielding 1988), as well as quantitative methods for synthesizing research findings across studies (Wolf 1986; Hunter and Schmidt 1989).

Although metatheorists are quite self-conscious, there does not seem to be a corresponding self-awareness among metamethodologists and meta-data-analysts. The self-consciousness of the latter groups is likely to increase, especially if the linkages to each other as well as to ongoing developments in metatheory are made clear. The ultimate hope here is a dialogue between, and even partial integration of, metatheory, metamethods, and meta-data-analysis.

Conclusions

The objective in this chapter has been to explain the recent coming of age of metatheorizing in sociology. Three sets of factors have been employed to help us account for this development: factors internal to sociological theory, factors internal to sociological metatheorizing, and factors external to theory and metatheory. This, then, constitutes a metatheoretical effort to explain the rise of interest in sociological metatheory; it demonstrates the utility of a metatheoretical approach.

Although metatheorizing is coming of age in sociology, it is certainly not arriving as a fully developed approach. The various forms of metatheorizing will require careful critique, development, expansion and perhaps drastic revision. The ultimate form of metatheorizing in sociology will be very different from its first explications in the last few years. Its form will change and evolve, but it is likely that the reflexiveness of metatheory, as well as of metamethods and metasociology in general, will become an established and accepted part of the sociological landscape.

This growth will need to overcome some powerful opposition, even from many sociological theorists. Much of this antagonism is difficult to understand. No matter how many defenses one marshals on behalf of metatheorizing in sociology, a continuing, if not escalating, cacophony of critiques can be anticipated. So be it! Although I am anxious to defend metatheorizing against its critics and to utilize useful derivatives from their critiques, I am also resigned to, and even welcome, a continuation of the attacks. The ire of some of the critics makes it clear that metatheoretical work is touching a raw nerve among some sociologists; it is doing something, perhaps many things, right. It is a lack of response, rather than critique, that would be the most damning to metatheorizing. Thus, let the critics have at metatheoretical work. At one level, their diatribes will only serve to bring greater (and deserved) attention to metatheorizing. At another, more important level, the criticisms will further goad metatheorists into sharpening their perspectives and improving the quality of their work. In the end, the critics will help rather than hinder what I see as the inevitable institutionalization of metatheorizing (and other forms of meta-analysis) in sociology. Such institutionalization is inevitable, because it involves simply the extension of the basic tools of sociology to the study of theory.

INTRODUCTION TO THIS VOLUME

The chapters included in this volume represent still more evidence of the theme of this introductory chapter—the maturation of sociological metatheorizing. Jeffrey C. Alexander and Paul Colomy (Chapter 2) propose a postpositivist model of knowledge cumulation in sociology. In so doing they reject the two major alternatives, the positivistic and the hermeneutic approaches, to the issue of the cumulation of knowledge. The positivistic model, emulating the natural sciences, sees sociology as making clear progress over time and contends that the future will bring with it still more progress. The hermeneutic approach, especially in its strongest forms, rejects the scientific model and the idea of scientific progress in sociology. Alexander and Colomy propose a postpositivist model that retains the idea of progress without accepting the untenable positions of the positivist and antipositivist positions. Thus we find in this ambitious chapter comparative analysis of three overarching metatheoretical orientations and the case made for a new postpositivist position. Walter L. Wallace (Chapter 3) is a firm believer in the positivistic model rejected by Alexander and Colomy. Working within this overarching metatheory, Wallace expresses deep concern over the lack of conceptual standardization in sociology. He, too, focuses on the issue of knowledge cumulation and argues that it is being greatly hindered by the absence of an agreed-upon language in sociology. If we cannot communicate adequately with one another, how can we hope to cumulate knowledge? Wallace offers a number of examples of profound differences in the way key concepts in sociology are defined. He then makes the case for conceptual standardization within sociology and argues that such standardization will greatly aid in the cumulation of knowledge within sociology.

Chapter 4 by Edward A. Tiryakian and Chapter 5 by Robert J. Antonio and Douglas Kellner also operate at the level of overarching metatheoretical perspectives. However, their metatheories are far narrower than those explored by Alexander and Colomy and by Wallace. Tiryakian sees metatheorizing as a radical inquiry that can liberate us from the hegemony of dominant metatheories and their range of underlying assumptions. Tiryakian metatheoretically analyzes the overarching perspective of the modernization paradigm, and proposes on the basis of an analysis of its weaknesses a neomodernization paradigm. He also demonstrates the convergences between the modernization and world-system paradigms, but concludes that what is needed for the realities of the 1990s is the neomodernization paradigm.

Antonio and Kellner focus on the metatheory that informs the views of classical theorists about modernity. They survey the work of a range of classical theorists and extract from it a metatheory of social modernity. This perspective is not found in its entirety in the work of any classical theorist, nor does it represent a conscious consensus on the part of those theorists. Rather, it is extracted from their theoretical work through the metatheoretical analysis undertaken by Antonio and Kellner. They see this metatheory of modernity as having come to be associated with positivism and as currently under attack by postmodernists. Like Alexander and Colomy, Antonio and Kellner reject the poles of positivism and antipositivism. They argue that classical theories of modernity can provide an alternative to these extreme metatheories. They argue that the need for metatheories of broad scope to analyze the new realities of the social world and the classical theories of modernity can be an important resource in constructing such wide-ranging perspectives.

Thus Chapters 2 through 5 are all working with overarching metatheoretical perspectives. In Chapter 6, Joseph Berger, David G. Wagner, and Morris Zelditch, Jr. also claim to be operating in this domain with their concern for *state organizing processes*. It is clear, at the minimum, that this perspective is of an entirely different order than the metatheories of concern in the four chapters discussed above. This difference should be seen in light of Berger et al.'s contention that metatheory is not an undifferentiated totality. Thus there are a number of different types of overarching metatheories in sociology varying greatly in scope. It is clear that the metatheory of state organizing processes is a far less general metatheory than positivism, hermeneutics, and postpositivism. It is also narrower than the metatheories of modernity offered by Tiryakian and by Antonio and Kellner. What is clearly needed is the development of a more precise sense of the range of overarching perspectives within sociology.

However, it seems to me that the key point in Chapter 6 relates to the process of metatheorizing. In my own recent work (Ritzer 1990b, 1991) I have tended to focus on the end-products of that process—greater understanding of theory, new theories, or new overarching perspectives. Berger et al. have begun to focus on the process in greater detail. They point out that although certain elements of their overarching perspective predated their substantive theory, other aspects of that perspective evolved in the course of their metatheoretical work and substantive theorizing. Thus metatheories are not merely produced and then etched in stone, but rather change over time as a result of further theoretical and metatheoretical work.

It is the process of metatheorizing that is of focal concern in the remaining chapters in this volume. Charles Lemert (Chapter 7) seeks to defend metatheorists from their critics, or what he calls their "cultured despisers." He looks at two broad types of critics and concludes that despite their protestations, both groups engage in the process of metatheorizing in the sense of studying and building upon the work of their predecessors. One group does this half heartedly, and therefore poorly, and the other does it quite well in spite of its overt aversion to metatheoretical work.

In a fascinating turn, Lemert proceeds to link the critics of metatheorizing within sociology to the cultured despisers of sociology who largely exist outside the discipline. His model here is James Coleman, who is not only a prominent critic (of Lemert's first group) of metatheoretical work but is also involved with a public group that is highly critical of a variety of social trends that are being manifested in many academic disciplines, including sociology. It is a defense of modernity, and an assault on postmodernity, that links these two types of critique. In linking these two types of assaults, Lemert is himself practicing metatheorizing designed to gain a greater understanding of theoretical developments (Ritzer 1988). More specifically, he is linking an internal-intellectual analysis of the critics of metatheory to an external-intellectual analysis of the critics of sociology. Lemert thus both analyzes metatheories and demonstrates the utility of metatheorizing.

Deena Weinstein and Michael A. Weinstein (Chapter 8) are also interested in postmodernity; the heart of their chapter lies in the contention that metatheorizing in sociology is linked to the more general rise of interest in postmodern thinking. They contrast metatheorizing to philosophical sociology. Philosophical sociologists make the case for various "foundations," or overarching perspectives, for sociology. In contrast, metatheorists are not interested in making the case for anything, but rather study the full range of sociological theories. Metatheorizing, like postmodernism, is also antifoundational in the sense that it does not stand for any specific attempt to impose a metatheoretical orientation on sociology. Those overarching perspectives produced by metatheorists are, at best, provisional rather than the permanent metanarratives produced by foundationalists.

Weinstein and Weinstein see metatheorizing as the product of a diverse, multiparadigmatic sociology. It is in such a context that one finds the greatest need to study the theoretical (and empirical and methodological) status of the discipline. Viewing metatheoretical work as legitimate within such a context, Weinstein and Weinstein, like Lemert, take on the critics of such work. Like Lemert, they see these critiques as part of the "culture wars of the contemporary academy." Linking metatheorizing directly with postmodernism, Weinstein and Weinstein see it as "liberated play with sociological theory." It is this play, even though it is quite serious and earnest, that so angers the positivists within sociology, especially because one of the things that metatheorists play with is positivism.

Stephan Fuchs (Chapter 9) analyzes the sociology of scientific knowledge (SSK) and relates it to the more specific issue of metatheorizing in sociology. Central to SSK is the relativism and reflexivity of all scientific work (including that done by sociologists of science). In Fuchs's view, scientific fields vary only in their degree of relativism and reflexivity. The degree of relativism and reflexivity becomes a dependent variable to be analyzed from the point of view of the theory of scientific organizations (TSO). TSO focuses on "the relationship between the structures of scientific groups and their cognitive styles and discursive practices." TSO thus becomes a meta-analytic tool to comparatively analyze scientific fields in terms of their degree of relativism and reflexivity.

Particularly relevant to the concerns of this book is the fact that Fuchs sees sociology as a weak, fragmented, and highly controversial field that, as a result, has a great deal of relativism and reflexivity. In other words (like the view offered by Weinstein and Weinstein), sociology is seen as a field that is particularly open to metatheoretical analyses. In contrast, strong, cohesive, and cognitively unified fields are characterized by lower levels of relativism and reflexivity. Practitioners in such fields are less aware or unaware of the relativism and reflexivity that exist within them. Thus they are less likely to produce meta-analyses by themselves and are therefore in greater need of meta-analyses done by outsiders (e.g., by sociological metatheorists and sociologists of science). In other words, the nature of sociology causes it to spawn its own metatheorists, whereas the nature of more settled sciences serves to prevent the emergence of indigenous meta-analysts. However, that does not mean that such fields are not in need of meta-analyses.

NOTES

1. This definition is based on the interpretation of "meta" as meaning "coming after," rather than "before" or "prior to," sociological theory (Radnitzky 1973; Turner 1986).

2. It should be noted that there is no clear dividing line between metatheory and theory, even though metatheory involves the study of theory and theory deals with the social world. As will be seen, many noted classic and contemporary theorists have also done metatheorizing, although such an orientation has generally only been implicit in their work.

3. For purposes of this discussion, metatheorizing will be discussed in an undifferentiated manner. There are, however, a number of types and subtypes of metatheorizing (Ritzer 1988, 1990b), but the employment of such a differentiation here would unduly complicate the analysis. The three major types are metatheorizing in order to (a) better understand theory, (b) create new theory, and (c) create an overarching theoretical perspective.

4. In a pure sense, this is actually an exercise in meta-metatheorizing, because the object of study is metatheory, not theory.

5. I also think that the more recent metatheoretical work is more sophisticated than its predecessors. This is implied in the critiques (see below) of earlier, explicit works in metatheory by Parsons, Furfey, and Gouldner.

6. Even the overarching perspectives produced by metatheorists tend to be limited and provisional (e.g., Ritzer 1981).

7. Other important metatheoretical works during these periods are those of Sorokin (1928, 1956) and Merton (1968).

8. Under the editorship, at first, of Talcott Parsons.

9. The citation of people like Münch and Helle in this discussion of the micro-macro linkage clearly indicates that some Europeans are involved in that debate, just as some Americans work on the agency-structure issue.

REFERENCES

Alexander, J., B. Giesen, R. Münch, and N. Smelser, eds. 1987. *The Macro-Micro Link.* Berkeley: University of California Press.

Alexander, J. and P. Colomy. 1990. "Neofunctionalism Today: Reconstructing a Theoretical Tradition." Pp. 33-67 in *Frontiers of Social Theory: The New Syntheses,* edited by G. Ritzer. New York: Columbia University Press.

Antonio, R. J. 1990. "The Decline of the Grand Narrative of Emancipatory Modernity: Crisis or Renewal in Neo-Marxian Theory?" Pp. 88-116 in *Frontiers of Social Theory: The New Syntheses,* edited by G. Ritzer. New York: Columbia University Press.

Archer, M. S. 1982. "Morphogenesis Versus Structuration: On Combining Structure and Action." *British Journal of Sociology* 33:455-83.

———. 1988. *Culture and Agency: The Place of Culture in Social Theory.* Cambridge, England: Cambridge University Press.

Bealer, R. 1990. "Paradigms, Theories, and Methods in Contemporary Rural Sociology: A Critical Reaction to Critical Questions." *Rural Sociology* 55:91-100.

Berger, J., D. G. Wagner, and M. Zelditch, Jr. 1989. "Theory Growth, Social Processes and Metatheory." Pp. 19-42 in *Theory Building in Sociology: Assessing Theoretical Cumulation,* edited by J. Turner. Newbury Park, CA: Sage.

Bernstein, R. J. 1971. *Praxis and Action: Contemporary Philosophies of Human Activity.* Philadelphia: University of Pennsylvania Press.

Brewer, J. and A. Hunter. 1989. *Multimethod Research: A Synthesis of Styles.* Newbury Park, CA: Sage.

Brown, R. 1987. *Society as Text: Essays on Rhetoric, Reason and Reality.* Chicago: University of Chicago Press.

———. 1990. "Social Science and the Poetics of Public Truth." *Sociological Forum* 5:55-74.

Burke, P. 1986. "Strengths and Weaknesses of the History of Mentalities." *History of European Ideas* 7:439-51.

Cohen, J., L. Hazelrigg, and W. Pope. 1975. "DeParsonizing Weber: A Critique of Parsons' Interpretation of Weber's Sociology." *American Sociological Review* 40:229-41.

Collins, R. 1981a. "Micro-Translation as a Theory-Building Strategy." Pp. 81-108 in *Advances in Social Theory and Methodology,* edited by Karin Knorr-Cetina and Aaron Cicourel. New York: Methuen.

———. 1981b. "On the Microfoundations of Macrosociology." *American Journal of Sociology* 86:984-1014.

———. 1986. "Is 1980s Sociology in the Doldrums?" *American Journal of Sociology* 91:1336-55.

———. 1988. "The Micro Contribution to Macro Sociology." *Sociological Theory* 6:242-53.

———. 1989. "Sociology: Proscience or Antiscience?" *American Sociological Review* 54:124-39.

Cook, K., J. O'Brien, and P. Kollock. 1990. "Exchange Theory: A Blueprint for Structure and Process." Pp. 158-71 in *Frontiers of Social Theory: The New Syntheses*, edited by G. Ritzer. New York: Columbia University Press.

Crombie, A. C. 1986. "What Is the History of Science?" *History of European Ideas* 7:21-31.

Effrat, A. 1972. "Power to the Paradigms." *Sociological Inquiry* 42:3-33.

Eisenstadt, S. N. and H. J. Helle. 1985. "General Introduction to Perspectives on Sociological Theory." Pp. 1-3 in *Macro-Sociological Theory*, edited by S. N. Eisenstadt and H. J. Helle. London: Sage.

Falk, W. and S. Zhao. 1989. "Paradigms, Theories and Methods in Contemporary Rural Sociology: A Partial Replication." *Rural Sociology* 54:587-600.

———. 1990. "Paradigms, Theories and Methods Revisited: We Respond to Our Critics." *Rural Sociology* 55:112-22.

Fararo, T. 1989. "The Spirit of Unification in Sociological Theory." *Sociological Theory* 7:175-90.

Fielding, N. 1988. *Actions and Structures: Research Methods and Social Theory*. Newbury Park, CA: Sage.

Fine, G. 1990. "Symbolic Interactionism in the Post-Blumerian Age." Pp. 117-57 in *Frontiers of Social Theory: The New Syntheses*, edited by G. Ritzer. New York: Columbia University Press.

Fiske, D. W. and R. A. Shweder, eds. 1986. *Metatheory in Social Science: Pluralisms and Subjectivities*. Chicago: University of Chicago Press.

Foucault, M. 1966. *The Order of Things: An Archaeology of the Human Sciences*. New York: Vintage.

———. 1969. *The Archaeology of Knowledge and the Discourse on Language*. New York: Harper Colophon.

Friedrichs, R. W. 1970. *A Sociology of Sociology*. New York: Free Press.

Fuhrman, E. R. and W. Snizek. 1990. "Neither Proscience nor Antiscience: Metasociology as Dialogue." *Sociological Forum* 5:17-36.

Furfey, P. H. [1953] 1965. *The Scope and Method of Sociology: A Metasociological Treatise*. New York: Cooper Square.

Gephart, Jr., R. P. 1988. *Ethnostatistics: Qualitative Foundations for Quantitative Research*. Newbury Park, CA: Sage.

Giddens, A. 1984. *The Constitution of Society: Outline of the Theory of Structuration*. Berkeley: University of California Press.

Gottdiener, M. and J. R. Feagin. 1988. "The Paradigm Shift in Urban Sociology." *Urban Affairs Quarterly* 24:163-87.

Gouldner, A. 1965. *Enter Plato: Classical Greece and the Origins of Social Theory*. New York: Basic Books.

———. 1970. *The Coming Crisis of Western Sociology*. New York: Basic Books.

Hunter, J. E. and F. L. Schmidt. 1989. *Methods of Meta-Analysis: Correcting Error and Bias in Research Findings*. Newbury Park, CA: Sage.

Jameson, F. 1984. "Postmodernism, or the Cultural Logic of Late Capitalism." *New Left Review* 146:53-93.

Jones, R. A. 1977. "On Understanding a Sociological Classic." *American Journal of Sociology* 83:279-319.

———. 1983a. "The New History of Sociology." *Annual Review of Sociology* 9:447-69.

———. 1983b. "On Merton's 'History' and 'Systematics' of Sociological Theory." Pp. 121-42 in *Functions and Uses of Disciplinary Histories*, Vol. VII, edited by L. Graham, W. Lepenies, and P. Weingart. Dordrecht, The Netherlands: D. Reidel.

———. 1985. "Presentism, Anachronism, and Continuity in the History of Sociology: A Reply to Seidman." *History of Sociology* 6:153-60.

Kellner, D. 1988. "Postmodernism as Social Theory: Some Problems and Challenges." *Theory, Culture and Society* 5:239-70.

———. 1990. "The Postmodern Turn: Positions, Problems, and Prospects." Pp. 255-86 in *Frontiers of Social Theory: The New Syntheses*, edited by G. Ritzer. New York: Columbia University Press.

Kuhn, T. 1962. *The Structure of Scientific Revolutions.* Chicago: University of Chicago Press.

———. 1970. *The Structure of Scientific Revolutions*, 2nd ed. Chicago: University of Chicago Press.

Laudan, L. 1977. *Progress and Its Problems: Toward a Theory of Scientific Growth.* Berkeley: University of California Press.

Lemert, C. 1990. "The Uses of French Structuralisms in Sociology." Pp. 230-54 in *Frontiers of Social Theory: The New Syntheses*, edited by G. Ritzer. New York: Columbia University Press.

Levine, D. 1989. "Simmel as a Resource for Sociological Metatheory." *Sociological Theory* 7:161-74.

Lovejoy, A. 1948. *Essays in the History of Ideas.* Baltimore: Johns Hopkins University Press.

Lyotard, J. 1984. *The Postmodern Condition.* Minneapolis: University of Minnesota Press.

Mannheim, K. 1936. *Ideology and Utopia: An Introduction to the Sociology of Knowledge.* New York: Harvest Books.

Mathews, F. 1989. "Social Scientists and the Culture Concept, 1930-1950: The Conflict between Processual and Structural Approaches." *Sociological Theory* 7:87-101.

Merton, R. 1968. *Social Theory and Social Structure.* New York: Free Press.

Mullins, N. 1973. *Theories and Theory Groups in Contemporary American Sociology.* New York: Harper & Row.

———. 1983. "Theories and Theory Groups Revisited." Pp. 319-37 in *Sociological Theory—1983*, edited by R. Collins. San Francisco: Jossey-Bass.

Münch, R. and N. Smelser. 1987. "Relating the Micro and Macro." Pp. 356-87 in *The Micro-Macro Link*, edited by J. Alexander, B. Giesen, R. Münch, and N. Smelser. Berkeley: University of California Press.

Nisbet, R. 1967. *The Sociological Tradition.* New York: Basic Books.

Noblit, G. W. and R. D. Hare. 1988. *Meta-Ethnography: Synthesizing Qualitative Studies.* Newbury Park, CA: Sage.

Osterberg, D. 1988. *Metasociology: An Inquiry into the Origins and Validity of Social Thought.* Oslo, Norway: Norwegian University Press.

Overington, M. A. 1979. "Doing What Comes Rationally: Some Developments in Metatheory." *American Sociologist* 14:2-12.

Parsons, T. [1937] 1949. *The Structure of Social Action*, 2nd ed. New York: Free Press.

Pope, W., J. Cohen, and L. Hazelrigg. 1975. "On the Divergence of Weber and Durkheim: A Critique of Parsons' Convergence Thesis." *American Sociological Review* 40:417-27.

Radnitzky, G. 1973. *Contemporary Schools of Metascience.* Chicago: Henry Regnery.

Ritzer, G. 1975a. *Sociology: A Multiple Paradigm Science.* Boston: Allyn & Bacon.

———. 1975b. "Sociology: A Multiple Paradigm Science." *American Sociologist* 10:156-67.

———. 1981. *Toward an Integrated Sociological Paradigm: The Search for an Exemplar and an Image of the Subject Matter.* Boston: Allyn & Bacon.

———. 1988. "Sociological Metatheory: Defending a Subfield by Delineating Its Parameters." *Sociological Theory* 6:187-200.

———. 1989a. "Metatheorizing as a Prelude to Theory Development." Paper presented at the meeting of the American Sociological Association, San Francisco, CA, August.

———. 1989b. "Of Levels and 'Intellectual Amnesia,' " *Sociological Theory* 7:226-29.

———. 1990a. "The Current Status of Sociological Theory: The New Syntheses." Pp. 1-30 in *Frontiers of Social Theory: The New Syntheses*, edited by G. Ritzer. New York: Columbia University Press.

———. 1990b. "Metatheorizing in Sociology." *Sociological Forum* 5:3-15.

———, ed. 1990c. "Metatheory: Its Uses and Abuses in Contemporary Sociology." *Sociological Forum* 5:1-74.

———. 1990d. "Micro-Macro Linkage in Sociology: Applying a Metatheoretical Tool." Pp. 347-70 in *Frontiers of Social Theory: The New Syntheses*, edited by G. Ritzer. New York: Columbia University Press.

———. 1991. *Metatheorizing in Sociology*. Lexington, MA: Lexington Books.

Rosenberg, A. 1988. *Philosophy of Social Science*. Boulder, CO: Westview.

Rosenberg, M. 1989. "Self-Concept Research: A Historical Review." *Social Forces* 68:34-44.

Schulin, E. 1981. "German 'Geistesgeschichte,' American 'Intellectual History' and French 'Histoire des Mentalites' Since 1900: A Comparison." *History of European Ideas* 1:195-214.

Seidman, S. 1985. "Classics and Contemporaries: The History and Systematics of Sociology Revisited." *History of Sociology* 6:121-35.

Shweder, R. A. and D. Fiske. 1986. "Introduction: Uneasy Social Science." Pp. 1-18 in *Metatheory in Social Science*, edited by D. Fiske and R. A. Shweder. Chicago: University of Chicago Press.

Skinner, Q. 1969. "Meaning and Understanding in the History of Ideas." *History and Theory* 8:3-53.

Skocpol, T. 1986. "The Dead End of Metatheory." *Contemporary Sociology* 16:10-12.

Sorokin, P. 1928. *Contemporary Sociological Theories*. New York: Harper & Row.

———. 1956. *Fads and Foibles in Modern Sociology and Related Sciences*. Chicago: Regnery.

Tiryakian, E. A. 1988. "Durkheim, Mathiez, and the French Revolution: The Political Context of a Sociological Classic." *European Journal of Sociology* 29:373-96.

Turner, J. 1985. "In Defense of Positivism." *Sociological Theory* 3:24-30.

———. 1986. *The Structure of Sociological Theory*, 4th ed. Chicago: Dorsey Press.

———. 1989a. "Introduction: Can Sociology Be a Cumulative Science?" Pp. 8-18 in *Theory Building in Sociology: Assessing Theoretical Cumulation*, edited by J. Turner. Newbury Park, CA: Sage.

———, ed. 1989b. *Theory Building in Sociology: Assessing Theoretical Cumulation*. Newbury Park, CA: Sage.

Vidich, A. J. and S. M. Lyman. 1985. *American Sociology: Worldly Rejections of Religion and Their Directions*. New Haven, CT: Yale University Press.

Wiley, N. 1988. "The Micro-Macro Problem in Social Theory." *Sociological Theory* 6:254-61.

———. 1989. "Response to Ritzer." *Sociological Theory* 7:230-31.

Wolf, F. M. 1986. *Meta-Analysis: Quantitative Methods for Research Synthesis*. Sage University Paper Series on Quantitative Applications in the Social Sciences, No. 07-059. Beverly Hills, CA: Sage.

Chapter 2

TRADITIONS AND COMPETITION
Preface to a Postpositivist Approach to Knowledge Cumulation

JEFFREY C. ALEXANDER
University of California, Los Angeles

PAUL COLOMY
University of Denver

INTRODUCTION

SOCIOLOGY ONCE ASPIRED TO BE a cumulative science. Its practitioners once sought to develop and continuously expand verified knowledge about social patterns, social processes, and their underlying causal dynamics. A generation ago, sociologists shared a fervent belief that such cumulation of scientific knowledge required only that scholars "work like hell" testing hypotheses and theories (Cressey, quoted in Laub 1983; Zetterberg 1955). The result of these labor-intensive efforts was a plethora of paradigms, models, concepts, and empirical investigations concerning virtually every imaginable facet of the social world. Like the natural sciences it emulated, sociology seemed to be making indisputable progress (Stinchcombe 1968).

Today, for a large and growing number of sociologists (e.g., S. Turner 1988), this vision of progress seems to have been a mirage. The contrast between the earlier generation's ardent faith in the possibility of

AUTHORS' NOTE: An earlier version of this chapter was presented at the Section on Theoretical Sociology, "Metatheorizing in Sociology I," at the annual meeting of the American Sociological Association, Washington, DC, August 11, 1990. This chapter is an initial and abbreviated statement of a larger project that outlines a postpositivist model of knowledge cumulation and decline in the social sciences (Alexander and Colomy unpublished).

scientific growth and the current cohort's profound uncertainty about
the ultimate product of their social science labors is stark and dramatic. Skepticism has supplanted faith, and words like malaise, pessimism, disintegration, and disillusionment increasingly color
discourse about contemporary sociology (J. Turner 1989a; B. Turner
1989; Collins 1986).

To account for this change is certainly important, and we hope that
one by-product of this discussion is the outline of an explanation that
adds something to those already offered (e.g., Wiley 1979, 1985; Collins
1986; J. Turner 1989a; S. Turner and J. Turner 1990). This is not,
however, our primary concern. This chapter is not an explanation but
a response to the demoralization of sociology's orthodox scientific
creed. An effective response, we argue, requires an alternative framework for understanding the nature of social science. The growth and
decline of social scientific knowledge must be assessed in terms of
new and more nuanced criteria than the earlier orthodoxy allowed.

Toward this end, we present the rudiments of a postpositivist
model that identifies and explains advances and declines in sociological knowledge. Resting upon an alternative conception of the relationship between theory and fact, the model develops a counterintuitive
assumption: it hypothesizes that sociological traditions are the critical
units of analysis for assessing the cumulation of social scientific knowledge. Building upon this tradition-bound framework, we outline
several distinct patterns of social scientific growth, using important
classical and contemporary cases of theoretical and empirical shifts to
illustrate the viability of our approach.

EXISTING THEORIES OF KNOWLEDGE CUMULATION
IN THE SOCIAL SCIENCES

At present, sociology is being pulled in opposite directions by two
competing theories of knowledge cumulation and decline: one a
continuing version of the "hard," quasi-natural science orthodoxy,
the other a reformulation of the "soft" approach to sociology as a
literary and humanistic enterprise. In an important sense this debate
revolves around the issue of boundaries between social science and
other disciplines.

In an intriguing set of papers Gieryn (1983) and Gieryn, Bevins, and
Zehr (1985) argue that scientists engage in "boundary-work" to

establish and reaffirm a positive public image for science. They do so by invidiously contrasting science with "nonscientific" intellectual activities. Gieryn shows that boundary-work is used strategically to legitimate a scientific discipline's professional claims to authority and its requests for tangible resources. The line demarcating science from nonscience, his studies demonstrate, is highly contingent and markedly responsive to changing historical circumstances.

Gieryn's imagery of a moving line between science and nonscience speaks directly to our concerns about the current condition of sociology. It should be emphasized, however, that these shifting boundaries have cognitive as well as ideological consequences, and we accord the former more attention. Furthermore, the pertinent boundaries are often multiple rather than singular, and proponents frequently frame their arguments in terms of social science's boundaries with two or more disciplines. Finally, intergenre boundary work may be positive as well as negative. Gieryn is primarily concerned with the negative boundary work involved in distinguishing science from nonscience. But it is also instructive, and this is particularly true in the case of the social sciences, to consider the positive boundary work manifest in attempts to forge powerful links between one set of intellectual activities and another.

Positivism (Toulmin 1953; J. Turner forthcoming) is the philosophical basis for the quasi-natural science view of sociology. Until very recently, positivism not only supplied the dominant theory of how knowledge cumulates and declines in sociology, but it also directly informed virtually all social science practice. Attempting to forge a strong identification with the natural sciences, its proponents asserted that if a boundary between the social and the hard sciences existed at all, it was minuscule. Sociologists were urged to embrace the methodological apparatus and procedures of the more mature sciences and to investigate "social facts" (Durkheim [1894] 1938) with the same dispassionate objectivity that hard scientists purportedly brought to their study of physical ones.

The Frenchman who invented the term *sociology*, August Comte, argued forcefully for the construction of a negative boundary between the science of society and speculative philosophy. Sociology was to be as devoid of metaphysical commitments as were the sciences of nature. This "positive science," as Comte called it, would consist entirely of propositions, laws, and causal statements; interpretations and value judgments would not intrude. As many have noted (e.g., Fuchs and Turner 1986) these efforts to wed the fledgling discipline of sociology to the more prestigious natural sciences represented, in part, a readily transparent maneuver to wrestle legitimacy, status, and material resources from both the established scientific community and the wider public. But "ideal" interests were at stake as well, and in the long run these proved (contra Mullins 1973) even more consequential.

In the century-long development of sociology (Eisenstadt and Curelaru 1976; Shils 1970; S. Turner and J. Turner 1990), this perspective was refined in various ways, and contrasting versions were elaborated. Nonetheless, a broad "positivist persuasion" (Alexander 1982a) continued to provide for sociology a unifying, if rarely articulated creed. That persuasion rested upon a series of postulates that continue to form the basis for its adherents today. First, it presumes that a radical break exists between empirical observations and nonempirical statements. Thus theory is a qualitatively different entity than fact. Second, positivism argues that more highly generalized intellectual issues have no fundamental significance for the practice of an empirically oriented discipline. In its most contemporary rendition, this argument holds that "metatheoretical" discussions and debates dissipate intellectual energies that could be employed more productively in "real" scientific work (see J. Turner 1985, 1989b,[1] in contrast with Ritzer 1988, 1990a, 1990b; Fuhrman and Snizek 1990). Third, the positivist persuasion holds that the elimination of nonempirical referents is a distinguishing feature of the natural sciences and, therefore, that a truly scientific sociology must follow suit if it is to assume an equally scientific stature (Stinchcombe 1968). Fourth, questions of a general theoretical nature, it is argued, can be adequately addressed only in relation to empirical observation. Several additional points follow. With regard to the formulation of social theories, the positivist persuasion argues that the process should be one of induction and generalization from observation, or specification through hypothetico-deduction. Critical empirical tests and falsification are enshrined as the final arbiter in theoretical disputes. Finally, it is held that there is no logical basis for generalized, ongoing, and structured types of scientific disagreement.

The revolutionary development of the natural sciences gave tremendous impetus to the positivist persuasion in social science. At an earlier period in the history of human thought, explanations of nature were deeply embedded in metaphysical and speculative themes. Before physics, there was natural philosophy; before astronomy, there was cosmology. If, as Barnes and Becker (1952) once asked, thinking about nature could make the transition to rationality and positive empiricism, why not thinking about society? Indeed, Durkheim's ([1894] 1938) influential methodological program was premised on the belief that this transition had already been made. In the 20th century, the growing power, prestige, and self-confidence of the natural sciences pushed social science even further in this direction. With the development in the postwar period of sophisticated methodological techniques borrowed directly from the natural sciences, this positivist dream seemed as if it were becoming a reality (e.g., Blalock 1976).

In recent years, however, developments in the history and philosophy of natural science (e.g., Toulmin 1953, 1972; Kuhn 1970) have thrown increasing doubt on the positivist persuasion. These broad intellectual developments have made positive ties between the sciences of nature and the human studies more difficult to sustain in consistent and unambiguous ways. Although there are important differences of emphasis within this antipositivist movement, there is a widely shared understanding that the match between scientific theories and external reality is much more problematic than the positivist persuasion envisioned; indeed, antipositivists hold that theories necessarily involve conjecture and highly contestable interpretations. These investigations have underscored the independent contributions that nonempirical and generalized elements make to the most respected scientific work. Not surprisingly, these trenchant criticisms of positivism have had tremendous ramifications for disciplinary communities (like sociology) that had used the hard sciences as a cognitive and legitimating exemplar (cf. Gouldner 1970). If positivism does not fully explain how knowledge grows in the sciences of nature, then how can it account for the growth of knowledge in sciences that hardly approximate their rigor, precision, and impersonal controls? If positivism does not adequately explain the cumulation of knowledge in the natural sciences, how can its precepts continue to be dutifully accepted as dictums for social science practice?

In sociology, positivism still has articulate and passionate defenders (e.g., J. Turner 1985, 1990, forthcoming; Collins 1975, 1988, forthcoming), and it continues to function as an orienting strategy for contemporary sociological work. Even its defenders, however, are well aware that the discipline's stance toward orthodox positivism has changed fundamentally, that what once could be readily assumed about the nature of sociological inquiry has recently become an object of skepticism, if not downright derision (J. Turner 1989a; Giddens and Turner 1988).

It is within this context of growing skepticism about positivism that reflections about the current "malaise" of sociology should be understood. The discipline's apparent transition from a single to a multiple paradigm science (Ritzer 1975) exacerbated the relativism and self-doubt that accompanied the loss of positivist self-confidence. The proliferation of apparently disconnected subfields (J. Turner 1989a; Dogan and Pahre 1989; Collins 1986) and the ostensible split between theoretical work and a multifarious array of substantive areas (J. Turner 1989b, 1990; B. Turner 1989) contrast sharply with the positivist alliance, shaky though it was, of functionalist theory and quantitative methods that characterized an earlier day.

In contrast with positivism, the other leading perspective about knowledge cumulation in the social science assumes a negative stance toward natural sciences and a positive relation to what it refers to as the "human sciences." Although this position has been available throughout the 20th century, outside of the exceptional German case it never posed a serious intellectual threat to the proponents of a positivist sociology. That in recent years it has acquired increasing stature and a wider audience must be understood in the context of positivism's decline and sociology's fragmentation.

Against Comte, the German philosopher Wilhelm Dilthey (1976) argued that between the human studies and natural science there stands an unbridgeable gulf. In a more constructive vein, Dilthey sought to build strong links between the social sciences and the arts and literary interpretation. According to what he called the hermeneutic position, social science consists of interpretations and descriptive models; if and when causal statements are attempted, they can emerge only from within the subjective world of the social scientist's own experience.

In this view, social science is a fundamentally different kind of activity from its counterpart in natural science. Its objects of investigation—"social facts"—are either states of mind or conditions that are interpenetrated with them. In order to construct the very objects of a social science, therefore, investigators must draw on their own life experience and on their personal understandings of other human beings. This places a premium not only on observation and measurement but on imagination and speculative thought experiments. Once the objects of social science are conceptually constructed, moreover, it is not easy to verify or falsify the social science theories that generalize from them in a definitive way. Because the personal experiences and evaluative standards of investigators are bound to differ, the embeddedness of social science in value judgments, different personal sensibilities, and political ideology is impossible to avoid.

The human studies position raises serious and unavoidable questions about the possibility of cumulating knowledge about the social world (Friedrichs 1970). Advocates of a hermeneutics approach argue that *understanding* rather than *explanation* should be the major goal of social inquiry. In its weak form (Giddens 1984), hermeneutics allows generalizations, although cautioning that they will be of a fundamentally more tentative character than those in the natural sciences. In its strong version, hermeneutics declares that the possibility of a universal, objective, and generalizing science is completely illusory and that the human studies should be restricted either to critical analysis from a moral perspective (Gouldner 1970; Haan, Bellah, Rabinow, and Sullivan 1983) or to descriptive accounts of unique or "idiographic" events (Winch 1958).

This alternative to mainstream positivism throws the cumulation of social scientific knowledge into doubt. Because research and theorizing are heavily dependent on the interpretive skills of the individual investigator, the dynamics of social studies are viewed as largely idiosyncratic and essentially unstructured. One logical conclusion is to celebrate subjectivity and relativism (Hollinger 1985) and to abandon the search for general principles that are applicable to a wide range of phenomena in favor of the pursuit of thick description (Geertz 1973) and moral interpretation (Friedrichs 1970; Haan et al. 1983). We will argue against this course.

A POSTPOSITIVIST APPROACH
TO KNOWLEDGE CUMULATION

Although the hermeneutic, human studies approach supplies a fundamental corrective to positivist orthodoxy, it embraces a framework about which we believe the social sciences must be extremely wary. Philosophically (Alexander 1990a, forthcoming; Toulmin 1972), this path leads to an extremely vulnerable form of relativism; socially (Alexander 1990b), it can lead to a dangerous and enervating distrust of reason itself.[2] An alternative paradigm that moves beyond both positivism and its antipositivist extreme is necessary if sociology is to avoid the difficulties associated with either of these positions.

In contrast to both of the approaches outlined above, we propose a substantially different model to examine both progressive and regressive developments in sociological knowledge. This perspective is a reaction to both the powerful critique leveled at orthodox positivism by philosophers and historians of science (e.g., Kuhn 1970; Lakatos 1968, 1970; Toulmin 1953) and to the severe limitations the human studies approach would impose on efforts to generate cumulative social knowledge. Unlike human studies, it suggests that social scientific knowledge can grow and, over the long run, certainly has grown. At the same time, its characterization of how knowledge advances and declines is quite different from conventional positivism. Our postpositivist alternative rests on four basic assumptions.

The first holds that sociological work is profitably analyzed as falling along a scientific continuum ranging from abstract, general, and metaphysical elements on the one end to the concrete, empirical, and factual on the other (Toulmin 1953; Alexander 1982a). Other elements of scientific discourse, including ideologies, models, concepts, laws, propositions, methodological assumptions, and observational statements, fall between these endpoints. Even though its overall form may be characterized more by one element than another, every social scientific statement contains implicit or explicit commitments about the nature of every other element on the scientific continuum. The nature and types of social scientific debate are limited by the distinctive character of these elements. The discussion and controversies that mobilize the profession focus on particular elements and emphasize certain kinds of discourse over others.

Second, these basic elements with which sociology is built cannot be formulated in an infinite variety of ways. Although social scientists usually accept one formulation or another without hard and definitive evidence in a natural scientific sense, they do not accept a position without argument and vigorous efforts at intellectual persuasion. Such efforts are rational in the sense that they refer to generalized criteria that themselves must ultimately be justified through open and uncoerced debate (Habermas 1984). Indeed, it is our contention that important social scientific debates largely consist of arguments over the criteria for evaluation that are immanent in different levels of discourse (e.g., criteria about presuppositions, ideologies, models, and methods).

Third, in the history of sociological thought the options available at each discursive level have been sharply limited. In terms of what they presuppose about human nature, for example, students of society have usually been preoccupied with the degree to which actors act in either an instrumentally rational fashion or with reference to moral rules or emotional need (Parsons 1937; Ekeh 1974; Alexander 1987a; Stinchcombe 1986). The options for ideological discourse are more historically bounded (Gouldner 1970), but in the modern era at least a continuous argument between relatively coherent conservative, liberal, and radical arguments can be observed. As for models of society (cf. Eisenstadt and Curelaru 1976), the axes of dispute have concerned the relative randomness or coherence of systems, on the one hand, and the relative dynamic versus equilibriating tendencies of systems, on the other. The conflict between interpretive and causal approaches has preoccupied general methodological disputes.

Fourth, although in principle there is no intrinsic relationship between the different elements arrayed across the scientific continuum, there is a clear tendency for certain kinds of commitments to hang together. Thus there are no empirical or logically compelling theoretical reasons for an interpretive methodology to be combined with the commitment to a nonrational or normative understanding of action. Yet, *structural* considerations of theoretical logic must not be confused with the *contingent* issue of historical and empirical probability. In the history of social thought, the commitments made at different scientific levels have not been randomly interrelated. To use a Weberian phrase, there has often appeared to be an "elective affinity" between some theoretical commitments and others (Eisenstadt and Curelaru 1976; Gouldner 1970). Conflict models of society, for example, tend to be more attractive to radical than conservative thinkers, and rationalistic presuppositions are more characteristic of liberals than conservatives. But an even more powerful contingent factor must be considered. Whatever the purely logical possibilities for intrinsic (as compared with elective) affinity between options at different levels, practicing social scientists usually *believe* that certain imperative linkages do exist. The reason is that social science practice unfolds within powerfully stated theoretical traditions, and every tradition stipulates the relationship between theoretical elements in a sharply defined way (Tiryakian 1979, 1986; Shils 1970; Wiley 1979; Seidman 1983).

In our view, the various forms of sociology are carried forward by traditions, which are typically called "schools."[3] We would define sociology, indeed, as a multilevel rational discourse about society and its constituent units, with the patterns and directions of that discourse being conditioned by the discipline's leading traditions. The elements of this definition form a paradox but not a contradiction. Traditions, of course, are patterns of perception and behavior that are followed not, in the first instance, because of their intrinsic rationality, not because they have "proven their worth," but because they are inherited from the past. The traditional status of social scientific schools confers upon them prestige and authority, which is reinforced because they are typically upheld by organizational power and supported with material resources (Mullins 1973; Fuchs and Turner 1986). These considerations do not, however, mitigate the rational aspirations of social science, its sharply delimited structure of debate, and its often extraordinary ability to approximate and understand social reality.

Like other traditions, the rational movements of social science are founded by intellectually charismatic figures, whose followers believe that their powerful attraction stems from their awe-inspiring scientific prowess. At the beginning of a discipline, such great intellectual figures are regarded as classical founders (Alexander 1987b); at later points, they are accorded quasi-classical status and are treated simply as the founders of powerful disciplinary traditions. This organizational fact shows in yet another way why social science practice cannot be understood simply as the confrontation between scientist and social reality. Social reality is never confronted in itself. Because perception is mediated by the discursive commitments of traditions, social scientific formulations are channelled within relatively standardized, paradigmatic forms. The matrix social scientists inhabit need not be drawn from a single tradition or be wholly of a piece, but inhabit it they must, aware of it or not.

Although traditionalism implies habitual behavior, it need not imply stasis or lack of change. In social science, this openness to change is intensified by the universalism of institutionalized standards that mandate impersonal rationality and push against the particularism of a traditionalist response (Merton [1942] 1973). Social science traditions define themselves by staking out theoretical cores that are highly resistant to change, but there are substantial areas surrounding these nuclei that are subject to continuous variation (Lakatos 1968, 1970; Kuhn 1970). In ideal-typical terms, changes in the peripheral areas of traditions can be conceived as proceeding along three lines: *elaboration, proliferation,* and *revision* (Wagner 1984; Wagner and Berger 1985; Berger, Wagner, and Zelditch 1989; Alexander 1979; Colomy 1986, 1990). Although these lines of development present themselves as loyally carrying out traditional commitments, they differ in the creativeness with which they pursue this task. Because elaborative and proliferative sociological work proceeds from the assumption that the original tradition is internally consistent and relatively complete, they aim primarily at refinement and expansion of scope. In revisionist work, by contrast, there is a greater sense of the vulnerabilities of the established tradition; in the guise of loyal specification, an often implicit effort is made to address these strains and to offer formulations that can resolve them (Alexander 1979; Colomy 1986, 1990).

Elaboration, proliferation, and revision are lines of specification that recur periodically in a tradition's history, not only in the period of routinization that immediately follows the charismatic founding but in the wake of the powerful reformulations that must emerge if a tradition is to remain intact. The latter possibility points to a fourth ideal-typical form of theoretical change. Insofar as cores themselves undergo substantial shifts—without abandoning their association with the overarching tradition—there occurs a theoretical activity that can be called *reconstruction* (Alexander and Colomy 1990b). Reconstruction differs from elaboration, proliferation, and revision in that differences with the founder of the tradition are clearly acknowledged and openings to other traditions are explicitly made. Reconstruction can revive a theoretical tradition, even while it creates the opportunity for the kind of development out of which new traditions are born (e.g., Habermas 1979).

The most far-reaching form of scientific change carries the reconstructive impulse farther still and brings us back full circle to the intellectually charismatic founders of sociological traditions. *Tradition-creation* involves generating new schools organized around historically distinctive cores. The essence of tradition-creation is the synthesis of elements drawn from several existing and often competing intellectual paradigms, with the aim of generating the theoretical core of a new school. Marx's reconfiguration of elements from Hegelianism, the Enlightenment, French socialism, and British political economy represents the best documented (Alexander 1982b) instance of this form of scientific change.

One should be careful not to see these ideas—elaboration, proliferation, revision, reconstruction, and tradition-creation—as presenting either a necessary historical sequence or a scale of theoretical significance. As for sequence, with one important exception to be noted below, different types of change weave in and out of both the history of sociology and the historical course of each particular tradition. As for significance, most of the greatest minds in social science never made the transition from reconstruction to tradition-creation. Many who attempted to make the transition, moreover, were much the worse for it. The works of Von Wiese are long forgotten; the writings of Gramsci, Lukacs, Mannheim, and Mauss continue to be intently pursued.

Traditions can also be destroyed (*tradition-deconstruction*). This does not happen because core and peripheral commitments are falsified in the narrow sense. It occurs because these commitments have become delegitimated in the eyes of the scientific community. Delegitimation leads to the withdrawal of trust from core commitments. Only after core commitments are abandoned can fundamental falsification be understood as having occurred. Even in this situation, however, traditions do not so much disappear as become latent; the possibility always remains (cf. Eisenstadt and Curelaru 1976) that they may be picked up again.

Elaboration, proliferation, revision, reconstruction, tradition-creation, and tradition-deconstruction describe the closeness of fit between subsequent theoretical and empirical work and an original tradition. It is important to emphasize that they do not describe the degree of real scientific advance. Elaboration, for example, may be thin or thick, to redeploy Geertz's (1973) ethnographic standard. Traditions may be enriched and elevated by the processes of theoretical change we have identified, but they may also be impoverished and simplified, robbed of their sophistication, and denuded of some of their most powerful intellectual sustenance. If social science change can be progressive, therefore, it can be regressive as well.

Over the long run, the dynamics of traditions within a disciplinary community (cf. Shils 1970)—the shifting fortunes of its theoretical positions—are not determined by the theoretical effectiveness and sophistication of the respective positions, nor by their objective empirical scope. Shifts in a discipline's "scientific sensibility" (Alexander 1986), usually precipitated by significant social and global developments (e.g., the anti-Vietnam-War movement, the Civil Rights struggle, and the push for democracy in Eastern Europe), put different questions on the floor; they place a premium on the creation of different modes of discourse. Indeed, it is often only after highly generalized and discursive commitments (e.g., Gouldner 1970) are made to a new approach that increased theoretical sophistication and empirical scope emerge. It is in this sense that one can speak less of social scientific "development" than of social scientific "movements."

Disciplines (contra Merton 1968) should not be understood as being organized primarily by specialties defined by their empirical objects of investigation (i.e., into middle-range subfields like deviance, political sociology, and stratification). The deep structure of a discipline (Toulmin 1972) consists of the networks and literatures that are produced by the contact between empirical objects, ongoing traditions, and new disciplinary movements.

TRADITIONS AND COMPETITION

Competition plays a critically significant role in the cumulation and decline of social scientific knowledge. Indeed, according to our model, social science does not grow simply because of the compulsion to understand empirical reality, nor can its growth be measured merely in relation to the expansion of empirical knowledge or conceptual scope. The primary motor of social scientific change is conflict and competition between and within traditions. The primary reference points for measuring scientific growth are established by the relations between traditions and by signposts internal to a given tradition itself. Instead of speaking about theoretical or empirical progress per se, one must speak of relative explanatory and theoretical success, vis-à-vis one's own tradition or competing ones (B. Turner 1989).

Every ideal-typical pattern of knowledge cumulation and decline is driven by competition. Implicitly or explicitly, every scientific statement claims to be more incisive or compelling on some point(s) than previous work. Accordingly, potential contributions are always partially assessed by comparison to earlier efforts.

Competition occurs in both discursive genres, and it occurs between and within traditions. At the level of generalized discourse, competition proceeds through disputes centered about a tradition's residual categories, its analytic and empirical breadth, its theoretical acumen in interpreting the classics, its avowed or implied ideological stance, its resonance with the epoch's reigning issues and social movements, its logical coherence (or lack thereof) as expressed through its conceptual schemes, and its utility for empirical investigation. At the level of research programs, competition is organized around rival attempts to explain empirical structures and processes regarded as significant by the discipline. In either case, a tradition advances when it issues statements deemed superior relative to comparable work produced by other schools.

At any given time, the field on which traditions compete is organized hierarchically.[4] Traditions are invidiously compared, and a small subset are accorded high levels of prestige. Such recognition is contingent on intermittent displays of scholarly virtuosity. Advantages accruing to those affiliated with prestigious traditions (e.g., greater publishing opportunities and a larger audience for those publications) unquestionably can facilitate the production of first-rate work. At the same time, however, the more renowned a school, the more likely its products will be subject to rigorous scrutiny. This disciplinary judgment that a tradition is especially illustrious encourages competing schools to frame their discussions as critical alternatives to the reigning approach. Proponents of less esteemed paradigms are constrained to demonstrate their tradition's relative merit by highlighting its theoretical and empirical strengths vis-à-vis more hegemonic paradigms. Thus a recent discussion of the Chicago school's "second generation" (i.e., the contributions of many of the sociologists who received their Ph.D.s from the University of Chicago's Department of Sociology between 1945 and 1960) indicates that Chicago sociology's generalized discourse as well as its research programs in role theory, deviance, social problems, the professions, formal organizations, and collective behavior and social movements were presented as critical responses to the then prominent functionalist tradition (Colomy and Brown forthcoming).

When a tradition is challenged, and especially when the challenge is regarded as legitimate and meritorious, its proponents are obliged to respond. For a variety of reasons, however, an insular strategy may be embraced with advocates presenting only occasional, perfunctory rebuttals or dismissing virtually all outside criticism as uninformed and unwarranted. In the short run, an insular strategy can sustain stability and some intellectual progress, primarily through elaboration and proliferation. In the long term, however, isolationism tends to delegitimate a tradition in the eyes of the disciplinary community and leads to its eventual eclipse.

Competition spurs incomplete or incipient traditions to devise more comprehensive formulations. Research programs that have not yet devised a complementary body of generalized discourse are highly vulnerable to metatheoretical critiques explicating the implicit and often restrictive assumptions upon which the research is premised. Thus despite the impressive empirical advances generated by the status attainment program, its failure to develop an explicit metatheoretical rationale led some to discredit it as atheoretical (e.g., Buroway 1977; Coser 1975) and others to suggest that the generalized discursive questions raised about the program have precipitated a crisis in status attainment research (Colclough and Horan 1983).[5] The most effective response to such charges, of course, is to articulate and defend the analytic grounds of the research program. Likewise, critics frequently assail incipient traditions that emphasize generalized discourse to the apparent neglect of empirical research. In this context, Giddens's analytically innovative and sophisticated structuration theory has been indicted for its failure to devise a compelling research program (Gregson 1989; Muller 1990). Again, the most viable rejoinder is to demonstrate the tradition's empirical fruitfulness by launching research programs in several specialty areas. This retort is most persuasive, moreover, if the new research proves superior to extant programs affiliated with long-standing traditions. For instance, Saks (1983) rebukes neo-Marxists and neo-Weberians for their continuing dependence on the patrimony of discursive attacks leveled against earlier functionalist and interactionist treatments of the professions rather than devising a viable research program of their own. For more established traditions, competitors' critiques and alternative explanatory models constitute a conceptual and research agenda that the focal school can address through elaboration, proliferation, revision, and/or reconstruction of both its genres. Recent revisions of the functionalist research program on social change, for example, are self-consciously presented as rejoinders to the charges leveled by the theory's critics (Colomy 1986; Alexander and Colomy 1990a).

Because established traditions constantly change and new schools frequently emerge, the boundaries linking and separating paradigms are regularly subject to reassessment. Typically cast as discussions of the similarities and differences between competing schools and usually pitched at the level of generalized discourse,[6] this intertradition boundary work—whether between symbolic interaction and ethnomethodology (Zimmerman and Wieder 1970; Gallant and Kleinman 1983), neofunctionalism and structuration theory (Muller 1990), feminism and Parsonian theory (Johnson 1988, 1989), Marxist and Weberian theory (Antonio and Glassman 1985; Wiley 1987), or postmodernist and critical theory (Habermas 1981, 1987; Kellner 1989, 1990)—can clarify and reaffirm existing divisions, introduce alterations in the intellectual core of one or more traditions, and/or, by highlighting previously unrecognized commonalities, lay the groundwork for syntheses of variable scope between approaches once regarded as largely irreconcilable.

As the preceding remarks imply, traditions are not hermetically sealed and competition between them can produce some convergence in both generalized discourse and research programs. When members of antagonistic schools address a similar problem and draw on some of the same intellectual resources to resolve it, their theorizing and research frequently reveal agreements alongside continuing differences. Highlighting common themes in the work of scholars affiliated with several rival approaches, Ritzer (1990c), for example, detects a diffuse, cross-tradition movement toward a synthetic position on the micro-macro issue. Commonalities can also emerge through expropriation, which occurs when proponents of a given approach openly appropriate an idea developed by competitors and employ it, usually with significant modifications, to extend their home traditions. Collins (1985, 1988), for instance, adopts the neofunctionalist notion of multidimensionality to advance a more inclusive version of conflict theory.

Over time, competition engenders significant changes on the disciplinary field. Established and highly regarded traditions are discredited and sometimes disappear, lowly ranked schools gain prominence, and new paradigms flourish. The alterations reflect schools' varying ability to fashion persuasive responses to both the critiques issued by rival traditions and shifts in disciplinary sensibility stemming from encompassing global and societal transformations. The difficulties in responding satisfactorily to these recurring challenges are enormous, and it is not surprising that most traditions experience periods of crisis or that many expire shortly after they are initiated. To persist, traditions must change and those that last for more than a generation are almost always substantially revised and reconstructed. Antonio (1990) suggests that Marxism has been periodically declared intellectually bankrupt only to renew and reconstitute itself and reappear phoenix-like on the disciplinary scene. We would add only that Antonio's characterization is applicable to every enduring social scientific tradition.

The discussion thus far has proceeded as if each tradition was an intellectually consensual community. By definition there is considerable consensus among a school's adherents, but this does not prevent serious disagreements from arising. Indeed, most schools contain two or more tradition segments[7] that although affiliated with the same encompassing framework and pledging scientific fealty to the same classic progenitor(s) nevertheless make disparate commitments at one or more levels of the scientific continuum. Although personal considerations undoubtedly play an important role and the availability of resources such as stable employment, students, funding, and publishing outlets exert a powerful conditioning effect, the fault lines along which tradition segments arise and the intellectual grounds used to support them are most readily understood as fundamental disagreements about the school's generalized discourse and research programs. For example, Meltzer and Petras (1970; see also Meltzer, Petras, and Reynolds 1975; Buban 1986; Reynolds 1990) maintain that though the (old) Iowa and Chicago schools of symbolic interactionism shared many assumptions about social action and order and acknowledged Mead as the founding figure of their school, their conflicting assumptions about methodology, determinism, and the nature of the self prompted the formation of distinct tradition segments.

Virtually every enduring tradition generates competing tradition segments; the longer a school persists the more segments it will create. Perhaps no social scientific tradition can stake a more rightful claim to longevity than Marxism and few if any have produced a larger number of segments, with distinctive renditions branching off at nearly every point along the scientific continuum (e.g., Alexander 1982b, p. 328-70; Bottomore 1975, 1978, 1988; Bottomore and Goode 1978; Anderson 1976, 1983; Antonio 1990; Aronson 1985).

Relations among tradition segments are always competitive, but the competition ranges from the friendly and mutually enriching type to more divisive forms that precipitate rancorous, public breaks and the formation of extremely hostile moieties. Even in the latter case, however, competition between segments can be among the most productive modes of scholarly exchange, resulting in significant contributions to every type of knowledge cumulation. Because all parties are well versed in the tradition's generalized discourse and research programs and are cognizant of the school's analytic and empirical shortcomings, disputants can prepare astute critiques and equally informed replies. In some instances, a segment's proponents may adopt an insular strategy in reaction to another's challenges, but such isolation is even more difficult to sustain among competing segments than it is between rival traditions.

The tendency to structure the disciplinary field hierarchically recurs among tradition segments. Depending on the number of competing segments within a school, there is a tendency to cast one or two segments in starring roles, while relegating others to much smaller parts. This invidious division places the intellectual burden of proof on the latter camp and in order to demonstrate their relative scientific prowess, insurgent segments can be expected to emphasize how their contributions account for anomalies more established segments purportedly cannot explain.

Founders of traditions that subsequently splinter into competing strands are usually associated with the school's most preeminent segment. So long as the founder continues to produce, it is unlikely that challengers will supplant his or her segment's privileged position.[8] Successful challenging segments more typically appear either after the founder's death or during dramatic shifts in disciplinary sensibility.

The disciplinary community as a whole tends to minimize differences between competing segments, treating a particular approach as a single and more or less coherent whole. Maynard and Clayman (forthcoming) note that despite the diversity within ethnomethodology, commentators usually treat it as a unitary perspective. Apart from the intellectual commonalities and personal relations that may bind adherents of rival segments, this disciplinary perception engenders an externally imposed sense of shared fate that encourages various forms of what might be called tradition teamwork (Goffman 1959) vis-à-vis the larger discipline. That teamwork is manifest in founding scholarly associations, securing official recognition for specialty areas deemed crucial to the tradition, engaging in collaborative publishing ventures, and defending the work of competing segments from criticism by adherents of rival traditions.

Finally, it is important to recognize that although competition generates winners and losers,[9] it is hardly an infallible mechanism for advancing knowledge. Competition between and within schools is as much a sociological process as an epistemological one, and the dynamics that propel it can impede genuine knowledge cumulation. Plainly put, the traditions or tradition segments that win in the social sciences do not always have the best arguments. The dynamics of fashion sometimes figure prominently in the rapid ascent of new traditions. Fashionable schools are not exempt from criticism—if nothing else scholarly communities are flush with critics—but the questions raised about the new approach may have little impact, at least in the short term, on the disciplinary community's assessment. On the other hand, the traditions or tradition segments that lose do not always advance the least defensible arguments. When debate is sharply divided and delegitimation of a rival school or segment becomes a primary objective, contrasting conceptions flourish and the focal tradition is often portrayed as devoid of any intellectual merit (Shibutani 1970). In a highly polarized context, the critique becomes stereotype, and the school under attack is known more by the litany of criticism leveled against it than by its own generalized discourse and research programs. Moreover, the intense commitments generated in these contexts erode the trust in mutual tolerance of disagreement that scholarly exchange requires (R. Turner and Killian 1987, p. 182) and render futile proponents' efforts to correct misrepresentations of their school. In short, a comprehensive account must acknowledge competition's crucial significance as a dynamic for advancing knowledge as well as its potential for undermining rational discourse.

CONCLUSION

By questioning the possibility of cumulative social knowledge, the recent wave of antipositivist thinking has raised fundamental questions about the very validity of a social science. Even the most articulate calls for a return to the discipline's founding faith concede that such a "bullish" position is premised on a willful inattentiveness to recent developments in the philosophy and history of science. It would seem as if the entire thrust of contemporary science studies must be bracketed if a social scientific theorizing that generates universal propositions and covering laws is to be pursued.

In an earlier period, Merton's (1968, 1987) middle-range strategy seemed to offer a way out of this kind of impasse. In retrospect, however, the very success of the Mertonian compromise may have been partially responsible for the fragmented character of social science today. Moreover, in light of the apparent gap between metatheory and empirical research noted by many contemporary observers, there is little available evidence to support Merton's prediction that progress in middle-range theory can serve as the foundation for building a viable general theory.

In the present period, one response to this dilemma would emphasize the importance of research programs rather than discrete empirical investigations, suggesting that such programs contain guidelines to connect an array of investigations in a limited number of substantive domains (Wagner 1984, forthcoming; Wagner and Berger 1985). This recommendation fails to appreciate the depth of the challenge that postpositivist science studies poses to contemporary social science. The critical effect of competition between perspectives is vastly underestimated, as is the role that general discourse plays in stimulating and framing the ongoing work within research programs.

If social science is once again to become a legitimate public activity, this crisis of confidence, which at its roots is no less than a crisis of confidence in reason itself (Alexander forthcoming), must be resolved. Our perspective offers the possibility that there are secure epistemological and, indeed, moral foundations for advances in the social sciences. For such a substantial conception of progress to be maintained, however, positivism must be fundamentally reconstructed and a new model of social scientific growth erected in its place.

NOTES

1. Recently, J. Turner (1990) has tempered his antipathy to metatheory and suggested that it is useful "when the goal is to produce scientific sociology" (p. 50). However, he remains highly critical of other forms of metatheory that in his view do not advance sociology as a science.

2. These broader ramifications are briefly discussed in the concluding section of this chapter and in much greater detail in Alexander and Colomy (unpublished).

3. This section elaborates an argument we have developed elsewhere (Alexander and Colomy 1990b).

4. Furthermore, competition is affected by the unequal distribution of material and symbolic resources across traditions that condition the production and reception of sociological discourse. These issues are examined in Alexander and Colomy (unpublished).

5. Horan (1978) disputes the contention that status attainment research is atheoretical. He contends that the program is premised on a functionalist conception of social structure—one he regards as analytically restrictive and, therefore, vulnerable to criticism on discursive grounds.

6. Intertradition boundary work also occurs at the level of research programs. Handel (1979), for instance, outlines a synthesis of functionalist and interactionist treatments of the structure and dynamics of social roles. However, in this case, as in many other efforts to integrate rival research programs, the proposed synthesis proceeds by specifying complementarities in the generalized theoretical logic of each program. Similarly, attempts to highlight differences between competing research programs—e.g., Collins's (1971) contrast between functionalists, and conflict theorists' studies of education—point to disparities in each program's underlying assumptions. The central point is that generalized discourse figures prominently in most intertradition boundary work, even when the connections or discrepancies between particular research programs are the primary concern.

7. The notion of tradition segments is adapted from Bucher and Strauss's (1961) discussion of professional segments. Their analysis highlights the diversity and conflict

within professions and suggests that competition between segments is an important source of change in professional communities.

8. When a splinter group competes on equal (or nearly equal) terms with the founder, it is often because the insurgent segment is itself organized around an intellectually charismatic challenger.

9. Competition can also produce stalemates. Focusing on rival research programs, Wagner (1984) argues that because competitors disagree about (a) the criteria appropriate for evaluating competing theories, (b) how to apply criteria they agree are appropriate, (c) the relevance of existing data, and (d) the interpretation of the data they agree is relevant, and because comparisons of competing theories tend to degenerate into irresolvable metatheoretical disputes, "competition is not a very efficient form of theory growth" (p. 75). It should be noted that in subsequent work Wagner has formulated a more comprehensive statement, arguing that in the context of contesting theoretical research programs competition can advance social scientific knowledge (Wagner and Berger 1985; Wagner 1984, pp. 104-5).

REFERENCES

Alexander, J. C. 1979. "Paradigm Revision and 'Parsonianism.' " *Canadian Journal of Sociology* 4:343-57.

———. 1982a. *Positivism, Presuppositions, and Current Controversies.* Berkeley: University of California Press.

———. 1982b. *The Antinomies of Classical Thought: Marx and Durkheim.* Berkeley: University of California Press.

———. 1986. "Science, Sense, and Sensibility." *Theory and Society* 15:443-63.

———. 1987a. "Action and Its Environments." Pp. 239-318 in *The Micro-Macro Link,* edited by J. C. Alexander, B. Giesen, R. Münch, and N. J. Smelser. Berkeley: University of California Press.

———. 1987b. "On the Centrality of the Classics." Pp. 11-57 in *Social Theory Today,* edited by A. Giddens and J. Turner. London: Polity Press.

———. 1990a. "Beyond the Epistemological Dilemma: General Theory in a Postpositivist Mode." *Sociological Forum* 5(4:531-544).

———. 1990b. "Between Progress and Apocalypse: Social Theory and the Dream of Reason in the Twentieth Century." Pp. 15-38 in *Rethinking Progress,* edited by J. Alexander and P. Sztompka. London: Unwin Hyman.

———. Forthcoming. "General Theory in the Postpositivist Mode: The 'Epistemological Dilemma' and the Search for Present Reason." In *Postmodernism and General Social Theory,* edited by S. Seidman and D. Wagner. New York: Basil Blackwell.

Alexander, J. C. and P. Colomy, eds. 1990a. *Differentiation Theory and Social Change.* New York: Columbia University Press.

———. 1990b. "Neofunctionalism Today: Reconstructing a Theoretical Tradition." Pp. 33-67 in *Frontiers of Social Theory: The New Syntheses,* edited by G. Ritzer. New York: Columbia University Press.

———. Unpublished. "The Structure and Dynamics of Traditions: Toward a Postpositivist Model of Knowledge Cumulation and Decline in the Social Sciences."

Anderson, P. 1976. *Considerations on Western Marxism.* London: NLB.

———. 1983. *In the Tracks of Historical Materialism.* London: Verso.

Antonio, R. J. 1990. "The Decline of the Grand Narrative of Emancipatory Modernity: Crisis or Renewal in Neo-Marxian Theory." Pp. 88-116 in *Frontiers of Social Theory: The New Syntheses*, edited by G. Ritzer. New York: Columbia University Press.

Antonio, R. J. and R. M. Glassman, eds. 1985. *A Weber-Marx Dialogue*. Lawrence: University Press of Kansas.

Aronson, R. 1985. "Historical Materialism, Answer to Marxism's Crisis." *New Left Review* 152:74-94.

Barnes, H. E. and H. Becker. 1952. *Social Thought from Lore to Science*, 2nd ed. Washington, DC: Harran Press.

Berger, J., D. G. Wagner, and M. Zelditch, Jr. 1989. "Theory Growth, Social Processes and Metatheory." Pp. 19-42 in *Theory Building in Sociology*, edited by J. Turner. Newbury Park, CA: Sage.

Blalock, H. 1976. "Implicit Theories Underlying Macro-Level Data Analysis: Measurement Errors and Omitted Variables." Pp. 76-100 in *New Directions in Sociology*, edited by T. Bottomore and R. Nisbet. Newton, MA: Abbott, David & Charles.

Bottomore, T. 1975. *Marxist Sociology*. New York: Holmes & Meier.

———. 1978. "Marxism and Sociology." Pp. 118-48 in *A History of Sociological Analysis*, edited by T. Bottomore and R. Nisbet. New York: Basic Books.

———, ed. 1988. *Interpretations of Marx*. Oxford, England: Basil Blackwell.

Bottomore, T. and P. Goode, eds. 1978. *Austro-Marxism*. Oxford, England: Clarendon.

Buban, S. L. 1986. "Studying Social Process: The Chicago and Iowa Schools Revisited." *Studies in Symbolic Interaction*, 2(Suppl.):25-38.

Bucher, R. and A. Strauss. 1961. "Professions in Process." *American Journal of Sociology* 66:325-34.

Buroway, M. 1977. "Social Structure, Homogenization, and the Process of Status Attainment in the United States and Great Britain." *American Journal of Sociology* 86:618-29.

Colclough, G. and P. M. Horan. 1983. "The Status Attainment Paradigm: An Application of a Kuhnian Perspective." *The Sociological Quarterly* 24:25-42.

Collins, R. 1971. "Functional and Conflict Theories of Educational Stratification." *American Sociological Review* 36:1002-19.

———. 1975. *Conflict Sociology*. New York: Academic Press.

———. 1985. "Jeffrey Alexander and the Search for Multi Dimensional Theory." *Theory and Society* 14:877-92.

———. 1986. "Is 1980s Sociology in the Doldrums?" *American Journal of Sociology* 91:1336-55.

———. 1988. *Theoretical Sociology*. New York: Harcourt Brace Jovanovich.

———. 1989. "Sociology: Proscience or Antiscience." *American Sociological Review* 54:124-39.

———. Forthcoming. "Sociological Theorizing." In *Postmodern and General Social Theory*, edited by S. Seidman and D. Wagner. New York: Basil Blackwell.

Colomy, P. 1986. "Recent Developments in the Functionalist Approach to Change." *Sociological Focus* 19:139-58.

———. 1990. "Revisions and Progress in Differentiation Theory." Pp. 465-95 in *Differentiation Theory and Social Change*, edited by J. C. Alexander and P. Colomy. New York: Columbia University Press.

Colomy, P. and J. D. Brown. Forthcoming. "The Chicago School and the Specter of Functionalism." In *The Second Chicago School of Sociology*, edited by G. A. Fine. Chicago: University of Chicago Press.

Coser, L. A. 1975. "Presidential Address: Two Methods in Search of a Substance." *American Sociological Review* 40:691-700.

Dilthey, W. 1976. "An Introduction to the Human Studies." Pp. 159-67 in *Dilthey: Selected Writings,* edited by H. P. Richman. Cambridge, England: Cambridge University Press.

Dogan, M. and R. Pahre. 1989. "Fragmentation and Recombination of the Social Sciences." *Studies in Comparative International Development* 24:1-18.

Durkheim, E. [1894] 1938. *The Rules of Sociological Method.* New York: Free Press.

Eisenstadt, S. N. and M. Curelaru. 1976. *The Forms of Sociology: Paradigms and Crises.* New York: John Wiley.

Ekeh, P. K. 1974. *Social Exchange Theory: The Two Traditions.* Cambridge, MA: Harvard University Press.

Friedrichs, R. W. 1970. *A Sociology of Sociology.* New York: Free Press.

Fuchs, S. and J. H. Turner. 1986. "What Makes a Science Mature? Organization Control in Scientific Production." *Sociological Theory* 4:143-50.

Fuhrman, E. and W. Snizek. 1990. "Neither Proscience nor Antiscience: Metasociology as Dialogue." *Sociological Forum* 5:17-31.

Gallant, M. J. and S. Kleinman. 1983. "Symbolic Interactionism Versus Ethnomethodology." *Symbolic Interaction* 6:1-18.

Geertz, C. 1973. "Thick Description: Toward an Interpretive Theory of Culture." Pp. 3-30 in *The Interpretation of Cultures,* by C. Geertz. New York: Basic Books.

Giddens, A. 1984. *The Constitution of Societies.* Oxford, England: Polity Press.

Giddens, A. and J. Turner. 1988. "Introduction." Pp. 1-10 in *Social Theory Today,* edited by A. Giddens and J. Turner. Oxford, England: Polity Press.

Gieryn, T. F. 1983. "Boundary-Work and the Demarcation of Science from Nonscience: Strains and Interests in Professional Ideologies of Scientists." *American Sociological Review* 48:781-95.

Gieryn, T. F., G. M. Bevins, and S. C. Zehr. 1985. "Professionalization of American Scientists: Public Science in the Creation/Evolution Trials." *American Sociological Review* 50:392-409.

Goffman, E. 1959. *The Presentation of Self.* New York: Doubleday.

Gouldner, A. 1970. *The Coming Crisis of Western Sociology.* New York: Basic Books.

Gregson, N. 1989. "On the (Ir)relevance of Structuration Theory to Empirical Research." Pp. 235-48 in *Social Theory of Modern Societies: Anthony Giddens and His Critics,* edited by D. Held and J. B. Thompson. Cambridge, England: Cambridge University Press.

Haan, N., R. N. Bellah, P. Rabinow, and W. N. Sullivan. 1983. *Social Science as Moral Inquiry.* New York: Columbia University Press.

Habermas, J. 1979. "Toward the Reconstruction of Historical Materialism." In *Communication and the Evolution of Society,* edited by J. Habermas. Boston: Beacon Press.

———. 1981. "Modernity Versus Postmodernity." *New German Critique* 22:3-14.

———. 1984. *Theory of Communicative Action,* vol. 1. Boston: Beacon Press.

———. 1987. *Lectures on the Philosophical Discourse of Modernity.* Cambridge, MA: MIT Press.

Handel, W. 1979. "Normative Expectations and the Emergence of Meaning as Solutions to Problems: Convergence of Structural and Interactionist Views." *American Journal of Sociology* 84:855-81.

Hollinger, R., ed. 1985. *Hermeneutics and Practice.* South Bend, IN: Notre Dame University Press.

Horan, P. M. 1978. "Is Status Attainment Research Atheoretical?" *American Sociological Review* 43:534-41.

Johnson, M. M. 1988. *Strong Mothers, Weak Wives.* Berkeley: University of California Press.

———. 1989. "Feminism and the Theories of Talcott Parsons." Pp. 101-18 in *Feminism and Sociological Theory*, edited by R. Wallace. Newbury Park, CA: Sage.

Kellner, D. 1989. *Critical Theory, Marxism, and Modernity*. Cambridge and Baltimore: Polity Press and John Hopkins University Press.

———. 1990. "The Postmodern Turn." Pp. 255-86 in *Frontiers of Social Theory: The New Syntheses*, edited by G. Ritzer. New York: Columbia University Press.

Kuhn, T. 1970. *The Structure of Scientific Revolutions*, 2nd ed. Chicago: University of Chicago Press.

Lakatos, I. 1968. "Criticism and the Methodology of Scientific Research Programmes." *Proceedings of the Aristotelian Society* 69:149-86.

———. 1970. "Falsification and the Methodology of Scientific Research Programmes." Pp. 91-196 in *Criticism and the Growth of Knowledge*, edited by I. Lakatos and A. Musgrave. New York: Cambridge University Press.

Laub, J. L. 1983. "Interview with Donald R. Cressey." Pp. 131-65 in *Criminology in the Making*, by J. L. Laub. Boston: Northwestern University Press.

Maynard, D. W. and S. E. Clayman. Forthcoming. "The Diversity of Ethnomethodology." *Annual Review of Sociology*.

Meltzer, B. N. and J. W. Petras. 1970. "The Chicago and Iowa Schools of Symbolic Interactionism." Pp. 3-17 in *Human Nature and Collective Behavior*, edited by T. Shibutani. New Brunswick, NJ: Transaction.

Meltzer, B. N., J. W. Petras, and L. T. Reynolds. 1975. *Symbolic Interactionism: Genesis, Varieties, and Criticism*. London: Routledge & Kegan Paul.

Merton, R. K. 1968. "On Sociological Theories of the Middle Range." Pp. 39-72 in *Social Theory and Social Structure* (enlarged ed.). New York: Free Press.

———. [1942] 1973. "The Normative Structure of Science." Pp. 267-78 in *The Sociology of Science*, edited by N. W. Storer. Chicago: University of Chicago Press.

———. 1987. "Three Fragments from a Sociologist's Notebooks." *Annual Review of Sociology* 13:1-28.

Muller, H. 1990. "Neofunctionalism or Structuration Theory." Paper presented at the annual meeting of the International Sociological Association, Madrid, Spain, July 11.

Mullins, N. 1973. *Theories and Theory Groups in Contemporary American Sociology*. New York: Harper & Row.

———. 1983. "Theories and Theory Groups Revisited." *Sociological Theory*. 1:319-37.

Parsons, T. 1937. *The Structure of Social Action*. New York: Free Press.

Reynolds, L. T. 1990. *Interactionism: Exposition and Critique*. Dix Hills, NY: General Hall.

Ritzer, G. 1975. *Sociology: A Multiple Paradigm Science*. Boston: Allyn & Bacon.

———. 1988. "Sociological Metatheory: A Defense of a Subfield by a Delineation of its Parameters." *Sociological Theory* 6:187-200.

———, ed. 1990a. *Frontiers of Social Theory: The New Syntheses*. New York: Columbia University Press.

———. 1990b. "Metatheorizing in Sociology." *Sociological Forum* 5:3-15.

———. 1990c. "Micro-Macro Linkage in Sociological Theory: Applying a Metatheoretical Tool." Pp. 347-70 in *Frontiers of Social Theory: The New Syntheses*, edited by G. Ritzer. New York: Columbia University Press.

Saks, M. 1983. "Removing the Blinkers? A Critique of Recent Contributions to the Sociology of Professions." *Sociological Review* 31:1-21.

Seidman, S. 1983. *Liberalism and the Origins of European Social Theory*. Berkeley: University of California Press.

Shibutani, T. 1970. "On the Personification of Adversaries." Pp. 223-33 in *Human Nature and Collective Behavior*, edited by T. Shibutani. New Brunswick, NJ: Transaction.

Shils, E. 1970. "Tradition, Ecology, and Institutions in the History of Sociology." *Daedalus* 99:760-825.

Stinchcombe, A. L. 1968. *Constructing Social Theories*. New York: Harcourt Brace Jovanovich.

———. 1986. "Reason and Rationality." *Sociological Theory* 4:151-66.

Tiryakian, E. A. 1979. "The Significance of Schools in the Development of Sociology." Pp. 211-23 in *Contemporary Issues in Theory and Research*, edited by W. E. Snizek, E. R. Fuhrman, and M. K. Miller. Westport, CT: Greenwood.

———. 1986. "Hegemonic Schools and the Development of Sociology: Rethinking the History of the Discipline." Pp. 417-41 in *Structures of Knowing*, edited by R. Monk. Lanham, MD: University Press of America.

Toulmin, S. 1953. *The Philosophy of Science*. New York: Harper & Row.

———. 1972. *Human Understanding*, Vol. 1, *The Collective Use and Evolution of Concepts*. Princeton, NJ: Princeton University Press.

Turner, B. 1989. "Some Reflections on Cumulative Theorizing in Sociology." Pp. 131-47 in *Theory Building in Sociology*, edited by J. H. Turner. Newbury Park, CA: Sage.

Turner, J. H. 1985. "In Defense of Positivism." *Sociological Theory* 3:24-30.

———. 1989a. "The Disintegration of American Sociology." *Sociological Perspectives* 32:419-33.

———. 1989b. "Can Sociology Be a Cumulative Science?" Pp. 8-18 in *Theory Building in Sociology*, edited by J. H. Turner. Newbury Park, CA: Sage.

———. 1990. "The Misuse and Use of Metatheory." *Sociological Forum* 5:37-53.

———. 1991. *The Structure of Sociological Theory*, 5th edition. Belmont, CA: Wadsworth.

———. Forthcoming. "The Promise of Positivism." *In Postmodernism and General Social Theory*, edited by S. Seidman and D. Wagner. New York: Basil Blackwell.

Turner, R. H. and L. Killian. 1987. *Collective Behavior*, 3rd ed. Englewood Cliffs, NJ: Prentice-Hall.

Turner, S. P. 1988. "The Strange Life and Hard Times of the Concept of General Theory in Sociology: A Short History of Hope." Paper presented at the Albany Conference on General Social Theory and Its Critics: Contemporary Debates. Albany, NY, April 15 and 16.

Turner, S. P. and J. H. Turner. 1990. *The Impossible Science: An Institutional Analysis of American Sociology*. Newbury Park, CA: Sage.

Wagner, D. G. 1984. *The Growth of Sociological Theories*. Beverly Hills, CA: Sage.

———. Forthcoming. "Daring Modesty: On Metatheory, Observation, and Theory Growth." In *Postmodernism and General Social Theory*, edited by S. Seidman and D. Wagner. New York: Basil Blackwell.

Wagner, D. G. and J. Berger. 1985. "Do Sociological Theories Grow?" *American Journal of Sociology* 90:697-728.

Wallace, W. L. 1983. *Principles of Scientific Sociology*. Chicago: Aldine.

Wiley, N. 1979. "The Rise and Fall of Dominating Theories in American Sociology." Pp. 47-79 in *Contemporary Issues in Theory and Research*, edited by W. E. Snizek, E. R. Fuhrman, and M. K. Miller. Westport, CT: Greenwood.

———. 1985. "The Current Interregnum in American Sociology." *Social Research* 51:179-207.

———, ed. 1987. *The Marx-Weber Debate*. Newbury Park, CA: Sage.

Winch, P. 1958. *The Idea of Social Science and Its Relation to Philosophy*. London: Routledge & Kegan Paul.

Zetterberg, H. 1985. *On Theory and Verification in Sociology*. New York: Free Press.

Zimmerman, D. H. and L. Wieder. 1970. "Ethnomethodology and the Problem of Order: Comment on Denzin." Pp. 287-95 in *Understanding Everyday Life*, edited by J. Douglas. Chicago: Aldine.

Chapter 3

METATHEORY, CONCEPTUAL STANDARDIZATION, AND THE FUTURE OF SOCIOLOGY

WALTER L. WALLACE
Princeton University

TWO TYPES OF METATHEORY

THE TERM *METATHEORY* **IN SOCIOLOGY** has been applied to a wide range of subject matters: "Metatheory is concerned . . . with the study of theories, theorists, communities of theorists, as well as the larger intellectual and social contexts of theories and theorists" (Ritzer 1988, p. 188; see also p. 190). The present chapter, however, will say nothing about the study of "theorists" or "communities of theorists," and nothing about the study of their "larger intellectual and social contexts"—leaving all that to the history and sociology of sociology. I shall focus, instead, on what I regard as metatheory proper, namely, the narrowly descriptive (and sometimes prescriptive) study of theories per se.

Such study has taken two main directions so far: *Synthetic* metatheory sorts whole theories into two or more overarching categories.[1] *Analytic* metatheory parses each theory into two or more components and then sorts these components into categories representing various types of assumptions, observable variables, and causal relations among such variables.[2] Although acknowledging that synthetic metatheory makes important contributions to sociology (chiefly to

AUTHOR'S NOTE: My thanks to Gene Burns, to Jack Gibbs, and to the graduate and undergraduate students who over the years have participated in my courses on sociological theory, for their many helpful reactions to ideas expressed in this chapter.

formulating the dependent variables on which the sociology and history of sociological theory focus—and, of course, to textbook writing), this chapter concentrates on analytic metatheory.

Normally, analytic metatheory sorts the deductively lowest level constituents of a theory into categories that have *empirical* referents (either directly or indirectly)—although it has recently been claimed that the categories should have *nonempirical* referents. My own assertion that "sense-based intersubjective verification is indispensable to every natural science [including sociology]" (Wallace 1983, p. 357) stands on one side of this issue; Alexander's (1982b) assertion that we should bring sociology "closer to nonempirical standards of objectivity," together with his proposed "requirements for achieving objectivity in a nonempiricist context" (pp. 115, 114) stand on the other side—although there is reason to doubt that he holds this position in its literal sense.[3]

The significance of requiring the lowest level categories of analytic metatheory to have empirical referents is well expressed by Carnap's (1966) "Consider the law: 'When iron is heated, it expands.' Another law says 'When iron is heated it contracts.' . . . The first law is accepted, rather than the second, only because it describes a regularity observed in nature" (p. 199, italics removed). To this it is essential to add that in the sciences the regularity in question must be observed by different investigators who, because they share a common technical language, are in position to confirm, question, or disconfirm each other's observations (see Popper 1961, pp. 44-48). Both these points are central to what follows.

THE CONTRIBUTIONS
OF EMPIRICAL ANALYTIC METATHEORY

Empirical analytic metatheory can contribute to (a) systematic cumulation of the *end-product* of sociological investigation (namely, collectively validated empirical knowledge about social phenomena); (b) systematic construction of new versions of the principal *means* employed in generating that end-product (namely, collectively shared theory and method); and (c) disciplinary *solidarity* among sociologists of all specializations—and, one hopes, eventually among social scientists of all disciplines. Let us consider these contributions more closely.

Cumulation of Sociological Knowledge

The obvious first point here is that knowledge can only cumulate when new knowledge of a given phenomenon is added to old knowledge of that *same* phenomenon (or more precisely, to the extent that no phenomenon is ever repeated exactly, that same type of phenomenon).

Such cumulation may occur both randomly and systematically. The key to random or chance cumulation of knowledge is simply duration. Given the random acquisition by different investigators of separate bits of knowledge across enough time, all possible knowledge cumulations will eventually occur. In the process, however, all possible *non*cumulations (i.e., discumulations, irrelevancies, and redundancies) will also occur. Consequently, *efficiency* in knowledge cumulation—wherein the time and energy required to achieve any given cumulation is minimized by deliberately reducing the incidence of noncumulations—devolves upon systematic cumulation.

The key to systematic cumulation of knowledge is *communication:* Only the passing to investigator B of the exact identity of the phenomenon investigator A has examined, together with the exact results of that examination, can make it possible for investigator B systematically to add new knowledge to that knowledge.[4] To enable that communication, the investigators must agree[5] on some set of common concepts, plus common rules for connecting the concepts to each other—which is to say, they must share a common *language.* Here it is important to note Durkheim's (1951) stress on the special cumulation-facilitating ability of concepts that have empirical ("objective") referents: "Conceptions with some objective foundation," he says, "are not restricted to the personality of their author. They have an impersonal quality which others may take up and pursue; they are transmissible. This makes possible some continuity in scientific labor—continuity upon which progress depends" (p. 36).

Basic Concepts in Sociology. Now it may be thought that we already share a common language in sociology, but by virtually all accounts, each of our two most basic concepts—namely, *social structure* and *culture*—signifies very different kinds of phenomena to different sociologists.

Social structure has been said to be "so fundamental to social science as to render its uncontested definition virtually impossible" (Udy 1968, p. 489), to attract "little agreement on its empirical referents" (Warriner 1981, p. 179), and to possess a meaning that "remains unclear" (Turner 1986, p. 407). Blau (1975) says, "The concept of social structure is used widely in sociology, often broadly, and with a variety of meanings. It may refer to social differentiation, relations of production, forms of association, value integration, functional inter-dependence, statuses and roles, institutions, or combinations of these and other factors" (p. 220). Gibbs (1989) says, "Sociologists use the term [social structure] in diverse ways, each of which is either so vague as to preclude empirical application or so broad as to include virtually all collective features of human behavior" (p. 234). And as recent evidence of this diversity, where Smelser (1988) claimed that "for sociologists, the units of social structure are conceived of . . . as *relational* characteristics" (p. 105, italics added), Coleman (1990) now refers to a type of "social structure" in which the participants "have *no relations*" (p. 276, italics added).

A similar history marks the term *culture*: In 1973, Schneider said that "by now just about everything has been thrown into 'culture' but the kitchen sink," and then reflected that "the kitchen sink has been thrown in too" as part of "material culture" (p. 119). Wuthnow, Hunter, Bergesen, and Kurzweil (1984) pointed out 11 years later that "theorists of culture remain sorely divided on how best to define culture" (p. 3); currently, Coleman (1990) refers to "values, orienta-tions, customs, language, norms, [religion,] and culture" (pp. 603, 604)—as though "culture" were somehow different from all these. No wonder Gibbs (1989) simply (but I believe, wrongly) gives up hope on "culture": "*Any* definition," he says, can promise "only negligible empirical applicability" (p. 275, italics in original).

Systematic knowledge cumulation at a discipline-wide level under such conditions is virtually nonexistent, even though there have long been important cumulations at subdisciplinary levels—that is, within research traditions, specialties, and subspecialties, and especially within individual careers and, of course, individual research pro-jects—where concepts specific to each level often have common and consistent meanings. This seems to be the likely, but unstated, basis for the claim that "sociological *traditions* are the critical units of analysis for assessing social scientific cumulation," and that "instead of speaking about theoretical or empirical progress per se, one must speak of . . . success vis-à-vis *one's own tradition*" (Alexander and Colomy 1990, pp. 2, 17, italics added).[6] That is to say, what needs stating here is that no tradition or specialty or subspecialty within a discipline can cumulate knowledge systematically unless it develops standard concepts (sometimes pejoratively called a *jargon*) for communicating knowledge among followers of the tradition. Indeed, it is just that set of standard concepts that constitutes the tradition.

The same requirement of concept standardization that applies to the tradition level also applies to the across-traditions, discipline-wide level of knowledge cumulation. And of course, it must eventually also apply to the across-disciplines, science-wide level of knowledge cumulation when we reach it centuries hence.[7]

Moreover, once concept standardization is achieved in the discipline as a whole, we may reasonably expect growing enhancement not only of the discipline-wide cumulation of knowledge, but of the discipline-wide planned pursuit of further knowledge. Here, Collins (1986) rightly says, "Precisely because of [its cumulation] science has hunches about what problems can now be tackled and what sorts of solutions are likely to emerge. Such continuity gives energy to research and enthusiasm to our intellectual work" (p. 1346). But what Collins leaves unsaid is crucial: Without standard concepts, neither systematic knowledge cumulation nor shared knowledge projection can exist. With such concepts, however, we can have them both.

Systematic Theory Innovation

The first contribution of empirical analytic metatheory, then, is to the efficient cumulation and shared projection (and, let us note with due emphasis, the teaching) of sociological knowledge along *existing* theoretical lines. Its second—and no less indispensable—contribution is to the creation of *new* theory.

By reducing existing theories to ordered sets of common types of constituents, empirical analytic metatheory instantly allows us to see that even the totality of all sociological theories proposed so far comes nowhere near exhausting the vast number of ways in which the elements in question can be interrelated. Thus empirical analytic metatheory facilitates not only comparing existing theories but also constructing new theories—systematically rather than haphazardly. (One is reminded of how the periodic table of chemical elements and the theory of chemical bonds suggest new chemical compounds that may be synthesized, and how dictionaries and grammatical rules suggest new sentences that may be constructed.)

Disciplinary Solidarity

The third contribution of empirical analytic metatheory is to the solidarity of sociologists. Gibbs (1989) says, "Sociology's fragmentation has accelerated since the 1950s . . . because of a proliferation of seemingly irreconcilable perspectives. . . . Never before has sociology been so fragmented, not just in North America but also in Europe" (p. 11). Arriving at similar conclusions, Turner (1989) says, "American sociology is 'falling apart' and losing . . . intellectual coherence" (p. 420); Smelser (1989) says "the current status [of sociology is] all periphery, no core" (p. 855); Collins (1986) says "we have become congeries of outsiders to each other, unable to see what the rivalries actually are in . . . fields [other than our own in sociology]" (p. 1340); and Rossi (1980) says the American Sociological Association is "paralyzed intellectually" by the "diversity of viewpoints among our members and [the] accompanying pluralism of substantive and professional paradigms" (p. 7).

It seems blindly self-destructive to continue holding our collective head in the sand any longer, hoping against hope that somehow this sense of fragmentation and paralysis will blow over, or that it really does not matter, or that some fantastic new theory will come thundering out of nowhere and bring us all to our feet, cheering. In my judgment, there cannot yet be a Newton or Darwin in sociology; no universally compelling general theory can yet be invented in our discipline. The reason is embarrassingly sociological: We do not yet possess enough of a common language in which such a theory must be formulated in order to be understood, tested, debated, and finally accepted across the discipline.

It is also this common language that can dramatically mitigate our growing sense of disciplinary fragmentation—as common languages have long been known to do in many other collectivities.

PAST ANTICIPATIONS AND PRESENT OPPOSITIONS

The idea of a common language in sociology is in no sense new. Durkheim's insistence on our having common definitions of the phenomena we investigate will be cited just below, but Weber's hope for the standardizing role of the "ideal type" warrants equal attention.

"An ideal-typical concept," Weber (1975) says, "is developed to facilitate empirically valid interpretation in the following way: the given facts are compared with a possible interpretation—an interpretive scheme" (p. 189; see also Weber 1949, pp. 43, 90). Thus, all who adopted a particular interpretive scheme would share a common understanding of whatever facts were compared to it—in just the same way that all who adopt a particular scale of spatial or temporal measurement (e.g., the gram, the meter, the minute) share a common understanding of the facts that are compared to it. And in order to achieve this common understanding, Weber (1949) is careful to say, ideal types must be constructed out of "the *most unambiguously intelligible concepts*" (p. 43, italics in original)—that is, unambiguously intelligible to *all*.

It is conceivable that Durkheim and Weber, though I believe them right on this, were ahead of their time; a few more decades of idiosyncratic poking around in the sociological vineyards may have had to take place—just as millenniums of informal usage were prerequisite for the first standardizing glossaries of natural languages. But in pursuing this preliminary exploration—exciting and fruitful as it was—we may have mistakenly come to believe that we do not need any discipline-wide standardization of concepts, and even if we needed it, we cannot achieve it. Let us consider these possibilities in turn.

We Do Not Need Conceptual Standardization

Durkheim's (1982) clear rejection of this idea, and his insistence on the indispensability of common definitions of the phenomena we sociologists investigate, goes as follows:

> Every scientific investigation concerns a specific group of phenomena which are subsumed under the same definition. The sociologist's first step must . . . be to define the things he treats so that we may know—he as well—exactly what his subject matter is. This is the prime and absolutely indispensable condition of any proof or verification. (p. 74)

In apparent accord with this view, Kroeber and Parsons (1958) warned that the "confusion among anthropologists and sociologists about the concepts of culture and society . . . has made for . . . confusion as to what data are subsumed under these terms . . . [and] impeded theoretical advance as to their interrelation," and called for achieving "consensus between and within disciplines" on both concepts (p. 582).[8]

Seeing no progress along these lines after 21 years, Blalock (1979) put forward a more comprehensive proposal—itself ignored for 12 more years. "What seems required [in sociology]," Blalock wrote,

> is a *self-conscious and coordinated* effort to focus on the basic concepts in the field, their clarity, overlap, inclusiveness, and implications for measurement strategies. The technical tools for theory building and data analysis are reasonably available, but many kinds of slippery and elusive conceptual problems remain at least as formidable as they were several decades ago. Here is where progress must be made if we are to achieve a true integration of theory and research. (p. 134)

In short, there appear to be some very good reasons for rejecting the belief that we do not need conceptual standardization in sociology.

We Cannot Achieve Conceptual Standardization

The belief that conceptual standardization cannot be *achieved* (no matter how much it may be *needed*) seems to rest on one or more of the following premises:

1. Social phenomena are too intrinsically complex and too inexplicably changeful; no standard way of classifying any one of them as similar to any other can be devised.
2. Sociologists are too individualistic in their thinking; pride would never permit us to reach consensus on any standardization—even if one were desirable and possible.
3. Sociological concepts are too dependent on the theoretical contexts in which they appear. Conceptual standardization would require discipline-wide acceptance of some particular theory—taken as an absolutely unique, indivisible, untranslatable.

Social Phenomena Are Too Complex and Too Changeful. Regarding the first part of this claim, it is difficult to ignore Weber's (1975) profound conjecture that

> *every* individual event, no matter how simple it may appear, includes an intensively *infinite* multiplicity of properties—if, that is, one *chooses* to conceive it in that way. It follows that no matter how complex a course of human "actions" may be, "objectively" it is in principle impossible for it to include *more* "elements" than could be identified in [any] single event in the physical world. (p. 124)

Regarding the second part of the claim, it is also difficult to ignore Durkheim's (1951) steadfast call to arms:

> The human mind would suffer a grievous setback if this segment of reality [i.e., human social phenomena] . . . should escape it even temporarily. There is nothing necessarily discouraging in the incompleteness of the results thus far obtained. They should arouse new efforts, not surrender. . . . Sociology should, then, renounce none of its aims; but, on the other hand, if it is to satisfy the hopes placed in it, it must try to become more than a new sort of philosophical literature. Instead of contenting himself with metaphysical reflection on social themes, the sociologist must take as the object of his research groups of facts clearly circumscribed . . . [for] by such concentration, real laws are discoverable. (pp. 36, 37)

Clearly, if we take these remarks of Weber and Durkheim at face value, we must reject the idea that social phenomena are in principle less liable than any other phenomena to investigation through the use of standardized concepts, and we must take seriously the fact that all the disciplines studying those other phenomena rely on such concepts.

Sociologists Are Too Individualistic in Their Thinking. This claim, of course, is an empirically testable one, but unfortunately the only publications I know of that seem directly relevant to it are my own discursive analyses of unsystematic samples of the classical and contemporary sociological literature (see also Wells and Picou 1981, pp. 107-24). These analyses have led me to conclude that we sociologists actually do share (but almost entirely without our knowing it) the same *generic* definitions of "social structure" and "culture." I contend that it is this consensus, however latent at present, that ultimately justifies calling ourselves a discipline rather than a mere heap of fundamentally incompatible traditions or specialties. Dispelling the long-standing manifest discord referred to earlier requires our becoming conscious and systematic about the nature of this consensus and promulgating it overtly.

For what it's worth, I allege these generic definitions to be the following: A *social structure* is defined as any observable interindividual *physical* behavior regularity—that is, people *doing* things together (in unison, exchange, or conflict with, or segregation from each other). A *cultural structure* (or culture) is defined as any observable interindividual *psychical* behavior regularity—that is, people *thinking/feeling* things together (in consensus, complementarity, or dissensus with or irrelevance to each other). There is much variability in the things people do together, and much variability in the things they think/feel together—and it is on this basis that we differentiate types of social structures and cultural structures (e.g., economic, political, educational, procreational). On the same basis, we then identify different types of substructures of social structures (e.g., superordinate, subordinate) and cultural structures (e.g., cognitive, affective), different types of substructures of these substructures, and so on. Add that all social and cultural structures and substructures manifest themselves in space and time, and we have defined sociological interest in their spatial location, extent, density, and patterning, as well as their temporal occurrence, duration, change, and stability. Finally, add that the *individuals* who participate in social structures and cultural structures may be nonhuman organisms as well as human ones, and we have defined sociological interest in owner-and-pet and horse-and-rider relations as well as sociobiological interest in such phenomena as slime molds, the Portuguese man-of-war, termite colonies, honeybee hives, fish schools, penguin crèches, elephant herds, and macaque, baboon, chimpanzee, and gorilla troops (see Wallace 1983, pp. 13-155, 1988, pp. 31-37).

The particular alleged generic definitions of social structure and culture that have just been cited, of course, may not be anything like the ones that should become standard in the discipline, and I may be wrong that there is already a latent consensus about these definitions, but they at least suggest the *possibility* of such definitions and such consensus.

Sociological Concepts Are Too Context Dependent. Garfinkel (1967) asserts that "a distinction between objective [i.e., context independent] expressions and indexical [i.e., context dependent] expressions is . . . unavoidable for whosoever would do science" and claims that the former are possible only in "the exact sciences"—of which sociology is not one (see p. 5). But an alternative possibility is that all expressions in all sciences—and in everyday talk, as well—are partly context independent and partly context dependent (and the proportions may depend not on the science but on the context one has in mind). Against Garfinkel, then, Durkheim (1982) emphasizes context independence:

> Since the definition . . . is made at the beginnings of the science its purpose could not express the essence of reality; rather it is intended to equip us in order to arrive

at this essence later. Its sole function is to establish the contact with things. . . . But it does not thereby explain them; it supplies only an initial framework necessary for our explanations. (p. 80)

Weber's (1949) emphasis is the same as Durkheim's: "The term 'social' . . . provides, when taken in its 'general' meaning, no specific *point of view*, from which the *significance* of given elements of culture can be analyzed" (p. 68, italics in original).

Steering between Garfinkel's position on the one hand and Durkheim's and Weber's on the other, it seems fair to conclude that although different theoretical contexts inevitably confer different connotations on the terms they use (thereby establishing some degree of context dependence), a common generic meaning is almost sure to underlie all usages of the same term in all theories (thereby establishing some degree of context independence). Otherwise, the requirements of communication soon compel us to define new terms if we wish to be understood.

Note, then, that it is only the generic empirical referents of concepts that should (or can) be standardized in sociology, or in any other discipline, or in everyday talk. This makes prior consensus on some particular theory unnecessary, as well as undesirable and infeasible. In any case, such consensus is certainly not being proposed here. In my judgment, to pursue consensus on a particular theory now would put the cart before the horse; in order to make an informed choice of such a theory, we should first be able to compare different alternatives in terms we can all understand.

THREE CAVEATS

In pursuing conceptual standardization in sociology, however, it seems important to bear in mind at least the following caveats. First, the discipline as a whole should concern itself only with standardizing (and periodically restandardizing) the handful of concepts used by the discipline as a whole—basic concepts such as *social phenomenon, society, social structure, culture, institution, status, role, norm,* and *value.* Too much conceptual standardization can choke off rather than systematize criticism and innovation.

Second, we should be self-consciously and perpetually tentative about any standardization we reach, and therefore permit nonconformity, encourage challenges, and welcome revisions.[9] Moreover, we should not exhaust ourselves trying to hit precisely the best standardization on our first shot. Pareto says, "Give me a fruitful error any time, full of seeds, bursting with its own corrections," and Bacon says, "Truth emerges more readily from error than from confusion." At this point in our history, any empirically referenced conceptual standardization will lead us out of confusion into fruitful error.

Third, there are undoubtedly many ways of achieving conceptual standardization in a scientific discipline, and no precedent in any other discipline can completely light the way for us. Nevertheless, the knowledge that the discipline of organic chemistry took more than 40 years of deliberate effort to reach this goal (they had many more concepts to deal with than we do) can give us a measure of confidence that the job is not impossible, that the pay-off is worth it, and that patience and fortitude will be useful (see Crosland 1962; Loening 1983; Lozac'h 1983).[10]

CONCLUSION

For all the reasons indicated above, the standardization of our basic concepts in sociology seems the single most important contribution we can make to the future of our discipline—not just for the next decade or two, but for many generations to come.

NOTES

1. Some synthetic typologies use categories based on the *time of origin* of different theories: Timasheff and Theodorson's (1976) typology includes "The Pioneers," "The Classical Writers," and "Major Contemporary Approaches to Sociological Theory"; Eisenstadt and Curelaru's (1976) typology includes "The First Two Stages of Institutionalization: Forerunners and Founding Fathers," "Sociology Between the Wars," and "Trends in Sociological Analysis and Activity After World War II." Some typologies use categories based on the *place of origin* of different theories: Bottomore and Nisbet (1978) include chapters on German, and American, sociology (see pp. 149-86, 287-320), and Gurvitch and Moore (1945) include chapters on French, American, British, German, Latin American, Italian, Spanish, Russian, and Eastern European sociology (see pp. 503-754). Some typologies use categories based on the central *substantive and/or causal imagery* of different theories: Turner's (1990) typology includes "Functional

Theorizing," "Conflict Theorizing," "Exchange Theorizing," "Interactionist Theorizing," and "Structural Theorizing"; Collins' (1988) typology includes "Evolutionism," "System Theories," "Political Economy," "Conflict and Social Change," and so on. Some typologies use *combinations* of time of origin and/or place of origin with thematic categories: Wiley's (1979) typology includes "the evolutionary period," "the Chicago school," "functionalism," and the "contemporary interregnum." Ritzer's (1983) typology includes "The Early Years" and "The Later Years," as well as "Structural-Functionalism and the Emergence of a Conflict Theory Alternative," "Varieties of Neo-Marxian Sociological Theory," "Symbolic Interactionism," and "Phenomenalism." Some typologies use *metamethodological* categories: Martindale (1979) classifies sociological theories according to whether they are "positivistic" or "nonpositivistic," and Martindale also uses *ideological* categories: "From time to time it makes sense to distinguish an Establishment sociology from an anti-Establishment sociology, or a radical sociology" (p. 23).

2. Whereas synthetic metatheory may concentrate on identifying the one or two *principal* assumptions, observable variables, and/or causal relations around which each whole theory is built and which it shares with other theories (e.g., functionalism, exchange, symbolic interactionism; see Note 1), analytic metatheory (ideally) identifies and then classifies *all* the assumptions, variables, and causal relations contained by a theory. I am aware of five sociologists now pursuing analytic metatheory. They, and the principal types of theory constituents they put forward, are Jeffrey C. Alexander (rational and nonrational "action," individualist and collectivist "order," and "the micro-macro dichotomy" [1982b, 1988; Alexander and Giesen 1987]); Donald N. Levine ("categorical frameworks, descriptive modalities, and explanatory logics" [1986, p. 275]), Jack P. Gibbs ("control" [1989]), James S. Coleman (individual and corporate "actors," "interests," and "rights" [1990]); and myself ("descriptive variables," "explanatory-predictive variables," and "causal images" [Wallace 1969, 1983, 1988]). Two important pioneers in analytic metatheory who focused on the assumptions and predispositions on which sociological theory rests are Friedrichs (1970) and Gouldner (1970).

3. This doubt affords hope for eventual discipline-wide consensus on an empirically referenced conceptual standardization of some kind, and the reasons for it therefore deserve brief examination here. The first of Alexander's (1982a) "nonempiricist" requirements calls for discipline-wide consensus about the "universal reference" of sociological theory, and although Alexander does not tell us what *kind* of "universal reference" he has in mind, it seems that it must be essentially *empirical* for the following reasons. If one refers (as Alexander once did) to sociology as a "science" and if one claims that "every scientific statement is the product of the interaction between . . . the *empirical* and the metaphysical" (pp. xviii-xix, italics added), it follows that no matter how much of any given scientific statement may be deemed "metaphysical" (and no matter what Alexander means by that term), *some* of that statement *must* be "empirical." Otherwise, according to Alexander's own argument, the statement cannot be scientific, and sociology, as the science Alexander and I both claim it is, cannot exist. I therefore conclude that what Alexander calls a "*non*empiricist context" is really an *empiricist* context—bearing in mind, of course, that no context can be *exclusively* empirical. On the latter point, Popper (1961) says, "If I am ordered: 'Record what you are now experiencing' I shall hardly know how to obey this ambiguous order. Am I to report that I am writing; that I hear a bell ringing; a newsboy shouting; a loudspeaker droning; or am I to report, perhaps, that these noises irritate me? . . . *A science needs points of view*" (p. 106, italics added; see also p. 280). As more recent evidence of Alexander's empiricism (self-denied though it may be), one notes Alexander and Colomy's (1990) claim, regarding "traditions" as sites of knowledge

cumulations in sociology, that "the most viable rejoinder [to critics] is to demonstrate the tradition's empirical fruitfulness" (p. 23).

4. In principle, the same requirement holds for investigator A's efficiently adding to his/her own knowledge: She/he must *remember* (i.e., self-communicate across time) the object and the knowledge already gained about it in order to be able to make a systematic addition to that knowledge.

5. More precisely, investigator B must agree with investigator A; A may be dead or otherwise prevented from agreeing with B.

6. Happily (from the present standpoint), the latter statement is immediately compromised by the phrase following it—"or competing [traditions]"—wherein the authors imply that one may, after all, speak (as I do here) about "theoretical or empirical progress per se" (i.e., progress across as well as within traditions).

7. Marx (1977) predicts that "natural science will in time incorporate into itself the science of man, just as the science of man will incorporate into itself natural science: there will be *one* science" (p. 98).

8. Bhaskar's more inclusive claim that "perhaps the most significant type of event in the history of *any* science is that in which it defines—redefines—its object of inquiry" (quoted in Fiske 1986, p. 73, italics added; see also Wigner, quoted in Fiske 1986, p. 74) is relevant here, too.

9. Thus it seems essential to recognize the welcome applicability to sociology of Loening's (1983) observation that "chemical nomenclature is not static; it changes with time just as the science of chemistry changes" (p. 54), and of Crosland's (1962) observation that "the independent attitude of individual chemists and of several national bodies has made the achievement of a uniform nomenclature only an imperfectly-attained goal" (p. 354).

10. The molecular biologists, too, are currently considering "a common language" to facilitate their "physical mapping of the human genome," and they are doing so under an assumption identical to that adopted here—namely, that "the importance of having a common language that would facilitate comparisons cannot be overemphasized" (see Olson, Hood, Cantor, and Botstein 1989, pp. 1434-35).

REFERENCES

Alexander, J. C. 1982a. *The Antinomies of Classical Thought: Marx and Durkheim.* Berkeley: University of California Press.
———. 1982b. *Positivism, Presuppositions, and Current Controversies.* Berkeley: University of California Press.
———. 1988. "The New Theoretical Movement." Pp. 77-102 in *Handbook of Sociology,* edited by N. J. Smelser. Newbury Park, CA: Sage.
Alexander, J. C. and P. Colomy. 1990. "The Structure and Dynamics of Traditions: Toward a Postpositivist Model of Knowledge Cumulation and Decline in the Social Sciences." Paper presented at the annual meeting of the American Sociological Association, Washington, DC, August.
Alexander, J. C. and B. Giesen. 1987. "From Reduction to Linkage: The Long View of the Micro-Macro Link." Pp. 1-44 in *The Micro-Macro Link,* edited by J. C. Alexander, B. Giesen, R. Münch, and N. Smelser. Berkeley: University of California Press.

Blalock, H. M. 1979. "Dilemmas and Strategies of Theory Construction." Pp. 119-35 in *Contemporary Issues in Theory and Research,* edited by W. E. Snizek, E. R. Fuhrman, and M. K. Miller. Westport, CN: Greenwood.

Blau, P. M. 1975. "Parameters of Social Structure." Pp. 220-53 in *Approaches to the Study of Social Structure,* edited by P. M. Blau. New York: Free Press.

Bottomore, T. and R. Nisbet. 1978. *A History of Sociological Analysis.* New York: Basic Books.

Carnap, R. 1966. *Philosophical Foundations of Physics.* New York: Basic Books.

Coleman, J. S. 1990. *Foundations of Social Theory.* Cambridge, MA: Harvard University Press.

Collins, R. 1986. "Is 1980s Sociology in the Doldrums?" *American Journal of Sociology* 91:1336-55.

————. 1988. *Theoretical Sociology.* San Diego, CA: Harcourt Brace Jovanovich.

Crosland, M. P. 1962. *Historical Studies in the Language of Chemistry.* Cambridge, MA: Harvard University Press.

Durkheim, E. 1951. *Suicide.* New York: Free Press.

————. 1982. *The Rules of Sociological Method.* New York: Free Press.

Eisenstadt, S. N. with M. Curelaru. 1976. *The Form of Sociology—Paradigms and Crises.* New York: John Wiley.

Fiske, D. W, 1986. "Specificity of Method and Knowledge in Social Science." Pp. 61-82 in *Metatheory in Social Science,* edited by D. W. Fiske and R. A. Shweder. Chicago: University of Chicago Press.

Friedrichs, R. W. 1970. *A Sociology of Sociology.* New York: Free Press.

Garfinkel, H. 1967. *Studies in Ethnomethodology.* Englewood Cliffs, NJ: Prentice-Hall.

Gibbs, J. P. 1989. *Control: Sociology's Central Notion.* Urbana, IL: University of Illinois Press.

Gouldner, A. W. 1970. *The Coming Crisis of Western Sociology.* New York: Basic Books.

Gurvitch, G. and W. E. Moore. 1945. *Twentieth Century Sociology.* New York: Philosophical Library.

Kroeber, A. L. and T. Parsons. 1958. "The Concepts of Culture and of Social System." *American Sociological Review* 23:582-83.

Levine, D. N. 1986. "The Forms and Functions of Social Knowledge." Pp. 271-83 in *Metatheory in Social Science,* edited by D. W. Fiske and R. Shweder. Chicago: University of Chicago Press.

Loening, K. L. 1983. "Standardisation of Chemical Nomenclature." In *Chemical Nomenclature Usage,* edited by R. Lees and A. Smith. Chichester, England: Ellis Horwood.

Lozac'h, N. 1983. "Nomenclature: The Way Ahead." In *Chemical Nomenclature Usage,* edited by R. Lees and A. F. Smith. Chichester, England: Ellis Horwood.

Martindale, D. 1979. "Ideologies, Paradigms, and Theories." Pp. 7-24 in *Contemporary Issues in Theory and Research,* edited by W. E. Snizek, E. R. Fuhrman, and M. K. Miller. Westport, CN: Greenwood.

Marx, K. 1977. *Economic and Philosophic Manuscripts of 1844.* Moscow, USSR: Progress.

Olson, M., L. Hood, C. Cantor, and D. Botstein. 1989. "A Common Language for Physical Mapping of the Human Genome." *Science* 245:1434-35.

Popper, K. R. 1961. *The Logic of Scientific Discovery.* New York: Science Editions.

Ritzer, G. 1983. *Contemporary Sociological Theory.* New York: Knopf.

————. 1988. "Sociological Metatheory: A Defense of a Subfield by a Delineation of Its Parameters." *Sociological Theory* 6:187-200.

Rossi, P. H. 1980. "The President Reports." *Footnotes* 8:1, 7.

Schneider, L. 1973. "The Idea of Culture in the Social Sciences: Critical and Supplementary Observations." Pp. 118-44 in *The Idea of Culture in the Social Sciences*, edited by L. Schneider and C. M. Bonjean. Cambridge, England: Cambridge University Press.

Smelser, N. H. 1988. "Social Structure." Pp. 103-30 in *Handbook of Sociology*, edited by N. H. Smelser. Newbury Park, CA: Sage.

———. 1989. "Reviewing the Field of Sociology: A Response." *Contemporary Sociology* 18:851-5.

Timasheff, N. S. and G. A. Theodorson. 1976. *Sociological Theory*, 4th ed. New York: Random House.

Turner, J. 1986. *The Structure of Sociological Theory*, 4th ed. Chicago: Dorsey.

———. 1989. "The Disintegration of American Sociology." *Sociological Perspectives* 32:419-33.

———. 1990. *The Structure of Sociological Theory*, 5th ed. Belmont, CA: Wadsworth.

Udy, S. H., Jr. 1968. "Social Structure: Social Structural Analysis." In *International Encyclopedia of the Social Sciences*, Vol. 14, edited by D. L. Sills. New York: Free Press.

Wallace, W. L. 1969. "Overview of Contemporary Sociological Theory." Pp. 1-59 in *Sociological Theory: An Introduction*, edited by W. L. Wallace. Chicago: Aldine.

———. 1983. *Principles of Scientific Sociology*. Hawthorne, NY: Aldine.

———. 1988. "Toward a Disciplinary Matrix in Sociology." Pp. 23-76 in *Handbook of Sociology*, edited by N. J. Smelser. Newbury Park, CA: Sage.

Warriner, C. K. 1981. "Levels in the Study of Social Structure." Pp. 179-190 in *Continuities in Structural Inquiry*, edited by P. M. Blau and R. K. Merton. Beverly Hills, CA: Sage.

Weber, M. 1949. *The Methodology of the Social Sciences*. New York: Free Press.

———. 1975. *Roscher and Knies*. New York: Free Press.

Wells, R. H. and J. S. Picou. 1981. *American Sociology: Theoretical and Methodological Structure*. Washington, DC: University Press.

Wiley, N. 1979. "The Rise and Fall of Dominating Theories in American Sociology." Pp. 42-79 in *Contemporary Issues in Theory and Research*, edited by W. E. Snizek, E. R. Fuhrman, and M. K. Miller. Westport, CN: Greenwood.

Wuthnow, R., J. D. Hunter, A. Bergesen, and E. Kurzweil. 1984. "Introduction." Pp. 1-20 in *Cultural Analysis*, edited by R. Wuthnow, J. D. Hunter, A. Bergesen, and E. Kurzweil. Boston: Routledge & Kegan Paul.

Chapter 4

PATHWAYS TO METATHEORY
Rethinking the Presuppositions of Macrosociology

EDWARD A. TIRYAKIAN
Duke University

IN A VOLUME DEVOTED TO "metatheorizing in sociology," it is incumbent on contributors to bring to bear their understanding of this theme prior to a more substantive discussion. George Ritzer (1988, 1990) has considerably advanced the attention given to metatheorizing, including his recent (1990) categorization of three main types as a function of their outputs. These, he argues, are (a) as means of attaining a greater level of understanding of a theory text, (b) as instrumental to theorizing proper, and (c) as source of metatheoretical perspectives (what Ritzer terms "perspectives that overarch sociological theory"). In the first section of this chapter, I take this as a point of departure for amplifying the discussion of metatheorizing, by advancing the argument that metatheorizing is, in one respect, a radical inquiry. In the second section, I propose the basis for recasting an overarching theoretical perspective in macrosociology, one that will be radical as a renovation of a frame of reference that was near paradigmatic a generation ago, was buried, and lay dormant for most of the following generation. I will term this *neomodernization analysis,* emphasizing here that I treat it as a frame of reference ("metatheory") rather than as a theory.

AUTHOR'S NOTE: This is a revised version of a paper presented at the annual meeting of the American Sociological Association, August 11, 1990, Washington, DC, session 71, "Metatheorizing in Sociology II": George Ritzer, organizer.

FORMS AND USES OF METATHEORY

In an earlier period of positivistic dominance, sociological theory or theorizing was seen as the endeavor to affirm objectively what may be called "the essential truth" of social systems in their becoming (structures and dynamics). Variations in theorizing occurred (as they still do) as a function of several factors, such as (a) what is taken to be the main independent variable(s) or causal factors producing the observed effects and (b) how inclusive of empirical phenomena, or levels of generalization, are the claims of the theorizing.

Concerning the latter, if theory T_1 claims that its propositions account for all salient characteristics of a given type of society S_1, irrespective of where S_1 is located in time and space, it claims a greater degree of generalization than theory T_2, which may claim to account for only some features of S_1 and/or at some points in time and space only. In the positivistic mode of theorizing, it is in the horizon of the theory project that at some finite point in the future, say t_j a complete theoretical account of the characteristics of types of social systems would be specifiable with a sufficient degree of empirical confirmation to enable the body of propositions to qualify as "scientific theory." The outcome of this theorizing would then be a set of coherent, consistent, interrelated propositions forming a logical system, on the one hand, and which, on the other hand, would be heuristic for empirical research and continuously validated by later observations. As part of this project of theorizing, the quest for "essential truth" was conducted in a framework of objectivity, because of a tacit tripartite equation: Scientific theorizing equals rational inquiry equals objectivity.

Sociological theorizing, if it was from the very first generation of sociologists (however broadly or narrowly we define that cohort from roughly 1820 to 1870), part and parcel of their sociological practice, did not itself constitute an object of sociological analysis until the present century. A landmark study here may be noted, namely, Sorokin's (1928) *Contemporary Sociological Theories*, which codified theories in terms of major schools and critically evaluated each major type and its underlying assumptions. That work may well qualify as one in sociological metatheorizing, and would qualify in terms of Ritzer's criteria, because Sorokin sought not only to evaluate the foundations of logically related works but also to point to a new theory that would be more consistent with empirical truths than previous theories.

Sorokin was very influential in making a new generation think of theory as a sociological domain in its own right, interdependent with substantive fields of research. Sorokin, after all, had this opportunity when he was called on to establish a new Department of Sociology at Harvard University. His first graduate student, Robert Merton (1967a, 1967b), certainly made the general relationships of theory and research the focus of two "classical" essays. But of course, for the discipline as a whole the person who made theorizing a specialty area in its own right as well as an implicit measure of theorizing in substantive fields was Talcott Parsons, initially a junior colleague of Sorokin's at Harvard, who by the next decade had eclipsed him in the national spotlight.

I would like to dwell on Parsons here for two major reasons: the linkage of theorizing to metatheorizing and his relevance to modernization and postmodernization analysis.

This section began with reference to an earlier "positivistic mode" of theorizing. Parsons and positivism have a complex relationship. In terms of giving centrality to values and norms as relating social actors to their situation, or more generally, in terms of the voluntaristic frame of reference that is central to *The Structure of Social Action* (1937) and all the later derivatives of his action theory, up to and including the last great essay published in his lifetime on the human condition (1978), Parsons must be situated at the antipode of positivism. One of his early essays (1935) may be read as a sort of antipositivistic manifesto, and his extensive discussion and critique of Durkheim's "early" (i.e., pre-*Elementary Forms*) positivism clearly indicate how incompatible Parsons thought positivism was with his own orientation.[1]

However, in theorizing as such, in reflecting about the nature of theorizing in sociology and for sociology, Parsons adopted a positivistic mode (unlike Sorokin, incidentally, who granted theorizing a multidimensional nature that allowed room for "intuition" and "insight" as part of his "integralist" mode of knowing the world). Consider in this context a very important transition essay (1945), in which Parsons posited the emergence of sociology into the privileged status of "a mature science." Crucial to this development is "a well-articulated generalized theoretical system" that is instrumental to codification and heuristic for research. Parsons's lengthy and detailed discussion of a theoretical system rested on a "frame of reference" as "the most general framework of categories in terms of which empirical scientific work 'makes sense' " (p. 44). His statement of the ultimate goal of scientific investigation to be the solution of problems of dynamic analysis (of interdependent variables), entailing causal explanation and the attainment of "laws," and the ensuing explication of structural categories in the treatment of dynamic problems of systems (pp. 46-49) provide the framework within an essentially positivistic discourse for an emergent "structural-functional theory of social systems" (p. 58).

It would be tangential here to examine the action frame of reference that Parsons laid out, and with it his strategy for theorizing about social systems in giving priority to the analysis of four levels of structural organization of "large-scale and complex societies" (Parsons 1959, p. 4; Alexander 1983). Nonetheless, I do wish to draw attention to a certain tension between the positivistic image of sociological analysis as "scientific theory" that Parsons embraced and the action frame of reference itself, the foundation of which is "phenomenological" (Parsons 1937, p. 750).

A phenomenological perspective takes objects as constituted in their perceived meaning for subjects (or actors), in subjects' lived experience of the world. Objects do not have an intrinsic meaning if by intrinsic is meant self-contained, apart from how they appear or are apprehended (and interpreted) by subjects. The subject (or actor) exists in a situation (i.e., in a meaningful environment)[2] consisting of a bounded field of objects, spatially and temporally structured. This standpoint, stemming from Husserl and Heidegger, blends into the well-known "social construction of reality" perspective that has diffused into sociology (Berger and Luckmann 1966).

In contrast to the positivistic quest for an "essential truth" of objective (social) reality that will be grasped by theory, new emphases of theorizing have become part of the intellectual landscape in the past 20 years or so. Much of this in the form of "hermeneutics," "deconstruction" or "poststructuralism" originates outside of sociology but is having echoes in sociological halls. Instead of providing accounts of social systems as objects to be explained, theorizing is about "texts," and perhaps it might be better to say that theorizing is about (con)texts and the interpretation of texts as an integral part of their constitution. In this respect, the new "postmodern," "poststructuralist" orientation has a deep-seated affinity with the key notions of reflexivity and indexicality in ethnomethodology, which ultimately derives from Garfinkel's (1967) readings of phenomenology (Husserl and Schutz) and of the early Parsons (Garfinkel 1967; Handel 1982; Leiter 1980; Mehan and Wood 1975).

Parsons had sought to develop general sociological theory as instrumental for making sociology a more exact science. He did succeed in making sociological theory a distinct specialty area, but the rejection of Parsonian theory as an objectively valid paradigm has of course led to an ambiguous situation of sociological theory. Although rejecting the Parsonian synthesis of major strands of sociological thought contained in *The Structure of Social Action,* sociologists have turned to new interpretations of the classical figures that Parsons allegedly misinterpreted,[3] to interpretations of *The Structure of Social Action* itself as a watershed in the history of sociological theory (Camic 1989; Tiryakian 1990a), and even to attempts to new general paradigms providing systematic micro-macro linkages (e.g., Coleman 1990). How successful these endeavors are in recasting sociological theory is beside the point, but what they are witnesses to is that a strong case can be made for Parsonian theory as a watershed in the history of sociological theorizing.[4] I will return to this in the second section of this chapter in dealing with modernization and modernity.

Metatheorizing has come into its own this past decade for various reasons and from various strands of analysis, several of which are linked to similar developments in other disciplines, including the humanities. A major external stimulus was new developments in the philosophy of science that reached the attention of sociologists, more or less at the same time that sociologists were rejecting the Parsonian "paradigm." A conjuncture of the widely read second edition of Kuhn's (1970) *The Structure of Scientific Revolutions,* the extension of Kuhn by Lakatos (1974) who gave a great deal of attention to the presuppositions of a "scientific research program" shared by a scientific community, and the collapse of a common language of sociological explanation with the rejection of "structural-functional analysis" led to a crisis of sociological theory during exactly the same period of national identity crisis in American society (approximately from 1966 to 1976). With the rejection of the theory canon, the discourse of metatheory stepped forward to fill the breach in the immediate post-Parsonian period. Let me propose some of the pathways out of Egypt to the promised land of renewed theoretical growth (assuming that metatheory is not an end itself but an activity instrumental to a higher level of theoretical explanation).

Given an emphasis on the structures that produce or underlie texts, one strand of metatheorizing is to be found in works that seek historical explanations or accounting of theory as text in terms of normative presuppositions. Gouldner's (1970) critique of Parsons was an important instance of this form of metatheorizing, which has as a basic perspective that texts (theories or theorists) are embedded in a social situation of domination, with the text having meaning as reflecting and/or maintaining that situation. Rather than this being a "secondary" meaning in making sense or explaining the text, it becomes a "primary" meaning for the critical theory or neo-Marxist analysis espoused by Gouldner, or more recently, for example, by feminists. A related metatheoretical historical analysis is that of Vidich and Lyman (1985), who examine the development of an underlying secularized Protestant orthodoxy in American sociological thought, which "as the successor to Protestant theology is compelled to assume the burden of providing a sociodicy" (p. 306).

Metatheorizing in the above vein of "uncovering" or "unmasking" the social context of dominance expressed in theories (of large-scale social systems of societies) has a well-recognized lineage in the Marxist tradition of the sociology of knowledge. It is in this sense a radical activity inasmuch as it seeks to lay bare class interests being maintained in the ideological or superstructural level of social organization; stated in other terms, metatheorizing may be viewed as an important liberating activity aimed against hegemony.

But this is too narrow a sense of *radical*. If we take the latter in its etymological sense, metatheorizing is a radical activity in bringing to light of rational inquiry the normative and axiomatic foundations layers of theory. It is not only the consciously held *suppositions* ("Given that . . . ," "Let us assume . . . ," etc.), but also a host of background, covert "domain assumptions" concerning the nature of the social order, reality, images of mankind, of what is sacred and profane, of the direction of history, and so forth. Together these sets of presuppositions provide the positive and negative heuristics of "scientific research programs" (Lakatos 1974) or the "tacit dimension" of knowing (Polanyi 1967). To elucidate these presuppositions or "deep structures" of theory is certainly instrumental to a clearer understanding of the power and limits of the theory, as Ritzer posited.

A second feature of metatheorizing is the rigorous examination of the intellectual, societal, and historical context of theory. This is where there is a major overlap between sociological metatheory and history of sociological analysis, taking note of Szacki's (1982) telling point that as a subfield, "the history of sociology is often less 'sociological' than is the history of other disciplines" (p. 366). To bring to the foreground the multidimensional context of even a single text of theory, as for example Parsons' (1937) *The Structure of Social Action* or Durkheim's (1965) *Elementary Forms*, or for that matter the theorist himself as text, as in the magisterial study of Lukes (1972), requires a very extensive effort that has few practitioners. To be sure, there is a great deal of partial elucidations of the context of theory, but this is done usually more as historical interpretation than as systematics oriented to theory development (Merton 1967a, 1967b).

There is another endeavor that I would consider metatheoretical, which if I read it correctly is the lesser discussed type in Ritzer's discussion (Chapter 1). Although he talks about one end-product of metatheorizing being a prelude to theory development, or alternatively the creation of new theory, he does not dwell on this. Let me suggest that metatheorizing in this aspect can prepare a new theory by two complementary strategies: the examination of sets of theories viewed as heterogeneous within sociology and the examination of sets of theories in other disciplines that may have a bearing on what sociological theory seeks to explain. So, let us say as an illustration of the first, sociological metatheory might examine the presuppositions of Durkheim's theory of anomie and Marx's theory of alienation and find an unexpected degree of compatibility. The metatheorizing would then examine other aspects of Marxist and Durkheimian theories and find structural similarities that have previously escaped attention. This and other products of this metatheoretical comparison might lay a foundation of common denominators suggesting the possibility of a new, more embracing sociological theory. I have sought to do this sort of metatheorizing in an essay discussing three successive "hegemonic schools" of sociology (Tiryakian 1986), which I considered as mutually compatible in terms of their presuppositions and cumulative in terms of theoretical content. Theorizing a new paradigm remains to be done, but at least this is an instance where what might appear to be a study in the history of sociology is really an endeavor of metatheorizing.

Finally in this regard, I would propose that Parsons' *The Structure of Social Action* may be viewed as the first modern work of sociological metatheory in the sense of metatheory discussed here. It was essentially the explication of a frame of reference based upon the examination of a set of theories, some located in sociology and some in other disciplines.

In the development of sociology, sociological analysis has frequently looked at other sciences and disciplines for models that might bring a more elegant explanation of pertinent social phenomena than otherwise available. Physiology and biology have been stimuli for the sociological imagination from the first (for Saint-Simon, Spencer, Durkheim) down to the more modern period (recall the extensive use Parsons made of homeostasis). Economics has been an equally important source of sociological models, with many adaptations of the utilitarian and neoclassical paradigm throughout the 19th and 20th centuries, right to the present in the form of rational choice models (Friedman and Hechter 1988). There has been a two-way exchange of conceptual frameworks between anthropology and sociology, often the result of organizational structure of joint departments or the training of sociologists in field research in collaboration with anthropologists. A good deal of "functional analysis" in sociology has an anthropological genealogy that can be traced to Malinowski and Radcliffe-Brown; sociological community studies (going back to the Lynds and to Warner) have a logic of inquiry based on an anthropological holistic approach, and this extends even to studies of industrial and corporate settings (e.g., Kanter 1977). The application of such anthropological notions as "liminality" and "rituals," to say nothing of "culture," to a wide range of sociological accounts of contemporary settings, institutions, and interaction processes also attests to the extensive use made of anthropology in sociological theorizing.

By and large this second strategy that I have briefly illustrated has not been rigorously and systematically carried out. Very often sociologists have taken not a theory or a model in a proper sense but only a concept, and even that when it is examined carefully is not so much an analytical concept as a metaphor. To explain a set of social phenomena in terms of what boils down to a metaphor is not to provide a (scientific) explanation but at best an image of the phenomena. *Metatheorizing here would be the critical examination of the adequacy of transferring or borrowing from another discipline theories or models or concepts used in sociological explanation.*

We may think in this context of metatheorizing as having a double function in relating sociological theory to other, extrasociological theories. The first, just mentioned, is to avoid misinterpreting or misusing concepts, theories, models, and so forth of other disciplines in sociological explanations. Metatheorizing here is to protect sociological theory from sins of commission—in other words, from invalid applications. The second is to avoid sins of omission, in the sense that a task of metatheorizing is to examine other disciplines (and not only the ones with which sociology has had extensive interchanges) for theories, models, concepts, and so forth that may have relevance for sociological explanation but that might otherwise be overlooked or neglected because their subject matter seems too "exotic." Such disciplines may range from humanistic ones (e.g., literary theory, hermeneutics) to natural sciences (e.g., cybernetics, neurobiology, cognitive psychology). Metatheorizing in this second function is to advance the systematics of theory by bringing to bear heuristics from other disciplines.

The dual "gatekeeping" function briefly discussed above is what I consider a promising area of expansion for sociological metatheorizing. To implement it calls for dialogues between sociologists and their colleagues in other disciplines. Necessary here is a training for sociological theorists in disciplines other than their own, at least to develop familiarity with the current literature and theorizing in one other discipline. Although a sociologist cannot have the "grammar" and "vocabulary" of a "native speaker," to have a dialogue or an understanding of the other's explanations does require a secondary training, and the sooner in one's academic career the better. This is easier said than done, because graduate training programs in sociology are more likely to be hermetic than open to other disciplines. It is hard enough at present for sociological theory to have a major place in the training of sociologists; to seek a place in the training program for metatheorizing (which, of course, should not be reduced to methodology) is really a radical demand. Let us hope that this volume and related activities by George Ritzer and his associates will enable this demand to get a favorable response.

METATHEORIZING MACROSOCIOLOGY: NEOMODERNIZATION ANALYSIS

Although the first section has covered a wide range of aspects of metatheory, this section will be concerned with just one, namely with what Ritzer views as the generation of "overarching perspectives." The perspective to be proposed as particularly appropriate for macrosociology in the 1990s may be termed *neomodernization analysis*.

From our earlier discussion, an "overarching perspective" is not a specific theory of social systems or societies but rather an orientation, or if you wish, a *Standpunkt* that situates a field of observations. Recall that Parsons designated this a "generalized conceptual frame of reference" consisting of a "frame of reference" and a set of "structural categories." Parsons generated such an overarching perspective (equals a generalized conceptual frame of reference), one that had several interrelated

themes that have been loosely used interchangeably and/or taken to
stand for the whole Parsonian theoretical enterprise: *structural-functional analysis, functionalism,* and *action theory.* Although Parsons was not
directly or primarily a contributor to what became called "modernization theory," he was instrumental in what became the first major postwar macrosociological paradigm of development. Let me make a point
at the onset of this discussion. I do not view "modernization" as a single,
unified, integrated theory in any strict sense of "theory." It was an
overarching perspective concerned with comparative issues of national
development, which treated development as multidimensional and
multicausal along various axes (economic, political, cultural), and which
gave primacy to endogenous rather than exogenous factors.

The modernization paradigm contained a number of axiological presuppositions that in the first phase of the paradigm's career (in the 1950s
and early 1960s) coincided with the hegemony of liberalism. So, for
example, the modernization paradigm took the evolutionary
developmentalism of Western societies toward modernity as tracing the
path and stages for newly arrived and arriving nation-states. Whether
demographic transition, economic transition to "take-off" mature econ-
omies, or even transition to a completely demystified world view (*secularization*), the various analyses focused on abstractions from the
Western historical process to arrive at principles of modernization.

There were many other value premises in the modernization paradigm, but to abbreviate the discussion let me forego discussing them.
I do want to pause to discuss one part of the Parsonian frame of
reference pertinent here, namely the structures of action that Parsons
(1951) called *pattern variables.* Derived from Tönnies, a set of five was
specified, each providing a key structuring of actors toward their
social situation. The pairing was grouped as follows:

A	B
diffuseness	specificity
affectivity	affective neutrality
particularism	universalism
ascription	achievement
collectivity-orientation	self-orientation

Although the above are structural categories of action space,[5] they
in fact became part of the conceptualization of modernization analysis in the sense that items under **A** were viewed as essential features
of "traditional society" and items under **B** as features of "modern
society." Modernization, taken broadly as an irreversible process of

transformation from "tradition" to "modernity," was a multilevel process of institutional change permitting actors to adopt a new, "modern" definition of the situation. For Parsons and the modernization analysts in various disciplines, it was self-evident that contemporary American society, its institutional structures, and its normative matrix was the society most advanced in modernity.

The modernization paradigm fell into desuetude in the late 1960s and 1970s under a barrage of neo-Marxist "underdevelopment" and "world-system" critiques, and even received a funeral oration at the end of that decade (Wallerstein 1979). Why, then, seek to exhume it?

Macrosociological models are always to some extent drawn up, validated and invalidated in relation to the sociohistorical environment. Macrosociologists seek to make sense of the world they live in and react to, not to an eternal, unchanging, constant social world. But they may also continue to operate in the world with the same set of presuppositions that framed macrosociological models and theories in an earlier historical setting, albeit real transformations have or are taking place in the world. Essentially, I propose that taken as a totality, the global setting of the 1990s is more suited to an overarching, revitalized modernization perspective than was the case in the 1970s or 1980s. At the end of this section, I will suggest that a metatheoretical analysis may even point to a reconciliation of modernization analysis and world-system analysis.

We are living in a period where there are immense structural and normative transformations taking place not only in different regions of the globe but of a global nature itself. This is widely felt, and dramatically so in a geopolitical sense as a result of the implosion of the Soviet empire in barely over a year, with individual components, including Russia, gravitating toward a market economy and the decentralization of political power.

If the "cold war" that marked the postwar world from 1946 to 1989 has ended, and with it the vision and world leverage of the Leninist-Stalinist interpretation of the historical process culminating in revolutionary socialism and embodied in the modernity of the Soviet state, does it imply that somehow this vindicates the presupposition that modernity lies with the United States, as specified two generations ago by modernization analysis? Hardly, and this for two reasons. First, there has been as much of a coming apart of American global dominance as of the Soviet one, exemplified in the United States becoming in the 1980s one of the largest debtor nations, dependent upon foreign investments to finance its government's chronic deficits. Second, internal changes in social and cultural values, which probably can be traced to various protest movements of the 1960s, make problematic or ambiguous specifying which of the pattern variables characterize structurally and normatively "modernity" and which "tradition." For instance, affirmative action as a general social policy to bring into the public sphere persons in previously disfranchised or underrepresented minority groups may be seen as giving "particularism" priority over "universalism." Equally, various American corporations seeking to become more competitive by raising productivity are becoming attentive to the Japanese model of organization stressing "collectivity orientation" over "self-orientation."

That we cannot equate American society, its values, and its institutions as the apex of modernity (or for that matter that we cannot specify one irreversible model of modernity) is why there is need to renovate "modernization analysis" and hence why I propose using the expression "neomodernization." But why use it at all?

We should use it because a macrosociology needs to treat collectivities not only as objects that are part of a system but also as collective subjects that react and act upon the world. The action frame of reference, viewing an actor as having contingent freedom to choose and select, rather than being determined or overdetermined by her or his environment, is more heuristic in making sense of changes that we have witnessed and experienced in the last 20 years, changes that cannot be accounted for in "structuralist" terms alone. So, for example, the emergence of East Asian/"Confucian" NICs (Newly Industrialized Countries) is indicative of a set of actors not determined by a "structure of dependency" or a world system that relegates them to a peripheral status. The rejection of authoritarian and totalitarian regimes, the desire to reconstruct society in accordance with popular collective aspirations, points to a new era of "nation-building" and rebuilding, but instead of a single outcome we will have a multiplicity of outcomes. Some will be relatively successful in achieving collective projects, and sad to say, some will not.

Structurally, then, we have entered a period similar to the 1950s and early 1960s when new large-scale sociopolitical entities attained autonomy. The world system of the period was politically structured by two major contending superpowers, which provided some space for interstitial, "Third World" countries. Today, structures of the world system have been significantly altered politically, economically, and technologically, with new powerful actors (e.g., East Asia/Japan and the European Community) emerging with new horizons and projects. Other actors who yesterday were silent voices in what appeared to be a monolithic empire based on coercion and corruption have found the courage to "live in truth" and make vehement demands for autonomy. The unexpected implosion of the Soviet empire stemming from the attempted reforms at modernization of Gorbachev—who seems increasingly to be cast in the mold of his predecessors, the modernizing czars of the previous century—has brought about a new wave of nation-building in Central and Eastern Europe, even in the USSR itself.

It is especially because we are in a new period of world history, if not in what Jaspers designated as an "axial age" (in reference to the period 600-500 B.C.), a period of extensive social, economic, political, and cultural restructuring—broadly speaking, a new cycle of modernization on a global basis—that I propose it is propitious to renovate a paradigm of neomodernization. Some of the presuppositions of this would be the following:

1. The nation-state is not the unique or privileged unit of macrosociology. More inclusive units would be empires (at the political level) and civilizations (at the cultural level). Other units, which may be more or less inclusive than nation-states depending upon the historical context, are ethnic groups and nation-groups (Nielsson 1985). The nation-state is a juridical actor but the nation-group (or nation, for short) is a more appropriate social category, one having objective as well as intersubjective features.

2. A collectivity (a nation) is not determined by its environment. It is interactive with its environment in the sense that the boundaries are not constant, and neither is the degree of control that one exercises vis-à-vis the other. Stated differently, adaptation to the environment is an interactive process.

3. The structures of the action space of a collectivity (a nation) cannot be reduced to one dimension, such as the economic, the political, or the cultural; rather, the interaction of these dimensions is always operative. Moreover, the action-space is increasingly global in terms of both constraints and resources, as is suggested in the key term of *global interdependence.*

4. It is also the case that societal change results from conflicting perspectives within each dimension: for example, class conflict within the economic, party conflict within the political, and religious and ethnic conflict within the cultural.

5. The projects or goal-seeking activities of nationhood are most of the time multiple, reflecting different standpoints of actors on the

economic, political, and cultural dimensions. There are some rare moments when there is a convergence of interests in a unified "nation-building" endeavor; this may often be preceded or attended by a period of "collective effervescence" in which the nation-group itself is endowed with charisma.

6. The processes of modernization are not unidirectional and irreversible; they are dialectical. Just as psychoanalysis came to realize the dialectics of personality development in terms of eros and thanatos, so also do we find processes of dedifferentiation that counter processes of differentiation, of disaggregation that counter processes of aggregation, of sacralization that counter processes of secularization.

7. Modernity as the telos of processes of modernization is not a final point in history. There is not an objective set of values, norms, and institutions that defines in an absolute sense what is "modern." However, there have been in earlier historical periods clusters of cultural, social, and technological innovations centered in specific locales ("centers of modernity") that have had long-term significance for the evolution of societies (Tiryakian 1985). The time and spatial frame for the comparative study of modernization and modernity is thus far vaster than what has typically been used (the 19th and 20th century industrial setting, or even the Western European setting from the 16th century to the present).

8. Modernization is not a continuous process, assured by attaining some threshold point of "takeoff." In the historical process, there are "slack" or "empty" periods when adaptation to the environment remains static or becomes increasingly ineffective, while during other periods, there is concerted collective action to upgrade the capabilities of the society in interacting with its environment. What accounts for these cycles may be empirically investigated but cannot be assumed a priori.

This is by no means a comprehensive set of presuppositions,[6] but it will give an indication of what I intend. What accounts for some collectivities succeeding in their projects of modernization while others do not achieve them, even though they may be operating in the same environment, is part of the comparative analysis that will make contributions to a renovated theory of modernization; we may expect that intersubjective factors will figure in such a theory as much as structural ones. But before we embark on new theorizing about macrosociology, we should return to the ontological and epistemological foundations, very much in the spirit of Giddens' earlier critique (1976) of the time-bound theory of industrial society still framing modern sociology. Metatheorizing today necessitates not only a hard look at the presuppositions of the past but also a hard look at our present world situation in order to frame a more adequate macrosociology of emergence.

POSTLUDE

Before concluding, it may be well to apply a metatheoretical focus to the two major macro paradigms of the past 30 years, modernization analysis and world-system analysis. These have been viewed by most sociologists as incompatible, although recently more nuanced discussions of modernization, dependency, and world-system paradigms are getting away from polemics and toward seeking bridges (Harrison 1988; So 1990). It is in the ecumenical spirit of the latter that I would like to return to an earlier point, namely metatheorizing as the examination of theories viewed as heterogeneous within sociology.

For purpose of the argument, I will take Parsons as the chief spokesman of modernization theory and Wallerstein as his counterpart for world-system theory. At first glance, they operate from seeming different presuppositions concerning the foundations of social systems: Parsons combines (I am using Parsons in the present for the sake of convenience) Weber's and Durkheim's emphasis on the normative foundations of a social order in giving primacy to value consensus and voluntarism in social action. Wallerstein, on the other hand, sees economic relationships of an involuntary, deterministic, and exploitative nature as being at the heart of a macro-historic system. Obviously, the inspiration for Wallerstein's presuppositions is Marx's model of historical materialism, with elements of Hobson's analysis of imperialism (1954).

However, if we examine certain texts of Parsons and Wallerstein, not as partisans but as disinterested metatheorists, we will find surprisingly that they are more complementary or congruent than anticipated. The texts in question are, for Parsons, *Societies: Evolutionary and Comparative Perspectives* (1966) and *The System of Modern Societies* (1971), and, for Wallerstein, *Processes of the World-System* (Hopkins and Wallerstein 1980) and *World-Systems Analysis* (Hopkins and Wallerstein 1982). What emerges from a metatheoretical analysis for the texts is that both macrotheories (a) stress a secular trend of globalization, (b) stress the emergence of the modern world order in the 16th and 17th centuries, and (c) stress minor reversals in the global trend that do not alter the basic evolutionary course.

So, for example, note Parsons' (1971) conclusion that "this directionality [of Western society having 'universal' significance] is one aspect of a threefold conception of the ways in which modern societies constitute a single system" (p. 139). And what are the other two aspects? A "single origin" and "the sense in which the modern system has been a differentiated system of [several] societies." Of course, Parsons is looking over the shoulders of Weber, but these presuppositions are fully consonant with those of world-system theory, for example in Hopkins and Wallerstein's (1982) conceptualization of the world-system perspective supposing "a single temporal, developing world, through its deepening synchronization, its chronologically ordered thrust, its cycles of expansion and contraction, and its secular trends" (p. 148).

The congruence of the two macrotheories lies in their contextual embededness in the intellectual and societal context of 19th century Western Europe. Western Europe, more precisely the Berlin-Paris-London triangle, formed the heartland of modernity. It was the repository of the Enlightenment with the legacy of "progress" transmitted by the twin-engines of scientific rationality and mastery of the environment and economic growth fueled by technology and the industrial mode of production. From this matrix as a single context for the development of (Western) macro theory came Marx, Spencer, Durkheim, and Weber, all with one accord viewing (in the wake of Hegel) a single world historical development having the industrial-enlightened European core at its epicenter. Of course they and their heirs differed as to the telos of the historical process, as to the motor force of modernity, and as to which nation was in the vanguard of modernity. Nonetheless, I would argue that they constitute a single genus inasmuch as they take modernity having a common beginning in post-Renaissance/Reformation Europe and in the dynamic forces of modernity emerging in the West and spreading outward so as to incorporate and homogenize the rest of the world (albeit a division of labor does not render the world uniform).

Neither modernization analysis of the 1950s nor world-system analysis of the 1970s is adequate for the premillennial period of the 1990s, but if we are correct that their presuppositions are compatible, the basis of a new macrotheory that will build on their respective strengths and omit their respective weaknesses may be in sight. A reconciliation of the two is even enhanced in a recent musing of Wallerstein (1990), which might be interpreted as opening the door to the interrelatedness and interdependence of the political and the cultural with the economic rather than the earlier monocausal emphasis on the economic. A "second phase" of world-system analysis and a second phase of modernization analysis may well turn out to be a collaborative enterprise in macrotheoretical concerns, for example, the study of cycles and clusters of transsocietal phenomena (including modernization itself) that are features of the globalization process.

NOTES

1. "Just as positivism eliminates the creative, voluntaristic character of action by dispensing the analytical significance of values, and the other normative elements by making them epiphenomena . . ." (Parsons 1937, p. 446).

2. For a recent theoretical discussion of the relation of action and environment, see Alexander (1988).

3. To qualify this, it is only Durkheim and Weber who have been extensively re-examined among the major figures whose writings were "data" for Parsons. Marshall and Pareto have received little if any recent sociological recognition.

4. It might be pointed out in passing that there is one other postwar sociologist who undertook general theory as a central task: Georges Gurvitch (for brief comparisons with Parsons, see Coenen-Huther 1989; Tiryakian 1990b).

5. It is crucial to keep in mind the phenomenological status of action space. The pattern variables have an intersubjective grounding in cultural values, but there is also existential choice made by actors (individuals or collectivities) as to which pole of the variable will structure the interaction with the social object. In brief, "structural categories" are embedded in social situations that are always defined and interpreted, and consequently subject to being reinterpreted.

6. For a parallel substantive discussion, see Tiryakian (1991). A congruent model of the self-transforming capability of society and its actors is presented in Sztompka (1991).

REFERENCES

Alexander, J. C. 1983. *Theoretical Logic in Sociology*, Vol. 4: *The Modern Reconstruction of Social Thought: Talcott Parsons*. Berkeley: University of California Press.

————. 1988. *Action and Its Environments: Toward a New Synthesis*. New York: Columbia University Press.

Berger, P. L. and T. Luckmann. 1966. *The Social Construction of Reality: A Treatise in the Sociology of Knowledge*. Garden City, NY: Doubleday.

Camic, C. 1989. "*Structure* After 50 Years: The Anatomy of a Charter." *American Journal of Sociology* 95(July):38-107.

Coenen-Huther, J. 1989. "Parsons et Gurvitch." *Sociologie et Sociétés* 21(April):87-96.

Coleman, J. S. 1990. *Foundations of Social Theory*. Cambridge, MA: Harvard University Press.

Durkheim, E. 1965. *The Elementary Forms of the Religious Life*. New York: Free Press.

Friedman, D. and M. Hechter. 1988. "The Contribution of Rational Choice Theory to Macrosociological Research." *Sociological Theory* 6(Fall):201-18.

Garfinkel, H. 1967. *Studies in Ethnomethodology*. Englewood Cliffs, NJ: Prentice-Hall.

Giddens, A. 1976. "Classical Social Theory and the Origins of Modern Sociology." *American Journal of Sociology* 81(January):703-29.

Gouldner, A. 1970. *The Coming Crisis of Western Sociology*. New York: Basic Books.

Handel, W. 1982. *Ethnomethodology: How People Make Sense*. Englewood Cliffs, NJ: Prentice-Hall.

Harrison, D. 1988. *Sociology of Modernization and Development*. London: Unwin Hyman.

Hobson, J. A. [1902] 1954. *Imperialism: A Study*. London: Allen & Unwin.

Hopkins, T. K. and I. Wallerstein, eds. 1980. *Processes of the World-System*. Beverly Hills, CA: Sage.

———. 1982. *World-Systems Analysis: Theory and Methodology*. Newbury Park, CA: Sage.

Kanter, R. M. 1977. *Men and Women of the Corporation*. New York: Basic Books.

Kuhn, T. 1970. *The Structure of Scientific Revolutions*, 2nd ed. Chicago: University of Chicago Press.

Lakatos, I. 1974. "Falsification and the Methodology of Scientific Research Programmes." Pp. 91-106 in *Criticism and the Growth of Knowledge*, edited by I. Lakatos and A. Musgrave. New York: Cambridge University Press.

Leiter, K. 1980. *A Primer on Ethnomethodology*. New York: Oxford University Press.

Lukes, S. 1972. *Émile Durkheim: His Life and Work*. New York: Harper & Row.

Mehan, H. and H. Wood. 1975. *The Reality of Ethnomethodology*. New York: Wiley Interscience.

Merton, R. K. 1967a. "The Bearing of Empirical Research on Sociological Theory." Pp. 156-71 in *On Theoretical Sociology*, edited by R. K. Merton. New York: Free Press.

———. 1967b. "The Bearing of Sociological Theory on Empirical Research." Pp. 139-55 in *On Theoretical Sociology*, edited by R. K. Merton. New York: Free Press.

Nielsson, G. P. 1985. "States and 'Nation-Groups:' A Global Taxonomy." Pp. 27-56 in *New Nationalisms of the Developed West*, edited by E. A. Tiryakian and R. Rogowski. Boston: Allen & Unwin.

Parsons, T. 1935. "The Place of Ultimate Values in Sociological Theory." *International Journal of Ethics* 45:282-316.

———. 1937. *The Structure of Social Action*. New York: Macmillan. Reissued in 1949 by Free Press, New York.

———. 1945. "The Present Position and Prospects of Systematic Theory in Sociology." Pp. 42-69 in *Twentieth Century Sociology*, edited by G. Gurvitch and W. E. Moore. New York: Philosophical Library.

———. 1951. *The Social System*. New York: Free Press.

———. 1959. "General Theory in Sociology." Pp. 3-38 in *Sociology Today: Problems and Prospects*, edited by R. K. Merton. New York: Basic Books.

———. 1966. *Societies: Evolutionary and Comparative Perspectives*. Englewood Cliffs, NJ: Prentice-Hall.

———. 1971. *The System of Modern Societies*. Englewood Cliffs, NJ: Prentice-Hall.

———. 1978. "A Paradigm of the Human Condition." Pp. 352-433 in *Action Theory and the Human Condition*, edited by T. Parsons. New York: Free Press.

Polanyi, M. 1967. *The Tacit Dimension*. Garden City, NY: Doubleday.

Ritzer, G. 1988. "Sociological Metatheory: A Defense of a Subfield by a Delineation of Its Parameters." "Sociological Theory 6(Fall):187-200.

———. 1990. "Metatheorizing in Sociology." *Sociological Forum* 5(March):3-15.

So, A. Y. 1990. *Social Change and Development, Modernization, Dependency, and World-System Theories*. Newbury Park, CA: Sage.

Sorokin, P. A. 1928. *Contemporary Sociological Theories*. New York: Harper & Row.

Szacki, J. 1982. "The History of Sociology and Substantive Sociological Theories." Pp. 359-74 in *Sociology: The State of the Art*, edited by T. Bottomore, S. Nowak, and M. Sokolowska. London: Sage.

Sztompka, P. 1991. *Society in Action: The Theory of Social Becoming*. Chicago: University of Chicago Press.

Tiryakian, E. A. 1985. "The Changing Centers of Modernity." Pp. 131-47 in *Comparative Social Dynamics: Essays in Honor of Shmuel N. Eisenstadt*, edited by E. Cohen, M. Lissak, and U. Almagor. Boulder, CO: Westview.

———. 1986. "Hegemonic Schools and the Development of Sociology: Rethinking the History of the Discipline." Pp. 417-41 in *Structures of Knowing*, edited by R. C. Monk. Lanham, MD: University Press of America.

———. 1990a. "Exegesis or Synthesis? Comments on 50 years of *The Structure of Social Action*." *American Journal of Sociology* 96:452-55.

———. 1990b. "Gurvitch et Parsons: Maître et Maître d'Ecole." *Sociologia Internationalis* 28(1):19-25.

———. 1991. "Modernisation: Exhumetur in Pace" (Rethinking Macrosociology in the 1990s), *International Sociology* 6 (2): 165-90.

Vidich, A. J. and S. M. Lyman. 1985. *American Sociology: Worldly Rejections of Religion and their Directions*. New Haven, CT: Yale University Press.

Wallerstein, I. 1979. "Modernization: Requiescat in Pace." In *The Capitalist World-Economy*, edited by I. Wallerstein. Cambridge and Paris: Cambridge University Press & Editions de la Maison des Sciences de l'Homme.

———. 1990. "World-Systems Analysis: The Second Phase." *Review* 13(Spring):287-93.

Chapter 5

METATHEORIZING HISTORICAL RUPTURE
Classical Theory and Modernity

ROBERT J. ANTONIO
University of Kansas

DOUGLAS KELLNER
The University of Texas at Austin

JUST AS "WORLD IMAGES" serve as "switchmen" determining the "tracks" for day-to-day struggles over concrete interests (Weber [1922/23] 1958, p. 280), highly generalized conceptions of the social world set boundaries of the contested terrain in scientific, hermeneutic, and critical practices. They play an important role in shaping the methodological and normative standards of judgment, the general direction of debate and inquiry, and even the range of "facts" that are "worth knowing." Under stable conditions, these social world-views provide a common background of taken-for-granted understandings about social reality. However, during great societal upheavals and transformations, the core meta-assumptions defining the fundamental social structures and processes and valid ways of knowing them are openly contested. Old practices no longer work, different aspects of social life become problematic, and new theories, techniques, and facts burst on the scene.

The meteoric rise of Western capitalism destroyed the social landscape of the *ancien régime.* By the later 19th century, revolutionary upheavals occurred so regularly and penetrated so many domains that a permanently posttraditional or "modern" era appeared to be dawning; instead of perpetually reproducing old ways, the quotidian itself became a continuous process of overturning and remaking. Addressing the radical rupture between the traditional world and new order, classical theorists forged broad, historically based "theories of society" that focused on a new, though usually implicit, theoretical object—"modernity." In the process, they rethought the assumptions, standards, and methods of their Renaissance and Enlightenment heritage, providing new cognitive maps, styles of discourse, standards of evaluation, modes of inquiry, and ideas for managing the emergent structures, processes, and sensibilities arising from modernity's stunning innovations (e.g., the rise of big capital, state bureaucracy, organizational and associational complexity, social and cultural pluralism, high speed travel, instant communication, and mass spectacle).

Yet their enthusiasm about creating a rigorous "science" of society led classical theorists to repeat some of the errors of their Enlightenment predecessors. They spoke too glowingly about the powers of their new science, and lacked sufficient sensitivity about its limits and consequences. Attempting to legitimate their practices in the face of lingering traditionalism, counter-Enlightenment opposition, and unconvinced publics, they often exaggerated the accessibility and coherence of the social world and overstated the rationality of their subjects. By contrast, however, classical theorists also developed an opposing critical epistemology suggesting a much more qualified, pluralistic, and self-reflexive version of their methodological meta-assumptions. Confronting the complexities, divergences, ambiguities, and irrationalities of modernity, social theorists began to question how precisely social reality could be represented; how the observer's social location complicates the already difficult task of grasping society's multitudinous sides; and how nonrational sentiments and unanticipated consequences make exact prediction and precise planning impossible. The contradictory play of these positivist and critical meta-assumptions generated tensions and problems throughout classical theory discourses on modernity.

In periods of turbulent change, metatheory helps clarify the meaning of empirical, interpretive, and political practices, and even establishes fresh bearings for them. It provides justification for new points of view and means for mediating the inevitable disputes over shifting assumptions, methods, and practices of attaining knowledge. Responding to the rise of modernity, classical theorists conducted epistemological debates over methodological, normative, and empirical aspects of their theories. However, the social world-view addressed in this chapter was not the product of a self-conscious metatheoretical project. Rather, it arose indirectly from classical theorists' efforts to address concrete features of the epochal rupture and new social formations. Their epistemological reflections were a part of the larger historical problematic of grasping the emergent social order. The metatheory elaborated below cannot be found in its entirety in the work of any individual theorist. Neither does it represent a substantive consensus among theorists. Instead, this metatheory portrays a convergence in the foci of major disputes as well as in important points of agreement within the discursive field of classical theory; it was implicit in the empirical and historical dialogues and debates between the theorists.

The metatheory of "social modernity" articulates a sweeping vision of the new epoch's fundamental social processes and structures. Although it incorporates a counter-conception of traditional society, the heart of the metatheory is constituted of interrelated subprocesses (i.e., specialization, rationalization, communication, cooperation, centralization, and individuation) of societal differentiation, their structural manifestations (e.g., division of labor, bureaucracy, voluntary associations, social selves), and a distinctive normative theory anchoring social criticism in the emergent features of the new social order. Finally, conflicting positivistic and critical epistemological features introduce ambiguities and contradictions into the approach. As will be evident below, our essay includes all three types of metatheorizing mentioned by Ritzer; we provide an "overarching perspective" to "deepen theoretical understanding" of classical theories and to stimulate "new theory development" (Ritzer 1990, pp. 4-5).

However, this chapter focuses on a distinctive type of metatheory addressing theoretical responses to fundamental challenges to taken-for-granted realities. This problematic follows from our critical epistemological stance, contending that the operative standards of validity, definitions of scope, and purposes governing the practice of social theory and, for that matter, all social science are anchored in socially based and historically variable methodological, normative, and empirical presuppositions. Accordingly, we hold that systematic metatheoretical reflection about these presuppositions and the larger cultural, social, and political contexts from which they spring is vital to understanding, guiding, and reconstructing sociological inquires about concrete realities.[1]

This chapter is part of a much larger project focusing on the discourses of modernity and the rise of social theory. Our ultimate aim is to address current claims by neopositivists and postmodernists about the bankruptcy of the classical style of global theorizing (Antonio and Kellner forthcoming). We argue that classical theorists, responding to the rise of the modern era, elaborated a new social world-view. Our chapter draws out the primary features, central tensions, and main contradictions of this perspective; probes its problematic aspects; and analyzes their significance for the positivist and postmodern broadsides. We intend to identify resources in classical theory that can be tapped for fashioning fresh ideas about the normative and political bases of specialized science and for creating new theories of society to address recent claims about sweeping changes or a "postmodern" rupture. The metatheory of social modernity is merely a starting point for analyzing contradictory features of current theoretical practices.

THE ANATOMY OF SOCIAL MODERNITY

Modernity Over Traditional Society

Classical theories chronicled a very long-term passage from simply structured traditional orders to complex differentiated society (e.g., *Gemeinschaft* to *Gesellschaft*, mechanical to organic solidarity, feudalism to capitalism, theological to positive society, militarism to industrialism, sacred to secular, traditional to rational authority). Societal differentiation produced a decisive break with the supposedly insular, homogeneous, static, and unreflective nature of traditional societies. However, few theorists located their models in specific historical time and space. They tended, instead, to speak of highly generalized evolutionary stages stretching from primordial times to the present. For the most part, their overarching theories of history served as backdrops setting off the distinct features of modernity and dramatizing the recent epochal rupture with traditional life. Thus they should be considered theorists of their own modern age.

Although premodern societies rarely exceeded a minimal level of complexity, classical theorists treated societal differentiation as an evolutionary process. Even the modestly differentiated social structures of the great empires of antiquity seldom extended beyond the borders of a few important cities and depended on ruthless plundering of the hinterlands. Except for a few fundamental bench marks (e.g., the rise of agriculture or of the ancient city), traditional societies tend to look alike when viewed from the panoramic lens of societal differentiation. In sharp contrast, late 18th and early 19th century capitalist development generated unparalleled levels of social and cultural complexity touching nearly every aspect of life. Social modernity's elaborate division of labor, radical technical innovations, specialized institutions, voluntary associations, high speed communications, pluralistic systems of value, and segmented knowledge systems constituted an entirely new complex order with structures and dynamics breaking qualitatively from all preceding societies.

Classical theorists viewed modernity as a liberating negation of the traditional world, implying that the fate of humanity depended on overcoming the material, cultural, intellectual, and, in particular, social impoverishment of traditional undifferentiated society. Marx's famous depiction of the French peasantry in *The 18th Brumaire* typifies the disdain for the parochial features of rural life. He claimed that their very simple and unspecialized modes of production leave peasants "isolated" from each other (Marx [1852] 1963, pp. 123-4, [1857] 1973, p. 589). Because they lack the creative power of organized collective action, peasant societies are wanting in social and cultural diversity as well as material abundance. By contrast, capitalism links people into huge, enriching social networks that destroy "the former natural exclusiveness" (Marx and Engels [1845-46] 1964, pp. 75-6, 91-5). Likewise, Cooley (1916, pp. 107-20, [1902] 1964, p. 147) praised the "liberation" from traditional society's "narrow" circles of interaction and "narrowness of consciousness." And despite his heralded pessimism, even Weber strongly affirmed modernity's technical advances, secular intellectual life, social diversity, and "free" individuality.

But societal differentiation initiated deep crises as well as new linkages and potentialities. Pointing to gaps left by the destruction of traditional social bonds and beliefs, classical theorists spoke of the waning of community and of increasing cultural fragmentation and alienation. Durkheim warned that the atomistic features of social modernity undermined social integration and threatened the very basis of organized society. And Marx's hopes for revolutionary unification of the proletariat and for a postcapitalist society of "associated producers" pointed toward a community and consensus reminiscent of premodern solidarity. But neither theorist believed that the old form of integration could or should be revived. Despite his warm accolades for communalism and excoriation of capitalist individualism, even Tönnies ([1887] 1963, pp. 228-35) understood that a return to *Gemeinschaft* was impossible and that social disintegration could be averted only by continuing on the modern track. Regardless of their many substantive disagreements, almost all classical theorists believed that any restoration of community must rely on the new resources of complex societies.

Specialization and the Discovery of Social Modernity

Praising "growing unity and breadth sustained by the co-operation of differentiated parts," classical theorists hailed a new principle of social "organization" (Cooley [1902] 1964, pp. 148-9). They considered specialization to be a primary modernizing force shattering social homogeneity and multiplying cultural possibilities. Although the process could be traced back to simple age and gender divisions of primeval hunting and gathering peoples, the decisive changes began with medieval commerce and exploded with the advent of the modern factory. Speaking of the dramatically "increased powers" of the capitalistic "division of labor," Smith ([1776] 1937, pp. 3-5) contended that a single worker, carrying out all the necessary steps of production, would be hard pressed to make one pin a day, whereas 10 specialists working together can produce as many as 48,000. Even with minimal division of labor, Marx ([1887] 1967, pp. 326-68) later held that 12 "co-operating" masons produce "much more" than one working singly for the same number of hours. However, by focusing activity, raising efficiency, and, ultimately, enlarging the role of science and planning, highly specialized production stimulates a vast material accumulation, making possible elaborate social and cultural differentiation. Marx's special contribution was that he identified complex cooperation explicitly as the secret "social force" propelling capitalist development and the rise of modernity.

Diverse forms of entirely new, nonlinear, and shifting layers of highly specialized organizations and associations extend complex cooperation throughout modern society. A huge ensemble of bureaucracies, voluntary associations, flexible informal orders (e.g., big communication networks and markets), and even looser collectivities based on shared interests and modes of collective identification (e.g., among feminists, workers, employees; see Simmel 1922, 1964, pp. 172-84) crisscross from the local to the international level. Rather than the fixity of self-enclosed familial and communal circles, modern social networks require fluid movement between different social settings (each constituted of changing groups) and link every person "with an almost infinite number of other individuals" (Mead [1934] 1964, p. 157). Because memories of traditional society's simple anatomy were still fresh, social modernity could hardly be taken for granted or reduced to aggregated individual characteristics as it often is today. Instead, classical theorists spoke effusively about discovering "sociological"

reality and about the need for a new "science" to map its fresh terrain
and unique potentialities.

But classical theorists also warned about new problems and dan-
gers. For example, Marx pointed to the alienating and despotic side
of capitalist specialization in the same pages that he praised its powers. Durkheim ([1893] 1964, pp. 353-73) spoke of an "anomic" unrav-
eling caused by hyperspecialized individuals and organizations
pursuing their own ends without considering wider consequences.
Revolution and counterrevolution, capital-labor struggles, deperson-
alization, and disorientation produced a sense of crisis heightened by
the fear that a modern facsimile of the absolute state might be imposed
if conditions went unabated. Still classical theorists spoke too optimis-
tically about the magic powers of societal differentiation, too one-
sidedly about its beneficial horizontal specialization, and too
uncritically of its unrelenting progressive path. It is not at all surprising that they underestimated the complexity, obduracy, and divisive-
ness of class, racial, ethnic, and gender hierarchies. All these problems
went hand-in-hand with the theorists' deeper assumptions about the
powers of their new science, the coherence of social modernity, and
the rationality of its subjects.

Voluntary Versus Compulsory Cooperation

Most classical theorists claimed that voluntary cooperation is the
leading organizational and normative principle of social modernity.
They celebrated the declining role of inherited status, narrow webs of
mandatory social expectations, and continuous face-to-face
surveillance characterizing traditional social orders dominated by
family and family-like relationships. Simmel ([1922] 1964) argued that
modern societies "enlarge the sphere of freedom" by making it "a
matter of choice with whom one affiliates and upon whom one is
dependent" (p. 130). Increased diversity, privacy, and flexibility
greatly expand the social space and resources for refining different
needs, tastes, and abilities. Democratic ideals spring, at least, in part,
from the needs of modern associations for flexibility and unforced
compliance and from consequent emphases on individual autonomy,
consensual give and take, and nonarbitrary standards of evaluation
and placement. Durkheim ([1893] 1964) held that modern organizational
environments favor the "spontaneous" play of "natural inequalities" (p.
377). For differentiated societies to function smoothly, people must be

allowed to choose roles consistent with their talents, training, and motivation and to use their resources freely in accord with their individual capacities and achievements. Even Marx's rage against the oppressive side of modernity was tempered by his often repeated point that capitalism multiplies needs, relationships, and possibilities, creating conditions for an emancipatory break that will extend voluntary cooperation far beyond current bounds.

However, theorists also recognized that big industrialists created highly centralized, rationalized, and impersonal command structures in response to increasingly elaborate specialization, intense competition, large work-forces, concentrated capital, and mechanization. Both Marx and Weber agreed that the compulsion of propertylessness forced workers into the factories and that the new organizations' unparalleled capacities for exactly calculating resources, regulating action, and centralizing power all focused on unrelenting capital accumulation. But even large bureaucracies deviate significantly from the direct, personal, and physical forms of premodern control, instituting distinctly voluntary features and employing democratic ideals to legitimate their coercive and extractive practices. Because it is entwined with expanded individual choice and is democratically clothed, compulsion is frequently mistaken for substantive freedom (e.g., "free" labor "chooses" to submit to the compulsion of the factory). Attacking Hegel for portraying the modern state as it claims to be rather than as it is, Marx ([1843] 1967) argued that social theorists must avoid this cardinal error of bourgeois thought. However, by failing to consistently separate the two forms of cooperation and to adequately theorize their complex relations, classical theorists, including Marx himself, were guilty of conflating justifications with reality and affirming the new modes of domination.

Although most theorists favored democracy, they did not concur about the nature and balance of equality and freedom, nor about strategies for realizing them (e.g., freer markets, increased state regulation, or more active public life). Because it contributed to corroding traditionalism, increasing efficiency, and growing abundance as well as to alienation and exploitation, classical theorists disputed how much compulsive cooperation could and should be reduced. A divide existed between thinkers such as Weber who stressed the unacceptable costs (i.e., incalculability and inefficiency) of deeper democracy and others like Dewey who argued that the modern system not only could withstand substantial increases in freedom and equality but that such reform was necessary to avert the centrifugal effects of a continued erosion of voluntary compliance. Big splits were manifested in intense debates over the respective roles of the state and market. Herbert Spencer argued that free market capitalism was enough; progress depended on keeping state activities to a minimum and allowing individuals maximal freedom to succeed or fail and to earn their just deserts. Marx, Dewey, and Durkeim insisted, conversely, that modernity would be crippled by conflict without equality of opportunity, which, in turn, required state intervention to increase substantive as well as formal equality. Only then would the compulsory attributes of large organizations and new hierarchies of merit be legitimate and subordinated to overriding societal democracy.

Much exaggerated claims about the leveling powers of social differentiation led classical theorists to make premature declarations about the inevitable end of class, race, ethnicity, and gender as primary modes of ascription, association, and identification and to overlook the fact that new organizations were nearly the exclusive domain of white males from the respectable strata. Faith that social science would produce noncoercive knowledge and transcend the blinders and one-sidedness of particular social locations fueled their rosy optimism about the extent and prospects for voluntary cooperation and democracy. Thinkers as diverse as Comte, Marx, Spencer, Durkheim, and Dewey implied that the new science of social modernity would provide means to identify unequivocally and eliminate unnecessary compulsion without a serious reduction in instrumental rationality. Science was the key to a more radical transformation completing the rupture with the ancien régime. Although they were sharply split over its form and how it would be deployed, theorists spoke ebulliently about the powers of their new way of knowing, seldom reflecting on limitations or on its possible role in the nascent forms of domination. The strong validation of science combined with a lack of specificity about democratic processes and institutions resulted in a technocratic bias that obscured and legitimated the new forms of compulsion.

Wider Communication and Richer Individuality

As Cooley (1916) pointed out, the communicative "régime of railroads, telegraphs, daily papers, telephones and the rest has involved a revolution in every phase of life" (p. 83). But even more profound structural developments underlie these important surface changes.

Durkheim, Simmel, Mead, Dewey, and many other theorists argued that increasing social complexity stimulates a movement from local, particularistic thought to more universal, relational systems of knowledge and value capable of coordinating diverse activities in highly differentiated substantive spheres. Cultural rationalization provides abstract modes of calculation, broader points of view, and common languages that overcome the isolation and self-enclosure of premodern communities. In contrast to the insular and "narrow" associations of traditional communities, each modern individual is "the point of intersection of an indefinite number of [social] circles." The accompanying "enlargement of communication" results in a much "wider" personal life and society (Cooley 1916, p. 107, [1902] 1964, pp. 147-9). By vastly increasing the scope of social relationships and the means, modes, speed, and extensiveness of communication, social modernity radically transforms the experience of space, time, and the social.

Diverse, semiautonomous, and changing organizational spheres produce geometric increases in the size and complexity of interactive networks. People must become accustomed to making abrupt and jarring shifts between sharply different social roles and settings outside the family circle. They are exposed daily to dramatic changes in expectations, perspectives, and activities (e.g., "going to work," "coming home," "going out"), moving back and forth from personal to impersonal social relationships, shifting between sharply different points of view, and considering conflicting contexts concurrently. In modern organizational settings, face-to-face interaction with diverse specialists requires deep background understanding of multiple layers of extremely abstract social actors, collectivities, and inter-organizational environments (e.g., "upper management," "low income clients," "the national office," "the state," "the economic climate"). Actors have to theorize typical interests, motives, and actions associated with distant, pluralistic, and complicated social locations. Although these nascent communicative capacities are taken for granted today (except during breakdowns), classical theorists argued that they nurture new types of subjectivity.

Societal complexity produces differentiated subjects. In social modernity, Simmel ([1922] 1964) held, "moral personality" is constituted "in an entirely new way" out of diverse "elements of culture" and "affiliations." A person's distinctive identity arises from the "point at which [his or her] many groups 'intersect' " (pp. 140-3). Classical theorists claimed that associative and cultural diversity produces socially responsible or "autonomous" individuality: modern intercommunicating subjects learn to balance their newfound freedom with choices that perpetuate a mutually beneficial societal interdependence. The increased receptivity to others' needs, tolerance of differences, and willingness to share collective costs and duties, deriving from the wider modes of communication and understanding, were supposed to animate the shift from compulsory to voluntary cooperation. But some theorists understood that the creation of such a being was a highly problematic proposition, because the new organizational environments created imposing blocks to communication as well as fresh interactive resources. For example, Weber ([1921] 1968) warned that "the modern means of communication" threatened to seal the already over-towering control of the great bureaucracies (p. 989), and Dewey ([1927] 1988) spoke of mass society's "bewildered" publics and "lost" individuals, of manipulation by highly rationalized modes of information control, and of the propagandistic powers of centralized media, states, and firms.

Still, according to Mead ([1934] 1964), social modernity's incredible complexity and copious voluntary features produce "a progressive social liberation of the individual." In addition to a "peculiar individuality" reflecting unique ensembles of diverse social relations, modern subjects develop "multiple personalities" each responding to different facets of their multisided group contexts. Although social life is usually integrated enough to provide these "elementary selves" with some unity, the "complete self" or "personality," like the social order, is an emergent and problematic "process" susceptible to "break up." Instead of a homogeneous, fixed, spectating Cartesian subjectivity, pragmatists such as Mead and Dewey envisioned a plurality of diverse selves, each with "its own particular and unique standpoint" and each ever emergent with their participatory practices and dynamic social locations (Mead [1934] 1964, pp. 141-4, 201-02, 221). Like all other individuals, even ultramodern scientific subjects cannot transcend the boundaries of their finite historical spaces. Rather than providing perfect pictures and timeless laws of essential reality, the science of social modernity offers a multiplicity of perspectives shaped by self-formative social activities and evaluated according to their consequences by intercommunicating subjectivities.

However, relatively few classical thinkers probed modern subjectivity in very much depth. Their overly optimistic hopes about autonomous individuality usually overlooked the centrifugal force of emergent inequalities and fragmentation created by the new hierarchies, formal organizations, and specialized disciplines. The theorists also far too quickly dismissed persistent modes of traditional dominance and association as well as the continuing force of affective and other nonrational factors in modern forms of identity and understanding. Entwined with their broader tendency to attribute too much consensus and rationality to modernity and to ignore systematically distorted communication, positivists treated the scientific subject as a transcendent spectator and, consequently, failed to grasp the highly problematic role of communication in their new science and the difficulty of achieving uncoerced consensus about important problems and "facts." Contrary to Simmel's and Mead's differentiated perspectival self, positivists heralded the rise of clear-eyed, hyperrational beings who, after tearing away the parochial veils of religion and metaphysics, are capable of precisely representing "objective" social reality. Durkheim's "revised" Cartesianism did not escape this dogmatic position, and, despite this strong antipositivist sentiments, Marx's Cartesian voice spoke loudly on the certainty of his materialist laws and collective emancipatory subject. Other theorists implied similar ideas with varying degrees of vulgarity in overblown claims about the reconstructive promise of positivistic social science.

Under warranty of "correct" methodology, hyperrational scientific subjects supposedly achieve a neutral vantage point unaffected by their social locations, somehow escaping the one-sidedness of ordinary observers. Positivist arguments privilege "scientific" methods and knowledge so strongly that they tower imperiously above all public discussion, providing ready-made rationales for expert planning, elite decision-making, and weak democracy. Breaking sharply with this technocratic vision, critical epistemological themes implied a much more modest version of subjectivity and representation. For example, Weber ([1904]1949) suggested a highly qualified idea of "objectivity" suitable for a pluralistic world, offering no antidotes to the divergent perspectives, conflicting interests, and clashing values of "unbrotherly" social modernity. Likewise, Dewey ([1929] 1988) substituted plural, partial, and uncertain "participatory" knowing for the ponderous truth claims of modern Western epistemology. Moreover, his enthusiasm about science and rationality was counterbalanced by an appreciation of the role of memory, feeling, and sympathy in modern social bonds and in modern modes of manipulation and resistance.

Antipositivists rejected hyperrationalism, objectivism, and epistemic certainty, implying that the gaze of science extended no further than the boundaries of their own communicatively mediated, historical social locations and that knowledge is always multisided, incomplete, open-ended, and subject to reformulation. For these thinkers, the enhanced powers of modern subjects derive from the growing awareness of their own radical historicity and of the consequent uncertainty of knowledge and limits to rationality. According to the epistemologically critical side of classical theory, capacities to see from many perspectives, to communicate with a wider circle of people than ever before, and to work together for a richer and more just social life all derive from discarding the Cartesian blinders and finally coming to terms with the complexity, pluralism, and uncertainty of modernity. Positivism's foundationalist obsession with exactitude and essentialist drive for static laws is a secular substitute for religion, whereas the highly qualified knowledge of critical epistemology expresses the disenchanted standpoint of social modernity.

However, like their bêtes noires, antipositivists still affirmed "scientific" means of attaining knowledge. Although it was communicatively mediated and completely dependent on intersubjective standards, these theorists believed that their new "science" still yielded much more than narratives. Although they did not concur about method, classical thinkers of all stripes generally agreed that social theories ultimately can be ranked and privileged according to the outcome of confirming or disconfirming historical-empirical inquiries. Moreover, thinkers like Durkheim and Dewey argued that a new social sphere of relatively autonomous communication and disciplined inquiry began with the world historical split of Renaissance science from the authority of the church and monarchs. They and many other theorists implied that the fate of modernity depends on extending this domain into a broader and more influential democratic public sphere, which, in turn, requires balancing the new awareness about the role of language and limits to knowledge with, at least, a conditioned idea of objectivity that maintains a decisive role for extranarrative factors.

Ethics of Interdependence:
Immanent Critique of Social Modernity

As part of the break with traditionalism, classical theorists rejected claims about enduring normative truths, usually implying that ideals and configurations of value arise in response to historically situated social needs, activities, experiences, dialogues, and struggles. The meaning of ideals is not neatly enclosed in a static identity logic, but instead arises from the consequences of their use in interpreting, regulating, and creating social life. Although normative conceptions bear strong imprints of past and present social contexts, they still point forward to unrealized possibilities. As Dewey ([1929-30] 1988) argued:

> There is danger in the reiteration of eternal verities and ultimate spiritualities. Our sense of the actual is dulled, and we are led to think that in dwelling upon ideal goals we have somehow transcended existing evils. Ideals express possibilities; but they are genuine ideals only in so far as they are possibilities of what is now moving. Imagination can set them free from their encumbrances and project them as a guide in attention to what now exists. But save as they are related to actualities, they are pictures in a dream. (p. 112)

The great rupture that produced modernity created a secular basis for universalistic social criticism. Rather than conjuring up transcendent ethical standpoints that ultimately mask narrow, earthly interests, modern theorists need only point to the contradictions between democratic legitimations and the actual social orders from which they arise.

Although critics hold that strong normative commitments are ruled out by the historical relativity of this sociological ethics, classical theorists' value perspectivism had limits. Thinkers, like Dewey, implied that rescuing the ethical domain from airy religious and philosophical formalism would animate normative discourse rather than plunge it into nihilism. Some theorists spoke as if they were giving voice to living ethical languages and beliefs arising from the communicatively mediated structure of differentiated society. For example, Durkheim ([1893] 1964) argued that social modernity is "not . . . a jumble of juxtaposed atoms" and that modern individuals have to "make concessions," "consent to compromises," and "take account of interests higher than . . . [their] own." According to this perspective, "co-operation . . . has its intrinsic morality"—the values of freedom and equality go hand in hand with the "mutual dependence" of differentiated and specialized social orders (pp. 227-8, 368, 406-9). Likewise, Dewey ([1929-30] 1988) claimed that "interdependence" calls forth a "new individualism" increasingly attuned to mutual rights, responsibilities, and needs (pp. 58-65, 75-76). And despite his stinging broadsides against bourgeois morality and democracy, Marx considered "real" freedom and equality to be immanent in capitalism's new "mode of cooperation" and to constitute the heart of class-conscious proletarians' revolutionary hopes.

Durkheim, Dewey, and Marx all argued forcefully that cooperative interdependence strongly favors the ideals of freedom and equality. The affinity was so strong that they thought the ideals would remain central to the most important societal aspirations, contradictions, and struggles for the foreseeable future. Furthermore, they did not take a neutral stance toward the ideals, but, instead, passionately embraced them in their own theoretical practices. They sided with what they believed to be the progressive possibilities of social modernity and with the majority of the populace whose needs and hopes were being shaped by the new conditions. On the basis of their implicit and sometimes explicit ethics of social interdependence, they executed an immanent critique of social modernity. Although each framed their criticism somewhat differently, all three theorists argued that heightened societal interdependence demands increased realization of freedom and equality to foster voluntary cooperation and to limit the reckless pursuit of individual and institutional self-interest. Each theorist pointed out the urgency of this contradiction, its social structural origins, and possible strategies to cope with it. And they all argued that the future of modernity hinged on overcoming or, at least, on significantly reducing this prime source of tension.

Classical theorists often appealed to this ethics of interdependence to criticize the repressive and fragmented features of modernity or to affirm forward-moving differentiation. Many were confident that increasing social complexity would eventually produce stronger social and cultural integration centering around the ideals of freedom and equality. Excessive optimism about social modernity sometimes was expressed in evolutionary warranties about the inevitable march of science and social progress. However, some theorists, such as William Graham Sumner, thought that democratic ideals were chimerical, and others, like Weber, argued that disenchantment opened the way for pervasive conflicts of interests and values that forbid wider democracy from ever holding sway. Weber was scathingly critical of "pseudohistorical" arguments that justify political values with bogus claims about the supposed direction of history. Yet against conservatives and socialists, Weber still defended what he considered to be the progressive features of modernity and contended that his own normative arguments were derived from a superior grasp of historical constraints and possibilities. Other theorists held that the rupture with traditional society transformed freedom and equality into more universal ideals and made possible, for the first time, their realization in an inclusive and just social order. They believed that their new science served these immanent values. Although others disagreed, social interdependence provided an ethical center to the project of classical theory.

CONCLUSION: CLASSICAL THEORY, METATHEORY, AND RUPTURE

After the rise of professionally specialized sociology, scientistic ("value-free") hyperempiricism made broader theorizing, including classical positivism, obsolete, banishing it mostly to "unscientific" subspecialty and interdisciplinary border zones. But however powerful and refined its arsenal of techniques, the new form of normal science was unequipped to deal with methodological pluralism and with the consequent conflicts between different paradigms (e.g., between empirical, formal, qualitative, and critical theorists). Neither was it reflective about its own guiding assumptions nor about how the problems and data within its purview came to be deemed significant while other matters were ignored. Metatheoretical languages are still needed to foster communication between positions based on different assumptions, to illuminate the taken-for-granted background of specialized practices, and, particularly, to bring their hidden social and political meanings to light in dialogue and critique. And as Weber ([1904], 1949) stated:

> All research in the cultural sciences in an age of specialization . . . will consider the analysis of data as an end in itself. . . . Indeed, it will lose its awareness of its ultimate rootedness in the value-ideas in general. . . . But there comes a moment when the atmosphere changes. The significance of the unreflectively utilized viewpoints becomes uncertain and the road is lost in the twilight. The light of great cultural problems moves on. Then science too prepares to change its standpoint and its analytical apparatus and to view the streams of events from the heights of thought. It follows those stars which alone are able to give meaning and direction to its labors. . . . (p. 112)

In short, metatheoretical dialogue is an especially important resource for understanding and coping with the necessary shifts in methodological, empirical, and normative perspectives during social transitions.

The problematic of modernity has reemerged again at the center of the most intense interdisciplinary theory debate of the last decade. Critics as diverse as Jean Baudrillard and Daniel Bell have spoken of new cultural ruptures, unparalleled fragmentation, and dramatic shifts in sensibilities. Post-Marxists, feminists, and other heterodox thinkers continuing the tradition of modern theory attack its foundationalist, essentialist, reductionist, and totalizing features in order to better grasp emergent social conditions. However, postmodernists herald a new epochal rupture that makes modern theory obsolete. They charge that (especially in radically pluralistic, postmodern contexts) social theory's core meta-assumptions—about "representing" external reality and about the existence of social "objects" (coherent social worlds) and "subjects" (selves capable of using theory to alter social life)—liquidate the local and the particular (obscuring difference) and contribute to social repression (e.g., Lyotard 1984). Yet as we have argued elsewhere, a well-aimed attack on positivistic ideas of exact representation, transparent social objects, and Cartesian subjects need not relegate the entirety of modern social theory to the intellectual scrapheap (Antonio and Kellner 1992). Instead, a metacritique of classical and contemporary approaches could begin a reconstructive effort to create more modest and solid bases for theoretical practices. In particular, we believe that (positivistic excesses aside) classical theory provides important resources for developing alternatives to both positivism and postmodernism.

Even in stable times, "theories of society" and metatheory are useful languages for discussing the meaning of specialized science, for keeping pressing problems of the day before it, for responding to new social conditions, for translating technical matters into public issues, and for guiding historically based social criticism. But, today, an unparalleled combination of overarching interdependency (e.g., internationalization of capitalist markets and production) and extreme social fragmentation (e.g., breakdown of the socialist bloc, deepening cultural crises in the West, and worldwide rekindling of ethnic and nationalist conflicts) raises the specter of new ruptures once again requiring sweeping theoretical vision. Classical theory's dynamics of societal differentiation and individuality, fragmentation and integration, and interdependence and justice provide a starting point for theorizing these conditions. And crucially, classical theorists asked the burning question of whether democratic pluralism can be preserved without realizing the potentialities of social modernity: that the ideals of rationality and democracy might need to be refashioned, revitalized, and more fully implemented to prevent social dissolution, the rise of absolutism, and an eclipse of individuality. This moot issue is still at the heart of the ongoing debate over modernity and postmodernity, and is no less pressing today. In order to avert a continued slide into insularity, professional social theory and metatheory must recover this critical dimension (i.e., immanent critique aiming at connecting science to public life and needs) implicit in the problematic of social modernity.

We believe that the current trajectory of change does not suggest, on the near horizon, an epochal shift to a postmodern age. Yet the social transition has already been very substantial (i.e., probably ending the post-World War II historical conjuncture) and is still ongoing. The current situation demands fresh forms of theoretical imagination—new substantive theories as well as a methodological break with the exhausted forms of postwar scientism and technocracy. In particular, critical theories of broad scope are needed to make sense of the present transformation (i.e., its properties, limits, and possibilities), to recover resources from past approaches that could once again be useful, and to encourage entirely new lines of inquiry fitted to the unique features of the emergent conditions. This project requires acute presuppositional or metatheoretical reflexivity, along with a strong empirical gaze.

NOTE

1. Neopositivists tend to view science as an unproblematic, transhistorical, and monistic enterprise, and, consequently, consider presuppositional inquiry a wasted effort. For example, Jonathan Turner (1990, pp. 38-40) contends that discourse about presuppositions ought to be avoided because it deflects energy away from science. By restricting metatheory to improving the procedures and content of his brand of normal science, Turner implies that correct methods are a given. In contrast, these matters become problematic when we confront science's social and historical character and pluralistic methods and practices (reflecting divergent existential domains, interests, goals, problems, and consequences). Critical epistemological discourse about presuppositional matters opens science to discussion, criticism, and revision on broader pragmatic grounds transcending the inwardly turned, procedural rules of particular, specialized, technical traditions. Although Turner's critique of metatheoretical navel gazing has some merit, heeding his call to give up presuppositional reflexivity would sharply diminish the resources for coming to terms with fundamental disagreements over methods (even in the natural sciences) and with the tendency of some specialists to treat their own techniques as apodictic truths. When "science's" basis in society and history is ignored, its practices easily degrade into self-referential and trivial pseudoscience.

REFERENCES

Antonio, Robert J. and Douglas Kellner. 1992. "The Limits of Postmodern Thought." In *Postmodernism and Social Inquiry*, edited by David Dickins and Andrea Fontana. Chicago: University of Chicago Press.

———. Forthcoming. *Theorizing Modernity*. London: Sage.

Cooley, Charles Horton. 1916. *Social Organization*. New York: Charles Scribners.

———. [1902] 1964. *Human Nature and the Social Order*. New York: Schocken.

Dewey, John. [1927] 1988. "The Public and Its Problems." Pp. 237-372 in *John Dewey, The Later Works, 1925-1953*, Vol. 2, edited by Jo Ann Boydston. Carbondale, IL: Southern Illinois University Press.

———. [1929] 1988. "Quest for Certainty." Pp. 3-250 in *John Dewey: The Later Works, 1925-1953*, Vol. 4, edited by Jo Ann Boydston. Carbondale, IL: Southern Illinois University Press.

———. [1929/30] 1988. "Individualism, Old and New." Pp. 45-123 in *John Dewey: The Later Works, 1925-1953*, Vol. 5, edited by Jo Ann Boydston. Carbondale, IL: Southern Illinois University Press.

Durkheim, Émile. [1893] 1964. *The Division of Labor in Society*. New York: Free Press.

Lyotard, Jean-François. 1984. *The Postmodern Condition: A Report on Knowledge*. Minneapolis: University of Minnesota Press.

Marx, Karl. [1852] 1963. *The Eighteenth Brumaire of Louis Bonaparte*. New York: International Publishers.

———. [1843] 1967. "Critique of Hegel's Philosophy of the State." Pp. 151-202 in *Writings of the Young Marx on Philosophy and Society*, edited by Lloyd D. Easton and Kurt H. Guddat. New York: Anchor.

———. [1887] 1967. *Capital*, Vol. 1. New York: International Publishers.

———. [1857] 1973. *Grundrisse*. New York: Vintage.

Marx, Karl and Frederick Engels. [1845-46] 1964. *The German Ideology*. Moscow: Progress.

Mead, George H. [1934] 1964. *Mind, Self and Society*. Chicago: University of Chicago Press.

Ritzer, George. 1990. "Metatheorizing in Sociology." *Sociological Forum* 5:3-15.

Simmel, Georg. [1922] 1964. "The Web of Group-Affiliations." Pp. 128-95 in *Conflict and the Web of Group-Affiliations*, edited and translated by Kurt M. Wolf and Reinhard Bendix. New York: Free Press.

Smith, Adam. [1776] 1937. *An Inquiry into the Nature and Causes of the Wealth of Nations*. New York: Modern Library.

Tönnies, Ferdinand. [1887] 1963. *Community and Society*, edited by Charles P. Loomis. New York: Harper & Row.

Turner, Jonathan H. 1990. "The Misuse and Use of Metatheory." *Sociological Forum* 5:37-53.

Weber, Max. [1904] 1949. " 'Objectivity.' " Pp. 49-112 in *The Methodology of the Social Sciences*, edited by Edward A. Shils and Henry A. Finch. New York: Free Press.

———. [1922/23] 1958. "The Social Psychology of World Religions." Pp. 267-301 in *From Max Weber*, edited by H. H. Gerth and C. Wright Mills. New York: Oxford University Press.

———. [1921] 1968. *Economy and Society*, Vol. 3, edited by Guenther Roth and Claus Wittich. New York: Bedminister.

Chapter 6

A WORKING STRATEGY FOR CONSTRUCTING THEORIES
State Organizing Processes

JOSEPH BERGER
Stanford University

DAVID G. WAGNER
State University of New York at Albany

MORRIS ZELDITCH, JR.
Stanford University

ONE OF THE INTERESTING ASPECTS of current work on theory in our field is the strong concern with the relation of metatheory to theory building. That metatheory plays a major role in theory building has, of course, long been recognized. What is most striking about some of the current concerns, however, is the attempt by some theorists to articulate in fairly precise terms exactly what that role is and should be. We see this in the work of Fararo and Skvoretz (1986) in their attempt to construct what they call a *theoretical method* for formulating specific theories. We see it also in the work of Lawler, Ridgeway, and Markovsky (unpublished) in their efforts to develop what they call a *theory program* for structural social psychology, and we see it in our own work on *state organizing processes* (a framework for the construction of theories of interpersonal processes; Berger, Wagner, and Zelditch 1985, 1989).

Our concern in this chapter is with state organizing processes as a metatheoretical conception. More specifically, we are concerned with determining exactly what we mean by this conception, what is its role in the construction of theory, and how such a conception differs from a specific substantive theory. Before turning to this topic, however, we want to make some general comments about metatheory and its relation to theory and theory building.

Many sociologists treat metatheory as all of one piece. Its virtues are extolled, its failings castigated, as though all metatheory had the same character and accomplished the same objectives. But metatheory is *not* all of one piece. It includes a diverse set of metamethodological and metatheoretical elements. These range from the most general substantive conceptions about the nature of man and society and the most general methodological conceptions about the nature of scientific inquiry to relatively specific and concrete conceptions as to how to do the work of science, or what might be called *working strategies*. (See Ritzer 1990 for a discussion of several different kinds of metatheory, which he differentiates largely in terms of the end products they produce.)

Thus to treat metatheory as an undifferentiated totality is problematic. It reifies the abstract idea of metatheory without consideration of its diverse character. It leads to disputes and conflicts at every level; every claim for the substantive importance of an idea (say "order") leads to a counterclaim for another idea against the original one; every argument for change or growth in our knowledge is met with challenge to its proposed character or even to its very existence. The result is a situation in which it is assumed that no standards can be applied to the comparison of metatheories and that therefore all metatheories are equally acceptable (or equally rejectable).

A more differentiated view of metatheoretical activity is in order. Understanding what metatheory is and what role it plays in our work requires a more specific focus on particular *elements* of metatheory rather than on metatheory as a whole. To help us develop a more specific understanding of metatheoretical activity in our own work, we restrict our concern here to those metatheoretical elements that are of the nature of what we call *working strategies*. That is, we are concerned specifically with questions of the relation of metatheoretical work to testable, empirical theorizing. In what specific ways are the two linked? How does one evaluate a metatheoretical conception and how does this differ from the evaluation of an empirical theory? Does such a conception change or evolve? Obviously, we cannot answer fully all of these questions here. But our basic premise is that to answer such questions we must first fix the relevant *metatheoretical unit of analysis*. There is every reason to believe that answers to such questions will depend upon the particular unit chosen for consideration and that we cannot meaningfully answer such questions about metatheoretical activity considered as a totality. In the first instance, the conclusions we draw concern the character and intent of working strategies.

Sociologists also usually think of metatheory as *preceding* work on theory building. However, we shall focus on ideas that have *evolved* in the course of our work in constructing theories and that have in turn shaped our thinking. It is indeed true that certain elements of our metatheoretical orientation do predate our work in constructing substantive theory. These include the idea of isolating different social processes and constructing abstract and general theories of them; the idea of testing and applying such theories; and the idea of formalizing such theories, if possible. For most of us, these ideas were there at the outset and have played a major role in shaping our work. Of greater interest perhaps is that some of the most important metatheoretical ideas we now use have been developed from experiences in actually constructing theories. Among the better known of these is the idea of formulating *scope conditions* as an explicit part of the structure of theory (Berger 1974; Walker and Cohen 1985); the *instantiation* of theory as a way of distinguishing the theoretical elements of an abstract formulation from the factual elements that are involved in applying a theory to a concrete social setting (Berger, Fisek, Norman, and Zelditch 1977); and the idea of conceptualizing different types of *theoretical research programs* as a scheme for understanding theoretical growth (Wagner and Berger 1985).

In this chapter, we describe one of the most important of these evolved ideas, that of our conception of a state organizing process. Before discussing the meaning and implications of that idea, we need to briefly review informally some of the key concepts and core principles of the status characteristics theory and the development of that theory.

STATUS CHARACTERISTICS THEORY[1]

The theory of status characteristics describes the evolution of a *status organizing process* in a task situation. A status organizing process is one in which evaluations and beliefs about the characteristics of actors become bases of observable inequalities in face-to-face interaction.

A crucial concept in describing such a process is that of *status characteristic*. A status characteristic is any characteristic around which expectations and beliefs about actors come to be organized. We distinguish two types of status characteristics, specific and diffuse. Key to this distinction is the difference between specific and general expectations. Expectations are specific if they refer to an individual's expectations to perform in a clearly defined and specified situation. They are said to be general if they are not restricted to any specified situation. Thus "mathematical ability" carries specific and "intelligence" carries general expectations. We say that a characteristic is a specific status characteristic if it involves two or more states that are differentially evaluated; associated with each state is a distinct specific expectation state. For example, reading ability may function as a specific status characteristic. We distinguish different levels of the characteristic that are differentially evaluated, and we associate with it beliefs about how individuals possessing the different states will perform specified tasks. We say that a characteristic is a diffuse status characteristic if it involves two or more states that are differentially valued; and associated with each state are distinct sets of specific expectation states, each itself evaluated; and associated with each state is a similarly evaluated general expectation state. Gender, race, ethnicity, educational attainment, occupation, and physical attractiveness each may be a diffuse status characteristic. Whether any of these are a diffuse status characteristic for a given group at a given time is a factual question, not a theoretical question.

The theory is applied to situations that satisfy certain conditions. Actors in the situation may be *interactants* or *referents*. The interaction process involves only two actors interacting with each other at any one period of time. These are the interactants. In the course of the interaction, who is interacting may change. A referent is an actor who is a noninteractant during a given period and whose status information is used by the interacting pair. There must be at least one valued collective task in the situation toward which interactants are oriented.

The core of status characteristics theory contains five principles. The first describes two conditions under which status information becomes *salient* to the actors. One of these is where the status characteristics are defined at the outset as relevant to the task, for example, as when tasks are sex typed as "masculine" and "feminine." The second is the situation where the status characteristic is a basis of discrimination in the group, for example, as would be the case in a mixed-gender or biracial group.

The second major principle argues that if a particular status element is not dissociated from the task then the interactants will act as if it is relevant. According to this *burden of proof* process, status characteristics and status advantages will be applied to every new task and every new situation as a matter of normal interaction unless their inapplicability is demonstrated or justified.

The third principle states that if new actors become involved during the interaction on a given task, then a restructuring of a situation will proceed in *sequence*. The status structure for the actor will further develop through the operation of the salience and burden of proof processes whenever he or she encounters a new interactant or starts a new task. At the same time, previously completed structures remain as long as the actor is in the given task situation.

The fourth principle claims that the actor combines all information that has become salient and relevant to the immediate task. Although in all likelihood the process by which this occurs is outside the individual's awareness, we can construct a model to describe it. In terms of this model, all status information leading to successful task outcomes is combined to determine a value of positive performance expectations. Similarly, all information leading to unsuccessful task outcomes is combined to determine a value of negative performance expectations. In this combining processes there is an *attenuation* effect. That is, there is a decrease in the increment of expectation values with the addition of each like-signed piece of information. The aggregated expectations for an actor are given by summing these two values. The actor's expectation advantage (or disadvantage) relative to another is equal to the aggregated expectation for self less that formed for the other.

The fifth argument states that an actor's position relative to another on the *observable power and prestige order* in the group is a direct continuous function of his or her expectation (dis)advantage relative to this other in the group. The observable power and prestige order of the group refers to the distribution of performance outputs, chances to perform, communicated evaluations, and influence among its members. Position A is higher than position B in this order if A is more likely than B to initiate performance outputs, to receive action opportunities, and to have performance outputs positively evaluated, but is less likely to be influenced in the case of disagreement with another.

The theory has evolved through three distinct stages in which each stage has been marked by an increase in its generality, empirical range, and deductive capacities. In the third version a graphic theoretical formalization has also been constructed (Berger et al. 1977). Since the version developed in the third stage, there have been major extensions of the theory (Wagner and Berger forthcoming). Two of these are of particular interest to us. There is an extension to the problem of how reward expectations are formed in status situations that makes use of the idea of referential structures (Berger, Fisek, Norman, and Wagner 1985). *Referential structures* are socially shared beliefs about the usual association between a valued social characteristic and levels of rewards. Examples of such beliefs are those linking, say, differences in gender, race, and ethnicity to the possession of valued status positions in American society. A second extension of interest to us is one that describes how expectations and behavior that develop in one task situation are transferred to and become inputs to a second task situation (Berger, Fisek, and Norman 1989). In addition, two distinct but related formulations of concern to us have been developed, one by Markovsky (1988) on the diffusion of status expectations through a population and one by Ridgeway (1991) on the social construction of status characteristics. For simplicity, we shall refer to this set of interrelated formulations as the status characteristics theory.

There are four bodies of such research that are relevant to the development of this theory. First, there is research done prior to its formulation that is part of its empirical background (see E. Cohen, Berger, and Zelditch 1972). Second, there is research in controlled experimental settings that is addressed to testing and extending the theory. Although a good deal of it has been done in a standardized experimental situation (Berger et al. 1977; Fisek, Norman, and Nelson-Kilger forthcoming), there is also significant experimental research conducted in other settings (see Webster and Driskell 1983; Bierhoff, Buck, and Klein 1986; Dovidio, Brown, Heltmann, Ellyson, and Keating 1988; Balkwell, Berger, Webster, Nelson-Kilger, and Cashen forthcoming). Third, there is research based on the theory and re-search that is accounted for by the theory that has been carried out in open-interaction settings (E. Cohen and Roper 1972; E. Cohen 1982; Fisek, Berger, and Norman 1991; Balkwell 1991). (See also B. Cohen and Zhou [1991] for research on the status process of enduring re-search and development teams in organizational settings.) Fourth, there is also collateral research, research that has not been specifically guided by the theory, but which nevertheless is relevant to the formu-lation (see Zimmerman and West 1975; Wood and Karten 1986;

Lockheed 1985). Although stressing as we do in this chapter the importance of metatheoretical ideas in the construction of theory, it is important to keep in mind that this is only part of the story. These different bodies of empirical research have each played a major role in shaping the evolution of the status characteristics theory.

The status characteristics theory is an abstract and general theory and to be used it must be applied to characteristics, which in a given population at a given time, represent status distinctions. The theory has been used to describe and explain the status organizing effects of a number of very basic status distinctions in our society. These include applications to gender (Lockheed and Hall 1976; Meeker and Weitzel-O'Neill 1977; Ridgeway 1982, forthcoming); applications to race (E. Cohen 1972; E. Cohen and Roper 1972; Lohman 1972; Webster and Driskell 1978; Hughes and Hertel 1991); applications to ethnic identities and differences (E. Cohen and Sharan 1980; Rosenholtz and Cohen 1985; Yuchtman-Yaar and Semyonov 1979); applications to physical attractiveness (Webster and Driskell 1983; Umbertson and Hughes 1987); and applications to reputed differences in reading ability in classroom situations (Tammivarra 1982; Rosenholtz 1985).

CONCEPTUALIZING STATE ORGANIZING PROCESSES

Our overall conception of a state organizing process and of the status characteristics theory as a theory within that framework is summarized in Figure 6.1.

Social Framework. At the very outset, in conceptualizing a state organizing process, we distinguish between what we call the level of the *social framework* and the level of the *situation of action.* A situation of action occurs within a social framework whose elements are more comprehensive and more enduring relative to those in an action situation. The elements in a social framework may be *cultural,* including such things as norms, values, beliefs, and social categories; *formal,* such as institutionalized and formalized roles and authority positions; or *interpersonal,* such as enduring networks of sentiments, influence, and communication.

This distinction generates two basic and related theoretical questions. First, of all the elements that can be part of the social framework, exactly

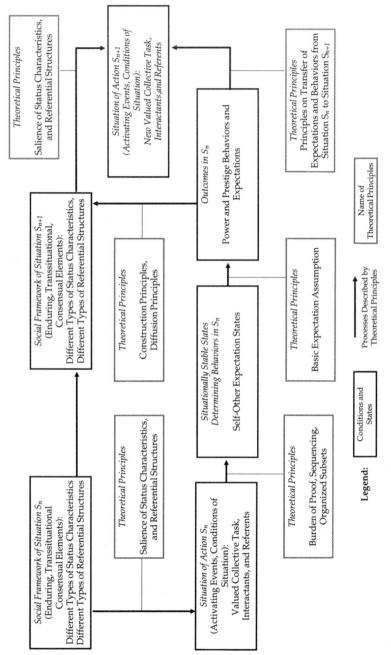

Figure 6.1 Status Characteristics Theory as a State Organizing Process

which elements are of concern to the theory? What is their nature and how can we identify them? Second, because these elements are not always significant in interaction, under what conditions will these elements be accessed by actors so that they are significant in their immediate interaction? In status characteristics theory the first of these questions is answered by conceptualizing and defining in abstract terms those elements of the social framework that are of concern to us: in particular, diffuse and specific status characteristics and different types of referential structures or referential beliefs. The second of these questions is answered by what in the status characteristics theory are called the *salience principles*. These theoretical principles describe how and under what conditions different types of status characteristics and referential structures become significant to the actors in their situation.

Situation of Action. Social processes occur in situations of immediate action that have stipulated properties and features. One of the most important components of such situations is what we call *activating events*. These are events or conditions that are the focus of the interaction process, the *goal states* toward which actors are oriented. In the status characteristics theory the activating events are collective tasks, the outcome states of which are capable of being evaluated in terms of team success or failure. In addition, the situation of action is described in terms of properties and components that define the *scope conditions* of the theory. In the status characteristics theory these include the conditions that there exist a number of actors in the situation, some of whom may be interactants and some referents; that some actors may possess different and others similar states of status characteristics; and that actors are task and collectively oriented. From the standpoint of the structure of the theory, these activating events and conditions are the theoretical *givens* of a situation of action.

Evolution of Process. Given the activating conditions, we assume that the social process will evolve: *behaviors* will occur that are addressed to the demands of the activating conditions, and *social information* will be used so that actors define their situation. The outcome of this process is the formation of *states*, which are stable structures that define the relations of the actors to each other within their immediate situation. Working within this perspective, the status characteristics theorist is confronted with some fundamental questions: How is the socially constructed information embodied in salient status characteristics and referential structures used by the actors to define their situation? How does redefinition occur during the course of the interaction with the addition or loss of interactants? If, as is often the case, such status information is multiple, complex, and inconsistent, how is it organized by interactants? In status characteristics theory, these questions are addressed in the *burden-of-proof, sequencing,* and *organized subset* principles. These theoretical principles describe how salient status information becomes relevant to goal states, how it is built up in the course of interaction, and how it is used by the actors to form situationally stable expectation states for self and other.

State Determined Behaviors. Once states are formed, these states determine the behaviors of the actors relative to each other and to the activating events. The relevant theoretical questions at this point are (a) exactly which behaviors are (and which are not) to be treated as state determined behaviors and (b) exactly how are expectations for self and other related to these state determined behaviors?

In status characteristics theory the concepts and theoretical principles that address these questions include the concept of the observable power and prestige order, which defines the behaviors that are status determined, and the concept of an actor's *expectation advantage* over another. The basic expectation argument is then used as the theoretical principle, which translates differences in expectation advantage into differences in power and prestige behaviors.

Transsituational Effects. Given that an episode in a situation of action is completed, that, say, the task has been dealt with by the actors, we think of the process as *deactivating.* In the case of status processes, this could mean that status distinctions that were significant and relevant in the situation become latent and that the power and prestige order dedifferentiates.

Furthermore, there may be *transsituational effects:* These may be outcomes from one interaction episode that become inputs to a succeeding episode, what might be called *succession* effects, or there may be outcomes from one or more interaction episodes that feed back to the level of the social framework, what might be called *construction* effects.

The relevant theoretical questions at this point are (a) how and under what conditions are expectations and behaviors that occur in one situation transferred to a succeeding situation, and (b) how and under what conditions do outcomes of the process on the level of the situation of action produce changes at the level of the social framework? Some of the most recent work in our program has dealt with just these transsituational effects. Recent work by Berger, Fisek, and Norman (1989) enables us to describe how expectations formed in one task situation affect expectations formed in succeeding task situations. In addition, Markovsky (1988) has constructed diffusion models that describe how changes in expectations toward members of disadvantaged status classes that are created in a specific task situation can diffuse through a larger population and thus produce macro-level changes. Ridgeway (1991) has formulated a theory that shows how, under specific conditions, effects occurring on the level of a situation of action can lead to changes on the level of the social framework. She describes how the status of an initially nonvalued characteristic can acquire from the status processes in situations of action status value and generalized expectations and thus become a status characteristic. These constructed status characteristics can then become elements of a new and altered social framework.

Before leaving this discussion, it is important to comment on the structure of this theory, as a theory. As may be clear from this analysis, there is a high degree of integration among its theoretical principles. Starting with given conditions, the process described by one principle creates conditions for a process described by a second principle, and as a set there is a distinct logical structure interrelating all these principles. What is not revealed by our analysis, but is also true, is that there is a high degree of conceptual coherence and predictive power in this formulation. This has much to do with the formalization of the current theory. Concepts such as the *relevance* of one status element to a second are constructed from more basic terms such as the *possession* and *expected possession* of status elements, and these concepts in turn are the building blocks for more developed ideas, such as the notion of different types of *path of relevance,* whose length, sign, and strength can be determined within the formal theory. Moreover, the formalization enables us to employ what Toulmin (1953) has called a representational system. In our case this involves the use of signed graphs and a set of functions on these signed graphs. With this representational system we can describe an extremely large number of simple and complex status situations, and we can predict the behavior of actors in these situations (see Humphrey and Berger 1981). It is important to keep in mind that such explanatory and predictive power would not exist within this theory without its formalization.

IMPLICATIONS OF THE CONCEPTION

Theory and Metatheory. We distinguish the conception of a state organizing process from a specific substantive theory of a social process. This conception is a metatheoretical framework within which substantive theory is constructed. Within this same framework we can construct different theories for the same process, for example, different theories of status processes. Similarly, within this same framework we can construct theories for different processes, such as theories, say, for social control and affect processes (see Berger 1988; Wagner 1988; Johnston 1988). There is not a one-to-one correspondence between metatheoretical conception and substantive theory. The reason for this is clear. A metatheoretical conception like the one we have described is a scheme that orients the theorist to a specific set of substantive questions. In the status theory, these are such questions as the following: Under what conditions do elements (already selected on theoretical grounds) from the social framework become salient to the actors? By what processes are situationally stable states formed? How do the outcomes of one episode influence the process within a second episode? It is in this sense that the scheme is a working strategy. But the questions must not be confused with the answers. While working within the terms of such a scheme, the theorist is directed to make theoretical decisions that he makes by formulating specific concepts and theoretical principles. These decisions as a set constitute the specific theoretical formulation. Because there are different kinds of decisions that can be made for the same set of theoretical questions, there are different theories that can be constructed. Consequently, there is no one-to-one correspondence between conception and theory.

There is a second sense in which a conception such as the one we have described and a specific substantive theory differ: in how they can be evaluated. In principle, a specific substantive theory can be directly evaluated in terms of its generality, empirical adequacy, deductive capacities, and its merits relative to competing alternatives, if any such exist. We believe, however, that a metatheoretical conception such as the one we have described is not evaluated directly, but that its evaluation is based upon the evaluation of the specific substantive theories constructed within this framework. Therefore the evaluation of the metatheoretical conception is in terms of its utility (or disutility) as a working strategy for the construction of theories that, by the criteria that we have already cited, are more or less successful. If these constructed theories are successful, the framework will be treated as a useful structure. If they are not, the utility of the framework can be brought into serious question.

Micro-Macro Relations. This conception of a state organizing process has certain features that imply particular ways of solving micro-macro problems in sociology. First, there is its abstract, general character, even at the theoretical (as distinct from metatheoretical) level. Second, there is its treatment of structure, action, system, and actor. Third, there is its treatment of scale.

Even at the level of theory, our concept of a state-organizing process is a guide for constructing abstract, general theories. Gender, race, ethnicity, education, and so forth are particular instances of abstract elements in the status characteristic theory. In some societies some of them are, in others some of them are not, status characteristics. Some may even change over time in such a way that what was once a status characteristic is no longer a status characteristic. But none of this alters the fact that *if* some particular social distinction is a status characteristic, then the theory describes how it affects behavior, how it maintains itself, and how it changes. Such a theoretical structure is *multiply interpretable,* that is, it has more than one possible application. This holds true even for the actors to whom the theory is applied, either persons or groups. Thus although no one has yet done it, the theory could be used to describe the status structure of a system of collectives, such as universities. The important point implied in the potential for multiple interpretation is that it is the application, not the theoretical structure, that is micro or macro. It does not require qualitatively different kinds of theory to explain micro and macro phenomena; the same theoretical structure may underlie both.

A second important feature of theories of state organizing processes is that they are interactor theories and describe such systems of interrelated actors both in terms of pregiven structure (the social framework) and action activated by initial conditions in situations of action. Thus they involve mixes of macro (system, structure) and micro (actor, action) elements. They reject equally the purely *structuralist* approaches where all action, say, is the enactment of institutional scripts (Meyer, Raminez, and Boli 1987), and the *radical interactionist* approaches where rules or meanings are being continually negotiated or invented (Strauss, Schatzman, Ehrlich, Butcher, and Sabshin 1963). Instead, state organizing processes have both "structural" or "system" principles and social psychological principles that link the structure of the system (the social framework) to action. Although admittedly this is the current fad in most solutions to the micro-macro problem, it is a fad that cannot fade away for theories of state organizing processes, because theories of such processes *consist* of theoretical principles that actually relate micro and macro elements for each specific theory constructed in terms of this framework of thought.

A third feature of state organizing processes is its treatment of scale. This follows from both the abstract, general nature of our theories and the fact that they are interactor theories. Scale is an important fact of social life, which makes a profound difference to the nature of social phenomena. A very small system behaves in quite different ways than a very large one. Thus it is not our intention to deny the distinction between micro and macro phenomena. Rather, it is our intention to deny that as a consequence there are two quali-tatively different kinds of theory necessary to explain the differences. The alternative is to formulate scale as a variable *in* theories, not a difference *between* them. The difference it makes is part of the analytic structure of theory, and in fact makes as much of a difference in very small systems, for example in differentiating two-person from three-person interaction, as in differentiating small from large systems.

In conclusion, we think it is important to stress one very general feature of working strategies such as our conception of a state organizing process that emerges from our analysis. Although these conceptions ordinarily may be more resistant to change than a substantive theory constructed within their terms, unlike (for example) Lakatos' (1968, 1970) program "core" they are not impervious to change. Whatever else is true of other types of metatheoretical elements, and given their diversity many different things may be true, these frame-works are capable of reflexive change, change in response to the success or failure of the theories developed within their terms. They can be explicated, elaborated, and modified in an effort to increase their utility as frameworks, and failing such efforts, they can even be abandoned as when researchers simply stop using them. We believe that this capacity for reflexive change reflects the fact that the essential component of such a working strategy is the set of specific theoretical questions it generates. By implication this capacity for reflexive change also reflects the fact, which is perhaps even more important, that not all theoretical questions that can be asked and answered are equally fruitful in the construction of substantive theories.

NOTE

1. This informal description of the status characteristics theory with changes is from Berger, Fisek, and Norman 1989. For a formal description of the theory, see Berger et al. 1977 or Humphrey and Berger 1981.

REFERENCES

Balkwell, J. W. 1991. "An Improved Postulate for Expectation States Theory." *American Sociological Review* 56:355-69.

Balkwell, J. W., J. Berger, M. Webster, Jr., M. Nelson-Kilger, and J. Cashen. forthcoming. "Processing Status Information." *Advances in Group Processes*, Volume 9, edited by E. Lowler, B. Markovsky, C. Ridgeway, and H. Walker. Greenwich, CT: JA1.

Berger, J. 1974. "Expectation States Theory: A Theoretical Research Program." In *Expectation States Theory: A Theoretical Research Program*, edited by J. Berger, T. L. Conner, and M. H. Fisek. Cambridge, MA: Winthrop. (Reprinted Lanham, MD: University Press of America, 1982.)

Berger, J. 1988. "Directions in Expectation States Research." Pp. 450-74 in *Status Generalization: New Theory and Research*, edited by M. Webster, Jr. and M. Foschi. Stanford, CA: Stanford University Press.

Berger, J., M. H. Fisek, and R. Z. Norman. 1989. "The Evolution of Status Expectations: A Theoretical Extension." Pp. 100-30 in *Sociological Theories in Progress: New Formulations*, edited by J. Berger, M. Zelditch, Jr., and B. Anderson. Newbury Park, CA: Sage.

Berger, J., M. H. Fisek, R. Z. Norman, and D. G. Wagner. 1985. "The Formation of Reward Expectations in Status Situations." Pp. 215-16 in *Status, Rewards, and Influence: How Expectations Organize Behavior*, edited by J. Berger and M. Zelditch, Jr. San Francisco: Jossey-Bass.

Berger, J., M. H. Fisek, R. Z. Norman, and M. Zelditch, Jr. 1977. *Status Characteristics and Social Interaction: An Expectation States Approach*. New York: Elsevier Scientific.

Berger, J., D. G. Wagner, and M. Zelditch, Jr. 1985. "Introduction: Expectation States Theory: Review and Assessment." Pp. 1-72 in *Status, Rewards, and Influence: How Expectations Organize Behavior*, edited by J. Berger and M. Zelditch, Jr. San Francisco: Jossey-Bass.

———. 1989. "Theory Growth, Social Processes, and Metatheory." Pp. 19-42 in *Theory Building in Sociology: Assessing Theoretical Cumulation*, edited by J. H. Turner. Newbury Park, CA: Sage.

Bierhoff, H. W., E. Buck, and R. Klein. 1986. "Social Context and Perceived Justice." Pp. 165-85 in *Justice in Social Relations*, edited by H. W. Bierhoff, R. L. Cohen, and J. Greenberg. New York: Plenum.

Cohen, B. P., J. Berger, and M. Zelditch, Jr. 1972. "Status Conceptions and Interaction: A Case Study of the Problem of Developing Cumulative Knowledge." Pp. 449-83 in *Experimental Social Psychology*, edited by C. G. McClintock. New York: Holt, Rinehart & Winston.

Cohen, E. G. 1972. "Interracial Interaction Disability." *Human Relations* 1:9-24.

———. 1982. "Expectation States and Interaction in School Settings." *Annual Review of Sociology* 8:209-235.

Cohen, E. G., and S. Roper. 1972. "Modification of Interracial Interaction Disability: An Application of Status Characteristic Theory." *American Sociological Review* 37:643-55.

Cohen, E. G., and S. Sharan. 1980. "Modifying Status Relations in Israeli Youth." *Journal of Cross-Cultural Psychology* 11:364-84.

Cohen, B.P. and X. Zhou. 1991. "Status Processes in Enduring Work Groups." *American Sociological Review* 56:176-88.

Dovidio, J. F., C. E. Brown, K. Heltmann, S. L. Ellyson, and C. F. Keating. 1988. "Power Displays Between Women and Men in Discussions of Gender-Linked Tasks: A Multichannel Study." *Journal of Personality and Social Psychology* 55:580-7.

Fararo, T. J. and J. Skvoretz. 1986. "E-State Structuralism: A Theoretical Method." *American Sociological Review* 51:591-602.

Fisek, M. H., R. Z. Norman, and M. Nelson-Kilger. forthcoming. "Status Characteristics and Expectation States Theory: *A Priori* Model Parameters and Test." *Journal of Mathematical Sociology.*

Fisek, M. H., J. Berger, and R. Z. Norman. 1991. "Participation in Heterogeneous and Homogeneous Groups: A Theoretical Integration." *American Journal of Sociology* 97:114-42.

Hughes, M. and B. R. Hertel. 1991. "The Significance of Color Remains: A Study of Life Changes, Mate Selection, and Ethnic Consciousness Among Black Americans." *Social Forces* 68:1105-20.

Humphrey, P. and J. Berger. 1981. "Theoretical Consequences of the Status Characteristics Formulation." *American Journal of Sociology* 86(March):953-83.

Johnston, J. R. 1988. "The Structure of Ex-Spousal Relations: An Exercise in Theoretical Integration and Application." Pp. 309-26 in *Status Generalization: New Theory and Research,* edited by M. Webster, Jr. and M. Foschi. Stanford, CA: Stanford University Press.

Lakatos, I. 1968. "Criticism and the Methodology of Scientific Research Programmes." *Proceedings of the Aristotelian Society* 69:149-86.

———. 1970. "Falsification and the Methodology of Scientific Research Programmes." Pp. 91-195 in *Criticism and the Growth of Knowledge,* edited by I. Lakatos and A. Musgrave. Cambridge, England: Cambridge University Press.

Lawler, E. J., C. Ridgeway, and B. Markovsky. Unpublished. "Structural Social Psychology: An Approach to the Micro-Macro Problem."

Lockheed, M. E. 1985. "Sex and Social Influence: A Meta-Analysis Guided by Theory." Pp. 406-29 in *Status, Rewards, and Influence: How Expectations Organize Behavior,* edited by J. Berger and M. Zelditch, Jr. San Francisco: Jossey-Bass.

Lockheed, M. E., and K. P. Hall. 1976. "Conceptualizing Sex as a Status Characteristic: Applications to Leadership Training Strategies." *Journal of Social Issues* 32(3):111-24.

Lohman, M. R. 1972. "Changing a Racial Status Ordering—Implications for Desegregation." *Journal of Education and Urban Society* 4(4):383-402.

Markovsky, B. 1988. "From Expectation States to Macro Processes." Pp. 351-65 in *Status Generalization: New Theory and Research,* edited by M. Webster, Jr. and M. Foschi. Stanford, CA: Stanford University Press.

Meeker, B. F. and P. A. Weitzel-O'Neill. 1977. "Sex Roles and Interpersonal Behavior in Task-Oriented Groups." *American Sociological Review* 42(1):91-105.

Meyer, J. W., F. O. Ramirez, and J. Boli. 1987. "Ontology and Rationalization in the Western Cultural Account." Pp. 12-37 in *Institutional Structure: Constituting State, Society, and the Individual,* edited by G. Thomas, J. Meyer, F. O. Ramirez, and J. Boli. Newbury Park, CA: Sage.

Ridgeway, C. L. 1982. "Status in Groups: The Importance of Motivation." *American Sociological Review* 47(February):76-88.

————. 1991. "The Social Construction of Status Value: Gender and Other Nominal Characteristics." *Social Forces*, 70.

————. forthcoming. "Gender, Status, and Social Psychology." In *Theory on Gender/Feminism on Theory*, edited by P. England. Chicago: Aldine.

Ritzer, G. 1990. "Metatheorizing in Sociology." *Sociological Forum* 5(1):3-15.

Rosenholtz, S. J. 1985. "Modifying Status Expectations in the Traditional Classroom." Pp. 445-70 in *Status, Rewards, and Influence: How Expectations Organize Behavior*, edited by J. Berger and M. Zelditch, Jr. San Francisco: Jossey-Bass.

Rosenholtz, S. J. and E. G. Cohen. 1985. "Activating Ethnic Status." Pp. 430-444 in *Status, Rewards, and Influence: How Expectations Organize Behavior*, edited by J. Berger and M. Zelditch, Jr. San Francisco: Jossey-Bass.

Strauss, A., L. Schatzman, D. Ehrlich, R. Butcher, and M. Sabshin. 1963. "The Hospital and Its Negotiated Order." Pp. 147-69 in *The Hospital in Modern Society*, edited by E. Freidson. New York: Free Press.

Tammivarra, J. S. 1982. "The Effects of Task Structure on Beliefs About Competence and Participation in Small Groups." *Sociology of Education* 55:212-22.

Toulmin, S. 1953. *The Philosophy of Science*. New York: Harper & Row.

Umberson, D. and M. Hughes. 1987. "The Impact of Physical Attractiveness on Achievement and Psychological Well-Being." *Social Psychology Quarterly* 50(3):227-36.

Wagner, D. G. 1988. "Status Violations: Toward an Expectation States Theory of the Social Control of Deviance." Pp. 110-12 in *Status Generalization: New Theory and Research*, edited by M. Webster, Jr. and M. Foschi. Stanford, CA: Stanford University Press.

Wagner, D. G. and J. Berger. 1985. "Do Sociological Theories Grow?" *American Journal of Sociology* 90(4):697-728.

————. forthcoming. "Status Characteristics Theory: Growth of a Research Program." In *Theoretical Research Programs: Studies in the Growth of Theory*, edited by J. Berger and M. Zelditch, Jr. Stanford, CA: Stanford University Press.

Walker, Henry A. and Bernard P. Cohen. 1985. "Scope Statements: Imperatives for Evaluating Theory." *American Sociological Review* 50:288-301.

Webster, M. A., Jr., and J. E. Driskell, Jr. 1978. "Status Generalization: A Review and Some New Data." *American Sociological Review* 43:220-36.

————. 1983. "Beauty as Status." *American Journal of Sociology* 89:140-65.

Wood, W. and S. J. Karten. 1986. "Sex Differences in Interaction Style as a Product of Perceived Sex Differences in Competence." *Journal of Personality and Social Psychology* 50(2):341-47.

Yuchtman-Yaar, E. and M. Semyonov. 1979. "Ethnic Inequality in Israeli Schools and Sports: An Expectation-States Approach." *American Journal of Sociology* 85:576-90.

Zimmerman, D. H. and C. West. 1975. "Sex Roles, Interruptions, and Silences in Conversation." Pp. 105-29 in *Language and Sex: Difference and Dominance*, edited by B. Thorne and N. Henley. Rawley, MA: Newbury House.

Chapter 7

SOCIOLOGICAL METATHEORY AND ITS CULTURED DESPISERS

CHARLES LEMERT
Wesleyan University

"IT MAY BE AN UNEXPECTED UNDERTAKING, and you might rightly be surprised that someone can demand from just those persons who have raised themselves above the herd, and are saturated by the wisdom of the century, a hearing for a subject so completely neglected by them. I confess that I do not know how to indicate anything that presages a fortunate outcome for me, not even the one of winning your approval of my efforts, much less the one of communicating my meaning and enthusiasm to you." (Schleiermacher [1799] 1988, p. 77)

These words were uttered nearly two centuries ago in 1799, just at the time when the first thrills of Enlightenment philosophies and the revolutionary era gave way to the sober reality of a changed world. They are the words with which the 19th century German theologian Friedreich Schleiermacher began his bold defense of what was then a subject of fashionable disdain. Schleiermacher's ([1799] 1988) essays, "On Religion, Speeches to Its Cultured Despisers," addressed a topic as unpopular in his day as sociological metatheory is in ours.

Schleiermacher's defense of religion, thereby, offers several considerations appropriate to today's topic. True, sociological metatheory is generally despised by a seemingly vast majority of cultured sociologists. But just as true, though not as apparent, those in our time who seek to defend metatheory may well have something to learn from Schleiermacher. We at least have the advantage of knowing how his story turned out. From this we can judge Schleiermacher's concern with religion in comparison to our concern with the future of our discipline. We know now what Schleiermacher could not have fully known—that he was rowing with too small oars against a current soon to become a torrent. He sensed, as any reasonable child of the Enlightenment must have, that the despisers of religion were great in number, whatever their culture; thus a defense of religion must be vigorous and imaginative, as his surely was. He proposed to wed elements of Kant's reasonableness and the emotions of his own Moravian piety to suggest that the divine elements in human creatures expressed and explained not only human reason but human emotion as well. Quite apart from its theological value, the argument was appealing because 19th century Europeans, faced with uncertainty on all sides, had feelings enough to go around. They knew enlightened rationality was insufficient to account for the dizzy experience of life in a changing world. Schleiermacher thus sought an enduring place for religion in modernity by uniting Enlightenment and Romanticism, the two most powerful cultures in Germany at the time.

This was a dramatic gesture that soon made him famous. But, by the time of Schleiermacher's death in 1838, Auguste Comte in Paris was well on the way to defining another view of religion—one that appeared to take religion just as seriously, but in fact made mockery of it. Comte's religion was a broken metaphor to justify his deeper, if somewhat screwy, ideas on science and sociology. By the end of the century, Durkheim and Weber held religion in Schleiermacher's same high regard, but without any real faith in it as such. For Durkheim, it was a last hope; for Weber, a hope lost. Schleiermacher could not have believed as he did had he fully realized what would come.

Just the same, we would be prudent to learn from his story, particularly because thought of Schleiermacher's apology for religion leads so naturally to recollections of those who defined our discipline, and defined it with great, if awkward, concern for his subject. Indeed, it may be that the hatred of metatheory in our time issues somehow from the preoccupations of sociology's founders with religion. Comte, Weber, and Durkheim had to set aside their various personal attitudes on religion in order to clear space for sociology. Young Émile Durkheim abandoning the line of rabbis to which he was heir is a convenient symbol of sociology's origins. If this, then would it not be so that cultured sociologists in our time might fear any hint that some of their colleagues still think in terms they consider too much like theology?

One might suppose that I am pressing the rhetorical case too heavily. But I think not. If we examine closely both the despisers of sociological metatheory and its defenders, we find many of the same general attitudes with which the early moderns troubled themselves. Surely, I yield the point that religion and theology are not, in themselves, at real stake in the metatheory controversy. But I do wish to argue that the most general attitudes are the same, and that they are because sociology has not become the science it dreamed of becoming once it separated itself from religion.

The cultured despisers of sociological metatheory are, it might seem obvious, always sociologists. Would that sociology were salient enough in the popular mind that, were it thought we were screwing up by doing too much metatheory, we might expect public outrage—perhaps even George Ritzer defending himself on ABC's *Nightline*. However, the general public is seldom outraged at sociology. Deans, colleagues in the sciences, and other academics sometimes are, but not the general public. At best, the public takes occasional amusement at us when the corporate elite at Washington University kills a department, or the guys at Harvard find another way to make bad news. No, it is only sociologists themselves who despise sociological metatheory.

Despisers of metatheory, so far as I can tell, fall into two camps: (a) those who think they do not do it, but do, half-heartedly and thus poorly; and (b) those who claim they do not but know they do, and in spite of themselves, they do it well. A brief look at both compels the conclusion that whatever we may call it, something like metatheory is difficult not to do.

Surely, the most honorable recent member of the first camp is the late George Homans (1967, 1984). To use a word he used, Homans nearly puked at the metatheoretical pretenses of colleagues at Harvard, Parsons especially. He hated, he said, "words about other people's words," and is reported to have once remarked: "Who cares what old Durkheim once said?" (Tilly 1990, p. 263).[1] Never mind that Homans cared quite a bit about what old Pareto said, the remark is sufficiently disingenuous on its face. George Homans loved pungent and occasionally shocking lines, of which this is one. What he meant to say was this: A real science ought not be *preoccupied* with what the dead have said.

Homans meant, thereby, pretty much the same thing James Coleman (1990) means in the very first lines of his recent book, *Foundations of Social Theory:* " 'Social theory,' as taught in the universities, is largely a history of social thought. An unfriendly critic would say that current practice in social theory consists of chanting old mantras and invoking nineteenth-century theorists" (p. xv). For those who have not looked at Coleman's book it is necessary to report that the first words, "social theory," appear inexplicably in quotation marks. This suggests right off that the book's title is a bit of a trick—that the book itself may have a lot to do with "foundations" but perhaps little with social theory as commonly conceived. The second sentence refers to "unfriendly critics" of social theory in a feigned third person as though the author, Coleman, is not one of them; yet, the reader soon realizes that proper social theorists of the kind Coleman has in mind would never describe their work as "chanting old mantras." (Notice, by the way, how religion lurks so near the surface.)

Those in camp with Homans and Coleman could not possibly mean what they are saying: that we should have nothing at all to do with those who precede us. Rather, I suppose, they intend to free us from bondage to tradition. This freedom from mystical incantations can be had only when social theory concerns itself with explanation, a term Homans used with elegant simplicity. In a like but less elegant manner, Coleman's first chapter bears the title "Metatheory" and the subtitle "Explanation in Social Science." In both cases, and most others in this camp, explanation is to the invocation of 19th century theories; as science is to religion. The first members of each analogue are progressive; the latter regressive. Scientific explanation is modern; sacred incantations are traditional.

Thus we see just how tricky members of this camp can be. Metatheory, to them, is regressive, traditional, and virtually religious, certainly unscientific. This conviction with respect to the foolishness of others whom they despise is derived logically, if not forthrightly, from their own very specific beliefs about science, modernity, and human progress. It is not surprising that both Homans and Coleman attempt to explain systems of social behavior with references to variants of very early 19th century doctrines. Homans argues the case for a vigorous methodological individualism, Coleman for a creative reconsideration of that doctrine.[2] The Homans-Coleman line has made fine contributions to our knowledge. This few would dispute. But it cannot be relied upon for wisdom about metatheory. Their denials aside, they too stand on the shoulders of giants. What concerns these people cannot be either metatheory or its interest in what others have said, but something foundational though fragile in their ideas of the nature of social science.[3]

The second camp of despisers differs slightly but importantly from the first. These are the despisers of metatheory who admit cautiously that they do it, but think they do it better. They are, on the surface, just as vigilant in their rebuke of metatheory as those in the previous camp. Jonathan Turner (1987), for example, considers metatheorizing "interesting philosophy and, at times, fascinating history of ideas, but it is not theory and it is not easily used in analytic theorizing" (p. 162). A similar view is expressed by Randall Collins (1986) who accounts the failures of current sociology to its scientific failure and attributes this failure in turn partly to metatheory. The trouble with metatheory, says Collins, is that it depends on "intellectual life elsewhere" and is not "creative in its own right."[4]

Collins and Turner both have in mind a kind of clearheadedness as the standard for good theory. Theirs is the ideal of the free-thinking, independent soul, an individual well-enough disciplined to resist temptations to study ideas just because they are "interesting" or "fascinating" (to recall Turner's remark). They reject these more expressive, hence traditional, intellectual values for those more creative, productive, and useful. If Homans and Coleman disguise their theoretical reliance on early 19th century utilitarians, Collins and Turner would seem to deny theirs on 18th century standards of a free-thinking, creative intelligence thoroughly susceptible to enlightenment. Other than this slight preference for one century over another, the real reason to distinguish the Collins-Turner camp from the Homans-Coleman camp is that the former, at least, is scrupulously honest and explicit in its borrowings from others. Members of this camp choose to call this practice by some name other than metatheory, and they have every right to do so. A name, however, is but a name; and practices are what they are.

I do not know any two sociologists who use the ideas of others more generously and creatively than do Collins and Turner. Both are serious students of 19th century social thought, and both develop theories on an inspiring range of topics in the closest possible connection with the work of others. Turner's behavioral theory of structures draws seriously and well on Durkheim, Freud, Mead, and Garfinkel, just as Collins's concept of interaction ritual chains would make no sense without the supposed Durkheimian side of Goffman. To claim, as does Turner, that this is analytic theorizing, not metatheory, is a right we can grant without being fooled; just as to tell us, as does Collins, that his relation to Goffman and Durkheim is not an act of "dependence" but one of free creativity is simply the prerogative of a truly creative thinker. Let them have their tastes. They depend like the rest of us on what others have said, even old Durkheim. What they want to reject by calling it metatheory is a disposition whereby some people derive pleasure shorn of utility from certain ideas. They want, in other words, to cleanse sociology of its prescientific impulses.[5]

Collins and Turner, like Homans and Coleman, read and write of the old, dead men, and honor them by using their ideas. If they represent two marginally different styles of annoyance with metatheory, they are close together in two respects: a strongly individualistic view of scientific work and an inclination to deny sociology's continuing reliance on pre- or extrascientific desires and interests. They are, in other words, similarly irritated by those who study Durkheim for no better reasons than pleasure or interest. This for them has too much the feel of a premodern disposition unable or unwilling to produce good science. So powerful is their concern (and we must respect it on this account) that they assert their own implicit 18th and 19th century metatheories without any reflex, not a pause to consider the historical necessities of their own choices.

Given that the despisers all do excellent work, useful and interesting to varying degrees to most sociologists, it is proper to ask, Why bother to make things worse by rebuking those who rebuke others? Does metatheory, after all, make that much difference? The answer, of course, is no. It is a fine thing for some to do, and to do as they please. It is also fine, just as well, for others to despise it. The only thing that makes a difference here is what the controversy tells us about the issues facing sociology, and thus about what we all should do, in our work, whatever it is, and what we think of our discipline. This is important because, we should recall, Schleiermacher's interposition in the controversy over religion, bold and imaginative though it was, did nothing at all in the long run to retard the eventual erosion of religious sentiment in the modern world. We do not yet know if the Age of Sociology is running the same course now that religion ran in 1799. Certainly, many think it is. The Washington University corporate academy (funded, if I am not mistaken, by a dog food company), or the Chicago school for the defense of Western civilization (founded by Alan Bloom and his friends) are the more visible external detractors of sociology. But we would be mistaken to assume they are the only ones. Sociology is poorly understood, and not always appreciated; and when deans get the idea that there is precedent and justification to get rid of something with a poor cost-benefit ratio, they know exactly what to do, and how to do it.

This, I think, is the larger historical perspective from which best to interpret the metatheory debate. The cultured despisers of metatheory within sociology are devoted to their discipline. But the cultured despisers of sociology outside the discipline are not; far from it. What can be learned from thinking about the despisers of metatheory is that brilliance, creativity, hard work, and other virtues of this sort are not sufficient in themselves. Schleiermacher was both brilliant and productive. He defended religion with exceptional creativity. But he could not save it. In our time, it is possible that both the despisers and defenders of metatheory in sociology are in the Schleiermacher position. One could argue that the defenders of metatheory very often do exactly as the despisers. They desire to defend the practice of metatheory on the grounds that a good metatheory makes a better science. This useful and helpful attitude, however, takes the despisers too seriously on their own terms and denies one special quality of metatheory—the sheer pleasure of reading and writing about interesting ideas and people. No doubt, as George Ritzer (1991) has demonstrated, metatheory has much to contribute to social scientific work. But to insist too much on the *utility* of theory—whether metatheory or mundane theory—is to put at risk the one unique value that metatheorists sometimes (not always) possess in greater amount than do despisers, whose attention to science is usually quite sober, even stern.

Metatheory, whatever we call it, is literally for "thinking about," thus reflecting upon, the ideas we use as such. It is, therefore, an activity unable to thrive in climates overly conditioned to hard work, progress, useful analytic theories, and the like. I have suggested that the most prominent despisers of metatheory in sociology cannot avoid being, at least, half-hearted metatheorizers. Even they reflect enough on their theories, and the theories of others, to incur real debts to tradition. They are, however, unable to find, or make, the time to "think after" the foundations of their own theories. Hence, to take the most salient current example, the astonishing witness of James Coleman—an accomplished modernist who scoffs at 19th century incantations, yet who invokes, across nearly 1,000 pages of text, a variant of 19th century doctrine[6] to explain the late 20th century, and possibly postmodern, world. He has every right to do what he wishes—and granting what it is, he does the thing brilliantly. Nonetheless, others are right to wonder if Coleman has thought after the connections between his implicit metatheory of modernity from which he derives his view of science, and, if he has, why he made the theoretical choices he made? If he has not, might he have chosen otherwise?

Yet, there are still other questions one can ask of Coleman directly, and in some instances of other of metatheory's despisers, indirectly.

In James Coleman's case, one might ask after the connection between his implicit metatheory, which evidently entails his view of the science of modernity, and his public association with groups like the National Association of Scholars that are concerned with bias and distortion in the university curriculum. The National Association of Scholars, on whose advisory council Coleman serves, campaigns aggressively against academic colleagues who, in the Association's words, wish "to eliminate allegedly 'Eurocentric' and 'patriarchal' bias in the curriculum." In particular this group contests the idea that "the 'canon' be revised to include more works by blacks, other ethnic minorities, and women."[7] Those who have seen the advertisement in *The Chronicle of Higher Education* in which these concerns are expressed will recall that the text, like Coleman's opening line in *Foundations of Social Theory*, liberally uses quotation marks and irony to make its point, namely: The alleged canon is only allegedly biased against women, blacks, and other minorities. Credit is due at least for honesty in naming women and blacks, but one shudders to imagine whom exactly they include under "other minorities." But there is no doubt that the statement is directed against Women's Studies, Afro-American Studies, Cultural Studies, and—to borrow their ploy—other programs in the University.

And so with this one illustration, the line of thought comes full circle. Those who consider programs in black, feminist, and minority studies a threat to the curriculum are not likely to have overlooked the extent to which these programs are very often programmatically and intellectually supported by sociologists, particularly younger or newer ones. In other words, at this precise point at least one sociological despiser of metatheory in sociology is in clear alliance with despisers of sociology in the academy. Though the alliance may be intentionally formed in some cases, its darker origins lie in the bowels of modernity itself.[8]

The despisers of metatheory disavow their own quietly whispered invocations of 19th century ideas from which they derive, just the same, a definite view of social science. The Coleman case is, again, instructive. He is perfectly consistent, and beautifully so, in pursuing the details of his largely unannounced metatheory—a metatheory he believes, one must assume, requires no announcement because it is taken for granted to be the theory that stands behind all theory, and all science. Thus his list of the "elementary actions and relations" constitutive of social theory reads like an index of cultural literacy in Enlightenment principles: Interest and Control, Rights to Act, Authority

Relations, Relations of Trust (Coleman 1990, Part I, passim). This is a perfectly fine list of elements, but a historically conditioned one. Coleman has made this choice. Others called upon to list the elements of a social theory might just as reasonably name Race, Class, Gender, Position in the World System, and Sexual Orientation—elements that do not figure in Coleman's theory of social theory.[9] How then do we decide, rationally, which is the better list? Can we decide? Perhaps not.[10] But is not this precisely the question put at issue by the National Association of Scholars to which Coleman lends support? Coleman, as author of the *Foundations of Social Theory*, develops a theory within a metatheory he does not name. Coleman, sponsor of the National Association of Scholars and, thereby, defender of the canon, in effect names and acts in the name of a metatheory of Western Civilization.

Today science and politics, like science and religion in Schleiermacher's day, are at considerable odds. Some people today, like those then, consider these odds good; others find them unfortunate. What is much beyond dispute is that the controversy exists, and that it has important implications for the future of science, social science, and all other forms of intellectual work in the university. No one seems to disagree on this point. Who then can reasonably claim there is no room for a historically grounded metatheory of social theory, including a frank avowal of the historical antecedents of that theory? Only, one supposes, those who disavow metatheory in their science in order, in their politics, to assert an authoritative right to act invoked as an appeal to trust the Tradition and its canon. This, one must believe, even they would admit is an unreasonable inconsistency.

Schleiermacher did not succeed in his defense of religion because history moved against him. Our situation is more complex. History may be moving against sociology. We cannot know for sure that it is, but we shall develop good theories of this history only if we develop good theories of those theories, and of the ways in which our unacknowledged debts to the past determine our present actions. It makes no difference what we call this practice. It only matters that we do it.

Schleiermacher concluded his first speech to the cultured despisers of religion with these words: "Now it is up to you to decide whether it is worth your while to listen . . . before you become still more entrenched in your contempt."

NOTES

1. Concerning his relations with Parsons and his use of "puke," see Homans (1984) and Lemert (1986).

2. Concerning Homans on methodological individualism, see *The Nature of Social Science* (1967). Coleman is known to have said on various occasions that his book is not generally well understood. It is in fact a complex argument, an admirable effort to revise not just this classic proposition but also the most important matters at issue in sociological theory (the famous macro-micro problem most notably). However poorly his critics may have appreciated his argument, certain of its foundational principles are beyond ambiguity. Though he clearly establishes the intent of orienting social theory to the explanation of the behavior of social systems with reference to their components (Coleman 1990, p. 27, compare p. 2), the social individual remains a theoretical foundation of his theory. Even where actors are defined without necessary reference to the social individual, it is clear that the individual's rights and freedoms ground "the internal analysis of system behavior" in a "humanistically congenial image of man" (p. 4). Thus Coleman's axiomatic statements must be read with reference to his attempt to generate a special variant of methodological individualism (p. 5); for example: "A minimal basis for a social system of action is two actors, each having control over resources of interest to the other" (p. 29). Nowhere is this more evident than in his definition of social capital (widely considered to be the most original and distinctive contribution of the argument): "The function identified by the concept 'social capital' is the value of those aspects of social structure to actors, as resources that can be used to realize their interests" (p. 305). Here, as throughout the book, Coleman cites Bourdieu favorably, but he could not possibly be farther from Bourdieu's intent to transcend the very Enlightenment oppositions—subject/object, individual/social structure—Coleman takes for granted. (See, for example, Bourdieu 1990, p. 34, among numerous other places.) It is surely Coleman's right to take for granted what he wishes, and to be understood or misunderstood on those terms. But it is quite something else to claim to do a social theory free of 19th century invocations (or transcendent of them) while using variants of 19th century metaphysics to claim social theoretical superiority to Marx, Weber, and Durkheim (Coleman 1990, pp. 6-10). To claim to be free of what one is not is an old mantra of its own sort.

3. Nor should we assume that all forthright despisers of metatheory are of the same theoretical inclinations as are Homans and Coleman. This general attitude toward metatheory so far exceeds their neoclassical line in social theory as to include writers like Theda Skocpol (1986) whose poisonous review of Alford and Friedland's *The Powers of Theory* bore the title "The Dead End of Metatheory." Skocpol's methodology is as little individualistic as one can get, yet she holds and defends a view of theory, including metatheory, nearly the same as that of her teacher, Homans.

4. Ritzer (1991) provides a genial rebuke of Collins' rejection of metatheory (cf. Ritzer 1989).

5. They are in this respect not much different from Talcott Parsons who began the late modern period in theory, and metatheory, with the question, Who now reads Spencer?, then defended his close reading of those he thought we should read with the insistence that historically occurring theories are, after all, data.

6. See Note 2.

7. *Is the Curriculum Biased?* is a paid advertisement by the National Association of Scholars, in the *Chronicle of Higher Education*, November 8, 1989, p. A23.

8. I wish to be as clear as possible on this point, most especially to respect the concerns of those (the National Association of Scholars prominently included) who claim there is too much politically correct cant in and behind much social theory today. It is not a question of inferring that despisers of metatheory, of whichever sort, are by that fact insensitive to the intellectual and moral claims of women, blacks, and minorities. They may or may not be. Some, in my opinion, clearly are. It is rather a clear question of the stakes at play in any flippant disavowal of metatheory in the name of science.

9. None of these concepts or their usual cognates is indexed. None is discussed seriously. In a brief section on slavery (Coleman 1990, pp. 86-88) neither race or gender is mentioned; in a section on nation-states in the world economic system (pp. 660-2) there is no mention of colonial or postcolonial circumstances; and so on.

10. Rorty (1989) thinks not.

REFERENCES

Bourdieu, Pierre. 1990. *In Other Words: Essays Towards a Reflexive Sociology,* translated by Matthew Adamson. Stanford, CA: Stanford University Press.

Coleman, James. 1990. *Foundations of Social Theory.* Cambridge, MA: Harvard University Press.

Collins, Randall. 1986. "Is 1980s Sociology in the Doldrums?" *American Journal of Sociology* 86:1336-55.

Homans, George. 1967. *The Nature of Social Science.* New York: Harcourt, Brace & World.

———. 1984. *Coming to My Senses, An Autobiography of a Sociologist.* New Brunswick, NJ: Transaction.

Lemert, Charles. 1986. "Whole Life Social Theory." *Theory and Society* 15:439-41.

Ritzer, George. 1989. "Collins Does Metatheory (Again) and He Does It (Pretty) Well." *Symbolic Interaction* 12:81-84.

———. 1991. *Metatheorizing in Sociology.* Lexington, MA: Lexington Books.

Rorty, Richard. 1989. *Contingency, Irony, and Solidarity.* New York: Cambridge University Press.

Schleiermacher, Friedrich. [1799] 1988. *On Religion, Speeches to Its Cultured Despisers,* translated by Richard Crouter. New York: Cambridge University Press.

Skocpol, Theda. 1986. "The Dead End of Metatheory." *Contemporary Sociology* 16:10-12.

Tilly, Charles. 1990. "George Caspar Homans and the Rest of Us." *Theory and Society* 19:261-8.

Turner, Jonathan. 1987. "Analytic Theorizing." In *Social Theory Today,* edited by Anthony Giddens and Jonathan Turner. Berkeley: University of California Press.

Chapter 8

THE POSTMODERN DISCOURSE OF METATHEORY

DEENA WEINSTEIN
DePaul University

MICHAEL A. WEINSTEIN
Purdue University

THE FOLLOWING DISCUSSION is a theorization of metatheory. Theory is necessarily reflexive in the sense that it presupposes a definition of what it is theorizing or at least an affirmation that what it is theorizing is ill defined. A theorization of metatheory, therefore, presupposes some judgment on the definition of metatheory.

Metatheory will be defined here after Ritzer (1988), as a concern with "the study of theories, theorists, communities of theorists, as well as the larger intellectual and social contexts of theories and theorists." Its object is the "underlying structure of sociological theory" (p. 188).

Ritzer (1990) places metatheory in a wider process of "metatheorizing," which includes at least three ways of undertaking "the systematic study of sociological theory" (p. 3). The types of metatheorizing are distinguished not so much by different thought processes or textual operations as by the possible aims of reflective practice. Metatheory proper is the aim of metatheorizing when that process is a means of achieving a deeper understanding of theory. But metatheorizing may also be undertaken as a prelude to the construction of new sociological theory, as for example, Marx did in his critical syntheses of idealist philosophy, classical positivism, and political economy; and Parsons (1949) did in *The Structure of Social Action* by synthesizing the contributions of Marshall, Durkheim, Weber, and Pareto. Alternatively, metatheorizing may be used to create perspectives that overarch sociological theory, achieving fresh theoretical integrations for their own sakes.

Metatheory proper is essential to the other two forms of meta-theorizing defined by Ritzer, because some understanding of the structure of extant sociological theory is necessary for both the generation of new theory from it and for the creation of overarching perspectives that synthesize all parts of it. In contrast, the generation of new theory and the creation of overarching perspectives are not essential to the constitution of metatheory, although they may be thought of as possible fruitions of it or, in the case of the overarching perspective, which is a provisional synthesis of theories, even as an aspect or, perhaps, the perfection or finality of it. Metatheory proper, therefore, will always be a product of metatheorizing, either as its express aim or as its necessary, though not always sufficient, condition, and as its inevitable by-product.

The first step in a theorization of metatheory is to acknowledge that metatheory is an element in the discourse formation of contemporary American sociology. It is an eruption within the professional discipline of sociology and it has a history within that discipline. One might easily conceive of informal sociology being done outside a professional discipline, but it is difficult to imagine informal metatheory. Metatheory has a complete dependence on the discipline of sociology because its object is the structure of theory in that discipline, which structure is the cultural form of the discipline itself. Metatheory is the study of the cultural form of sociology, in both its process of constitution and in its constituted forms.

Theory is the cultural form of sociology in the sense that it defines the categories through which the objects of sociology are described and the relative importance of those objects in relation to each other. At the very least theory provides the language in which sociologists justify rhetorically their other practices. At the most it conditions what is judged to be an object that qualifies to be investigated sociologically. The power of theory to give form to sociology probably lies somewhere between these two extremes, which is to say that to claim that theory is the cultural form of sociology is not to maintain that that form is unitary or even precisely definable.

A theorization of metatheory is itself a distinctive form of metatheorizing and an example of metatheory, because it considers metatheory as a set of disciplinary practices within sociology. A metatheorist is necessarily a theorist, a theorist of theory. A theory of theorizing theory is itself a theorization of theory. Hence, there is no infinite regress involved in theorizing about metatheory. There is no metatheory of metatheory: there is only more metatheory.

The definition of metatheory being used here is not neutral, but excludes a competing definition and confronts an interpretation of sociology that would exclude it from the discipline. A theorization of metatheory is logically compelled to be partisan and polemical. It must distinguish itself from, if not refute, its competitor, and it must defend its inclusion within sociology. The distinction and defense will bring out the "underlying structure" of metatheory by contrast effects, placing it within the possible discourse formations of contemporary American sociology.

THE DISTINCTION

As the study of the cultural form of sociology, metatheory is distinguished from another form of thinking that has sometimes been called metatheory, but that is more generally denominated as philosophical sociology. In the first half of the 20th century, when sociology was undergoing its formation as an independent discipline centered in the academy, a wide range of foundations were offered for it with the intent of fixing its aims, objects, and methods. Those programs or proposals for foundations were not internal to the discipline but sought to control its directions from the outside through metaphysical and epistemological principles. Philosophical sociology was an array of attempts to capture sociology for one or another broader philosophical project, including the vision of sociology as one of the positive sciences, disciplined by whatever epistemes interpreted the particular positivistic programs, since there were many of them.

Philosophical sociologies attempted to give structures to sociology rather than to investigate its extant structures. They were metaphysical theories of sociology, which contained subordinate metatheories, because they had to interpret sociological theories within their metaphysical and epistemological principles. Indeed, they tended to absorb sociological theories into philosophical propositions based in philosophical anthropology. Philosophical sociologies tended toward the notion that general sociology should support a philosophical vision, be it Marxism, behaviorism, organic naturalism, social-action theory, neo-Thomism, or existential phenomenology, among others. They were prescriptive even if they deployed the rhetoric of presence (Derrida, 1973) and placed sociology within an image of some privileged form of reality or interpretation of human nature.

It is deceptive, of course, to put the discussion of philosophical sociology in the past tense. Even as sociology became a free-standing discipline, the complexity of which, in practice, began to outrun any possible philosophical program to direct it, attempts continued to be made and still persist to bring it under such a program. Such attempts might even be considered to be normal if one follows Kuhn (1962) in holding that theories in the sciences are related to more general paradigms that include metaphysical and epistemological presuppositions. In that case any sociological theory will contain, at least implicitly, a philosophical sociology. That philosophical sociology will tend to be made explicit and self-reflexive when the theory bids for acceptance against competing alternatives. As long as sociology remains a multiparadigm discipline or a protoparadigm discipline there will be explicit endeavors to contrive philosophical justifications for theories, that is, to prescribe theories of and for sociology. Those prescribed theories will normally have a descriptive component; that is, they will elucidate some aspect of the extant structures of sociological theory in addition to legislating the structures that it should have. Philosophical sociology will, therefore, include some of what is defined in the present discussion as metatheory, but only as a reflection of its metaphysical or epistemological principles.

Where precisely is the distinction to be made between philosophical sociology and metatheory as defined by Ritzer and theorized in the present discussion? Turner (1986) contrasts metatheories that prescribe prerequisites for the conduct of theory to metatheories that study extant theories. Ritzer (1988, p. 187) follows Turner, but goes a step farther by excluding from metatheory "broader philosophical questions about what sociological theory ought to be doing" and by confining it to the "objective study of extant theories," including their underlying presuppositions. But according to Ritzer's definition of metatheory one of its objects is "the larger intellectual and social contexts of theories and theorists." There is a question, then, as to whether and, if so, how queries about what sociological theory ought to be belong to the larger intellectual and social context of theories.

On the face of it, attempting to prescribe the nature and limits of sociological theory is one of the ways in which theory is theorized in the discipline of sociology. From that viewpoint it must be included within metatheory as one of its objects of study. Ritzer does this when he describes its structure, but at the same time he excludes its practice from his definition of what metatheory is/ought to be. Metatheory has a built-in ambivalence. As a study of theorization in sociology it must include the study of attempts to prescribe for theory, but as a disciplinary practice its code must prescribe forbearance from prescribing for theory. Metatheory is the sociological variant of the more general postmodernist cultural tendency of "antifoundationalism."[1] Philosophical sociologies are foundationalist in the sense that they suggest or legislate rules for theorists to follow based on metaphysical accounts of reality, moral ideals, or epistemological standards. They criticize all competing foundationalist doctrines in terms of their own definitions of foundations, and they criticize antifoundationalism as a form of skepticism that will not admit to its own presuppositions. In contrast, antifoundationalism criticizes foundationalism itself, eschewing any attempt to impose a theoretical program on sociology.

Metatheory also has a kinship with European poststructuralism, especially with the variant of it presented by Jean-François Lyotard (1984).[2] Lyotard distinguishes between narrative and scientific forms of knowledge, the first of which functions to orient human beings to their social existence through the temporal frames provided by such discursive structures as tradition, common sense, myth, ideology, and metaphysics; and the second of which functions to provide denotative inferences about the objects it describes and orders into explanatory networks. In terms of the present discussion, philosophical sociology belongs on the side of narrative knowledge, providing what Lyotard calls "metanarratives," which claim to tell fundamental and all-encompassing stories about the place of human beings in historical reality. Lyotard (1984, p. xxiv) notes that, in contemporary culture, metanarratives, foremost among them the one that equates science with reason, have lost their privilege as the legitimators of and lawgivers to the sciences. He offers as an alternative to them a kind of thinking that abjures the imposition of totalities that pretend to systematize reality, and that is sensitive to differences and to fresh combinatory possibilities; that is, a kind of thinking that is similar to some of the operations of metatheorizing.

Lyotard provides a way of clarifying the difference between a philosophical sociology and what Ritzer calls an "overarching perspective" on extant theory. When metatheory is used as a means of synthesizing theories it does not produce accounts of the historical reality (metanarratives), but narratives of narratives; stories of theory, not the story of history. These stories of theory are always provisional because they are not founded on fixed metaphysical, epistemological, or moral principles, but as Ritzer (1990, p. 4) notes, are "derived from theory," the object of which changes and cannot be constrained by prior closure. Metanarratives are static frames for the flux of historical life, whereas the overarching perspectives created by metatheorizing are provisional totalizations of theory that have an indeterminate relation to any extratheoretical references.

Does metatheory presuppose that there are no possible metaphysical, moral, or epistemological foundations for sociology? If it does, then it falls into a dogmatic skepticism that is as certain of the impossibility of foundations as any foundationalism is of its account of foundations. But there is no reason for antifoundationalist metatheory to move to closure as a contrafoundationalism. An alternative to closure is a hyperreflexivity, whereby metatheory claims that no extant foundationalism has achieved general assent from sociologists or has successfully established its truth, and that unless one does either or both the way is open to pursue a wide range of inquiries into the structure(s) of extant theories. As a permission to study extant theorization, metatheory acknowledges its possible historical relativity. If either a consensus on the metaphysical foundations of sociological theory was achieved or sociology became a single-paradigm science through the hegemony of a grounded theory, then metatheory would collapse back into philosophical sociology. The ground for the possibility of metatheory is the multiplicity of theorization in sociology, which permits a second-level theorization about the process of constituting and the form of the theoretical object. Metatheory distinguishes itself from philosophical sociology by bracketing out any judgments on the truth or falsehood of any foundationalist claims. It will ordinarily be undertaken by theorists who are not convinced of the truth of any foundationalism, and it will be self-lucid if it suspends judgment on the issue of foundationalism rather than raising a skeptical defense against it.

Philosophical sociology treats the multiplicity of theorizations as an opportunity for the critique of error and the vindication of some presumed metaphysical, moral, or epistemological truth against opposition. Metatheory treats the multiplicity of theorizations as an opportunity for multiple operations of analysis and synthesis. It is the reflexive awareness of multiplicity based on a reasoned forbearance from efforts to reduce that multiplicity to unity through philosophical speculation. The same individual may, of course, be both a metatheorist and a philosophical sociologist as long as the two activities are kept reflexively distinct. In its distinction from its competitor, philosophical sociology, metatheory is an admission of theoretical multiplicity and a permission to study it in a variety of ways. One would not expect it to be undertaken by someone who believed with certitude in a foundationalist metaphysics of society or of science. It elucidates the structure of difference, not the unity of differences.

THE DEFENSE

As a response to the multiplicity of theorizations in contemporary sociology, metatheory studies those theorizations as social constructions and as cultural constructs with the aim of disclosing whatever structure(s) that they evince both singly and as a multiplicity. It does not prescribe structures for theorization but studies the prescriptions of philosophical sociologies as part of its field of objects, refusing to pass judgment for or against them while placing and interpreting them within its larger discursive field. Metatheory does not replace philosophical sociology or attempt to prohibit its practice but stalemates it by offering its own alternative secondary reflection on theory: Metatheory includes philosophical sociology as an object by excluding it as a practice. Historically metatheory is a postmodernist form of thinking that signals the liberation of secondary reflection from any metaphysical master discourse or metanarrative. It is the permission to clarify and provisionally order, enabled by forbearance from imposing philosophical foundations.

From the standpoint of cultural history metatheory is an intelligible development or emergent within a wider disciplinary practice that is characterized by theoretical diversity and competition. It is an effort to gain greater understanding of that diversity and competition, not by resolving it through metaphysical fiat, but by revealing its social conditions and by following the continuities and ruptures of its artifacts, sociological theories. Through conceptual clarification of presuppositions metatheory may effect convergences or even reconciliations among competing theories, just as well as it may show sharp differences among theoretical formations that seemed to be allied. It provides a clarifying service for theory as a whole, not for any particular theory, and, so, it transcends ordinary theoretical debate, which considers the structure(s) of theory as a whole only to plead a partisan case. Metatheory systematizes in a nonreductive way.

Understood as an intelligible emergent within the cultural history of sociological theory, there would seem to be no reason to argue against metatheory as one of the legitimate practices of sociological inquiry. What grounds could there be for claiming that there is something wrong with stepping back from the fray with a reflective gaze and mapping the field of play? Yet there is a widespread animus against metatheory within sociology. Nobody would think of arguing, for example, that the sociology of the family should not be practiced, but some do contend that metatheory should be abandoned. Metatheory must defend itself against the attack on it because that attack is itself an implied comment on the structure of theoretical discourse.

Theda Skocpol (1986) has made explicit the complaints against metatheory that are prevalent in the discipline. In her review essay, "The Dead End of Metatheory," she mocks "metatheoretical urges" to "classify the grounds of other people's arguments rather than pursue substantive problems" (p. 10). She then moves on to the more substantive point that "metatheoretical exercises risk creating artificial ideal-typical categorizations that obscure rather than illuminate the more fruitful tendencies in substantive theory and research" (p. 10). Although Skocpol does not develop her case against metatheory with any precision (if she did so she would be engaged in metatheorizing) her sentiment is obvious and her intent is discernible. From her standpoint, metatheory is a dead end because it diverts the energies of sociologists from substantive problems to classifying given arguments, and because the activity of classification tends to result in oversimplified distortions of ongoing theory and research.

Skocpol's two points are not logically dependent on each other and will be considered here separately. Her first claim, that metatheory draws energies away from substantive research, cannot be denied in the obvious sense that the time and effort spent on metatheorizing could be applied to other kinds of sociological inquiry. But, without any further elaboration, it begs the question of whether or not the time spent on metatheorizing is time well spent. An answer to that begged question has already been given above in the claim that metatheory provides for sociological theory a description and manifold analysis of its discursive field, liberated from the reductive descriptions and analyses of that field offered in ordinary theoretical debate and in the philosophical sociologies that grow up as ideological components of that debate. A consequence of the metatheoretical topology of the field of theory is to relativize the pretensions of any of the players on that field—that is, to make each of the players aware that there is a context in which they play that outruns adequate description in the terms of their own particular theoretical categories. The intellectual humility fostered in theory by metatheory works to moderate the claims of any specific theory, most importantly the claim to be able to theorize theory as a whole within the categories of any specific theory. Its primary function in the economy of sociology is to provide a reflexive and explicit antidote to theoretical absolutization, which it accomplishes, first of all, by classifying "the grounds of other people's arguments."

If one grants that the categories adequate for describing the discursive field of sociological theory outrun the categories for describing that field within any particular sociological theory, then the question becomes one of whether or not a special reflexive effort should be made to delineate, analyze, and explore that field as a whole—that is, whether it is wise, prudent, or legitimate to essay provisional totalizations of theory. In the absence of such a provisionally totalizing practice the context of theorization is left deliberately unclarified, which seems, on the face of it, to be a simple prohibition of rational inquiry. Politically, such prohibitions, as Skocpol surely knows, are imposed or recommended by those who stand to benefit from general ignorance of the nature and relativity of their presuppositions. What Skocpol implies is that theoretical debate in sociology can take care of itself very well, thank you, without a metatheoretical monitor. That is a social Darwinist understanding of theoretical discourse that favors those discursive formations that are able to mobilize the greatest support in the discipline. A metatheoretical name for Skocpol's position might be "disciplinary positivism," the view that the disciplinary practice of a science is/should be self-sufficient and self-determining, and has no need for any secondary reflection on its theorizations. That position is an alternative to metatheory on the skeptical flank. Like all skepticisms, it is self-refuting because it takes a position within the discourse that it claims to doubt.

The metatheoretical parry of disciplinary positivism yields an unsuspected characteristic or bias of metatheory, which further determines it as a distinctive discourse formation. If disciplinary positivism is social Darwinist, then metatheory, by taking up a reflexive position toward theory, tends to level the playing field by treating less popular or less successful theoretical alternatives as elements in the field, granting them legitimacy by analyzing their structure and presuppositions, and explaining, at least in part, their lack of success in terms of social conditions, for example, disciplinary power and status structures. Metatheory, then, is not thoroughly neutral, but includes a partisanship in its transcendence of ordinary theoretical debate. Simply by its totalizing practice it lends legitimacy to the socially (though not necessarily intellectually) weak in their struggle against the strong. It stalemates philosophical attempts to impose a theoretical program on sociology and it critiques the social Darwinist pretense of trusting in interperspective debate to let the truth will out. Its admission of multiplicity and its commitment to study it enhance theoretical pluralism and favor, though do not insure or presuppose, theoretical egalitarianism.

Skocpol's second point, that metatheoretical classification risks oversimplifying and distorting ongoing theory and research, is a much less significant claim than her first one. Abstraction always is effected at a sacrifice of complexity, but that sacrifice can lead as well to clarity of insight as to distortion. The question here is not one of whether metatheory should be undertaken at all, but one of distinguishing between good and bad examples of metatheory. Only if sociological theories are such uniquely qualitative entities that classifying them would destroy their nature can the argument be made that classifying them must distort them.[3] But theories are already abstractions from more concrete strata of inquiry. The damage is already done, if science damages, by theory. Here again, from the political viewpoint, the appeal to complexity against "artificial" categorizations is associated with a conservatism which protects vested interests by refusing to theorize about them. And, again, metatheory is revealed to work against the kind of intellectual domination that abjures reflection. Metatheory, then, is descriptive but it is not neutral. It critiques a dominant ideology of disciplinary positivism by naming it and giving it a place within the field of metatheoretical objects. In doing so it deprives disciplinary positivism of the social advantage that it gained by remaining implicit, and reveals its intellectual relativity as a self-negating negation of metatheory that stands on the same meta-level as philosophical sociology and metatheory itself.

THEORETICAL PLAY

Standing between philosophical sociology and disciplinary positivism, metatheory constitutes itself by borrowing some aspects of each one of them while excluding other aspects and, therefore, limiting each one's intellectual pretensions. From disciplinary positivism metatheory borrows a confidence in the empirical theories and methods of the sociology of sociology, which it uses to study the social processes through which theorists and groups of theorists within a disciplinary structure constitute theory. Metatheory's acceptance of the sociology of sociology is a precritical move; that is, metatheory will employ the sociology of sociology in the absence of any foundational certification of it from philosophy.[4] That, of course, is what disciplinary positivism does in every field of sociology. It does not wait for philosophical permission and direction before it goes to work on inquiry. But metatheory rejects the pretension of disciplinary positivism that the theories and methods of sociology are self-sufficient and self-justified. They are submitted by it to a critical and totalizing reflection that it borrows from philosophical sociology.

The philosophical play of metatheory consists in the clarification and provisional totalization or ordering of the discourse formations of sociological theory. Metatheory borrows from philosophical sociology all of the philosophical methods for analyzing, criticizing, and synthesizing sociological theories, which it uses to contextualize theoretical discourses in frames and structures of relationship and disrelationship that are not evinced by any single and extant discourse. Just as metatheory does not invent its own sociology but takes up the sociology of sociology in order to apply it to the constitution of theory; so metatheory does not invent its own reflective methods but uses all of the methods that philosophy has developed to study theories in its own reflection on sociological theories. But metatheory rejects the pretension of philosophical sociology to provide metaphysical, moral, or epistemological foundations for sociological theory. It does not seek to control and direct sociological theory with a master discourse, but simply to identify, describe, and contextualize "the underlying structure of sociological theory."

As a disciplinary practice within sociology, metatheory is an eruption of postmodernist forms of discourse in that discursive field. What is meant specifically by postmodernism here is anti-foundationalism, the suspension of judgment on the question of whether or not there are true propositions about what reality most fundamentally is that can control and direct theorization about the phases, aspects, or regions of that reality. Metatheory is the rejection of attempts to provide foundations for theory and the permission to do without such foundations. It does not seek its own definition of theory, so it uses, by turns, the definitions of theory that are extant in the discipline of sociology, playing them off against one another. But it is also reflexive enough to know that it may imply definitions of theory as it demarcates its field of objects, so it seeks to be explicit about such definitions, acknowledging, too, that they are provisional; for example, the definition of theory as the "cultural form of sociology" offered in the present discussion.

The antifoundationalism of metatheory is most clearly revealed by the split within it between the sociology of theory and the philosophical analysis of theories. Metatheory does not choose between disciplinary positivism and philosophical sociology but is the difference between them. As a branch of sociology it applies sociological empiricism to the practice of sociological theorization, making theorization a dependent variable that is relative to extratheoretical social processes. But as a clarifying and totalizing reflection on theory, it acknowledges the dependence of any description of extratheoretical social processes on some theorization of those processes that can be placed within a structure of other theorizations. Theory, then, is doubly relativized by metatheory, which constitutes itself as both a science of theory and a philosophy of theories, each of which cannot be reduced to the other but are related to each other. Metatheory talks about theory scientifically and about science nonscientifically, that is, purely theoretically. Its life is in the interplay, the *différance* (Derrida, 1973) that makes the differences, which it does not reconcile.

The distinctive historical feature of metatheory is its admission in a postmetaphysical academic culture of nonscientific forms of discourse. It is that feature that most accounts for the resistance to it from broad sectors of sociology. Skocpol, for example, does not mock the sociology of theory but reserves her derision for the "urge" to clarify theoretical presuppositions and then to classify those presuppositions into orders or structures revealing their conceptual relationships and disrelationships. The clarification and ordering of presuppositions comprise a distinctively philosophical form of discourse that has no direct empirical component but that is centered in the intellectual imagination.

The intellectual imagination is the legacy of modern philosophy to postmodernism. Divested of the project of defining totality through discovering foundations, philosophy does not give up a totalizing discourse but merely acknowledges that discourse to be dependent upon extant theorizations and, therefore, provisional. Metatheory, on its philosophical side, is the totalization of theories, not the totalization of society, which is what philosophical sociology attempts. As a series of provisional totalizations of theories, metatheory does not achieve closure in a description of the totality of theory, but it results in a reflexive review of extant theorizations that finds more or less unity among them, depending upon the theoretical objects given to it. It is totalization liberated from the presumption to totality, that is, a free play with theory, controlled neither by empirical observation nor by metaphysical legislation. The scientific side of metatheory treats the social construction of theory as an empirical process. The philosophical side of metatheory treats the constructed theories as objects of the intellectual imagination to be analyzed, criticized, and provisionally systematized or separated. The second side is not anti-positivistic, but it is nonpositivistic.

The two sides of metatheory cannot be unified with one another in a general theory of theory, but they can be coordinated. The constitution of theory within disciplinary power and status structures is the empirical referent for the field of discursive formations of theoretical objects. Those formations arise within that process of constitution and the sociology of that process yields measures of the social strength of discourse formations, of their power over disciplinary practice. Reciprocally, the philosophical contextualization of theories reveals the limits of alternative conceptualizations of the sociology of theory. In the first case theoretical dominance, the popularity or acceptance of theories, is held relative to social conditions. In the second case theorizations of social conditions are held relative to each other and to any structure(s) of intellectual relations discernible among them. The sociology of theory depends upon the philosophical categorization of theories for its dependent variable and for the clarification of its theoretical alternatives. The philosophical totalization of theories depends upon the sociology of theory to show it the nonintellectual conditions for the acceptance and rejection, and the popularity and unpopularity of theories, dispelling any illusion that hegemony, ascendancy, or consensus indicates truth.

Metatheory is, to use Claude Lévi-Strauss's (1966) term, a *bricolage*, a structure of the mind that is not unified by logical relations but by qualitative relations of opposition and similitude. By refusing to privilege either sociology of theory or the philosophical totalization of theories, or to promote any forms of thinking that are not already included within their practice, metatheory forbears from logical systematicity. But, unlike the bricolages of the Lévi-Straussian "savage mind," metatheory does not reconcile its divisions in a unifying myth. Rather, it is a work of a demystified savage mind, that is, of a postmodern mind that has renounced not only the quest for unity but nostalgia for unity and for its quest.

Within the economy of sociology, metatheory functions primarily to provide reflexivity about the alternatives for sociological theorization, their intellectual relations to each other, and the social conditions of their acceptance and rejection. If that function is to be affirmed as legitimate and, perhaps, valuable, then one must acknowledge that contemporary sociology is characterized by a multiplicity of theorizations that resist synthesis or genuine reduction in ongoing theoretical debate. Only under the condition of apparently irreducible plurality is the special move of metatheory justified, because that move embraces plurality in order to discover its underlying social and intellectual structure(s). For those who believe that only one theory is true, metatheory will be dissolved into philosophical sociology. For those who believe that ordinary theoretical debate should take care of itself, metatheory will be suppressed in the interests of disciplinary positivism. Metatheory cannot prove that the two rival beliefs to its own are refutable, but it can include them in its theorization by showing that they are elements in the extant plurality of theorization, irreducible to each other and to itself. From the viewpoint of its disciplinary function metatheory will flourish the more pronounced theoretical pluralization becomes and will decline the more theoretical consensus prevails. Its practice is contingent on the state of theoretical discourse. There would be no possibility for inquiring into an underlying structure of differences if a single theoretical paradigm characterized sociology, either through imposition of a program or the presently unlikely event of a single empirically grounded theory. But if there are competing programs and empirical theories, metatheory's provisional intellectual and empirical totalizations will be a live option, which, from a sociological standpoint, will probably be taken up by some sociologists.

Those who take up metatheory will find themselves engaged, simply by practicing their mode of inquiry, in the culture wars of the contemporary academy. The scientific component of their practice will provoke the opposition of the macrotheorists, such as functionalists and Marxists, who are bidding for hegemony over the discipline. The philosophical component of their practice will provoke the opposition of laissez-faire positivists who find that reflexivity about the relativity of theorizations provides at least some small check on the unbridled struggle among theoretical alternatives. There is no way of getting around the partisanship of metatheory's nonpartisan reflection. Simply by reviewing the entire field of theoretical discourse and by relating the ascendancy of theories to power and status structures, metatheory gives a significance to socially weaker alternatives that they would not have otherwise. Metatheory has an egalitarian bias, which, in the present configuration of sociological discourses, favors non- and antipositivist theorizations against positivistic discourse. It will, therefore, awaken its most pronounced opposition from disciplinary positivists, although it does not seek to replace positivism, but only to displace it by making it one of an array of live options. Metatheory is a participant in the culture wars and must conceive itself in terms of both functionalism (as a contributor to the disciplinary economy) and conflict theory (as an agent of change in that economy).

But metatheory is also something for itself, something distinctively postmodern, which gives it an unborrowed integrity despite its lack of foundations. Metatheory is liberated play with sociological theory, what Georg Simmel (1950) might call the "play-form" of theory or what Jacques Derrida (1973) means by deconstructive play.[5] Considering theories simply in terms of their social conditions, intellectual forms, and intellectual relations to each other, metatheory cuts off from empirical analysis of the wider society and from metaphysical accounts of the englobing reality, accepting direction neither from below nor above. It indulges in the pleasures of the texts and their circumstances, clarifying and continually reordering them in an indefinite play and interplay of provisional contextualizations. It is, finally, (just) the (just) dessert of sociology and not its desert; an open end, not a dead end. And, perhaps, this is the deepest reason for any resentment against it. While sociology works, metatheory plays. But its play is also the defense of sociology's autonomy from the pretension of any form of thought to impose a master discourse or metanarrative on theory and research. Metatheory rests its case on that contribution to its disciplinary home.

NOTES

1. For an explication of antifoundationalism and its relations to European poststructuralism, which has influenced contemporary philosophical debate in the United States, see Rorty (1979).

2. For the impact of poststructuralism and, more generally, postmodernism on the discipline of sociology, see Denzin (1986) and Murphy (1988).

3. We do not claim that Skocpol holds this position. It is the extreme claim in her line of argument.

4. Metatheory has the same relation to the methods of other descriptive human studies as it has to the sociology of sociology. For example, it will apply the methods of intellectual history and textual criticism to sociological theory without waiting for foundational certification from philosophy.

5. See our essay on the Simmelian and Derridian notions of play (Weinstein and Weinstein 1990).

REFERENCES

Denzin, N. K. 1986. "Postmodern Social Theory." *Sociological Theory* 4:194-204.

Derrida, J. 1973. "Différance." Pp. 129-160 in *Speech and Phenomena, and Other Essays on Husserl's Theory of Signs,* edited by J. Derrida. Evanston, IL: Northwestern University Press. (French ed. 1968)

Kuhn, T. 1962. *The Structure of Scientific Revolutions.* Chicago: University of Chicago Press.

Lévi-Strauss, C. 1966. *The Savage Mind.* Chicago: University Chicago Press. (French ed. 1962)

Lyotard, J-F. 1984. *The Postmodern Condition: A Report on Knowledge.* Minneapolis: University of Minnesota Press. (French ed. 1979)

Murphy, J. W. 1988. "Making Sense of Postmodern Sociology." *British Journal of Sociology* 39:600-14.

Parsons, T. 1949. *The Structure of Social Action.* New York: Free Press.

Ritzer, G. 1988. "Sociological Metatheory: A Defense of a Subfield by a Delineation of Its Parameters." *Sociological Theory* 6:187-200.

———. 1990. "Metatheorizing in Sociology." *Sociological Forum* 5:3-15.

Rorty, R. 1979. *Philosophy and the Mirror of Nature.* Princeton, NJ: Princeton University Press.

Simmel, G. 1950. "Sociability." Pp. 40-57 in *The Sociology of Georg Simmel,* edited by K. H. Wolff. New York: Free Press. (German ed. 1908)

Skocpol, T. 1986. "The Dead End of Metatheory." *Contemporary Sociology* 16:10-12.

Turner, J. 1986. *The Structure of Sociological Theory.* Chicago: Dorsey.

Weinstein, D. and M. A. Weinstein. 1990. "Simmel/Derrida: Deconstruction, as Symbolic Play." *Diogenes* 150:121-44.

Chapter 9

RELATIVISM AND REFLEXIVITY IN THE SOCIOLOGY OF SCIENTIFIC KNOWLEDGE

STEPHAN FUCHS

University of Virginia

EVER SINCE ITS INCEPTION in the mid 1970s, the sociology of scientific knowledge (SSK) has displayed a strong interest in philosophical discourse and epistemological critique.[1] At the core of this interest lies the "problem of representation," or the relationship between the word and the world. Of course, this problem does not only concern SSK but all of scientific discourse. In particular, the social sciences have always debated their ability to generate valid representations of the social world. The basic question is whether, and to what extent, our accounts and descriptions of some reality are determined by this reality or by other things, such as the transcendental categories of Pure Reason, the constructive operations of the intelligent mind, or some "social factors" that constrain our cognitive choices.

Historically, there have been, roughly, three answers to this question.[2] The *empiricist* answer is that there is a privileged system of discourse, science, whose rational methods assure that true statements are uniquely determined by the empirical evidence and by logic. Objective reality and true scientific statements are ontologically separate, but true statements "correspond" to reality. The *realist* answer is that scientific knowledge represents a combination of objective and subjective or social forces. True knowledge does, to some extent, correspond to reality, but is always "underdetermined" by the evidence, which leaves some room for forces other than reality itself to influence knowledge. The third answer, *idealism*, argues that our accounts of reality are the only reality there is. The very notion that there is such a thing as an external reality that can be mirrored by adequate representations is a socially and textually created fiction. The facticity of reality is the result of a skillful process of construction and negotiation, which then manages to conceal that any constructive work has been done.[3]

In SSK, there are two substantive levels at which the problem of representation occurs. The first level concerns the relationship between (natural) science and the physical reality it purports to capture in its true accounts. I shall call the problem of representation at this level the "problem of relativism." The second level has to do with the relationship between science and the descriptions of it given by sociologists of scientific knowledge. This is the "problem of reflexivity." Despite the emphasis on SSK, the problem of representation concerns all fields that produce knowledge; it is just that SSK makes the production of knowledge its explicit topic.

THE PROBLEM OF RELATIVISM

Ever since Kuhn's (1962/70) "paradigm incommensurability" thesis, the issue of relativism has been of major significance in SSK. Likening revolutionary paradigmatic transformations to social and political revolutions, Kuhn and his followers denied that there was a neutral and rational methodological algorithm, such as crucial experimental tests, that forced scientists into consensual acceptance of one "superior" paradigm. Rather, Kuhn suggested that during revolutionary scientific upheavals, competing paradigms were related like incompatible ways of life and doing science (see H. Collins and Pinch 1982; Shapin and Schaffer 1985). The choice between competing paradigms is not simply a choice between true and false, but one between conflicting scientific lifeforms and organizations. As a result, this choice is at least partly driven by social and political forces, such as power, reputation, and generational succession.

Postempiricist philosophers of science such as Rorty (1979) and Feyerabend (1975) radicalize Kuhn's argument to the point that the very idea of epistemology appears misguided and redundant. For Rorty, Kuhn's central message is that there never was any such thing as the "method of science." Rorty deconstructs the representational metaphor of science as a Mirror of Nature that was at the core of modern Western metaphysics. For Rorty, following Wittgenstein and the pragmatists, "truth" is a relationship between people, not between statements and the world. In this interpretation, "truth" is hardly more than a fancy epistemological label for statements so fundamental to our way of life that we are unable or unwilling to drop them easily.

Much of SSK has sought to substantiate relativism or, at least, realism through empirical research of scientists' actual practices. Laboratory ethnographies, for example, show that scientists at the workbench behave more like Garfinkelian sense makers than Popperian or Lakatosian rule followers (see Latour and Woolgar 1986; Knorr-Cetina 1981; Lynch 1985). Scientists are not observed to follow the universal rules of some preestablished methodology. Rather, they use the resources available at local labs to construct cultural artifacts in processes of social negotiation. Scientists construct natural reality much like mundane reasoners construct everyday reality. Knowledge is not a sudden revelation of nature's actual characteristics; it is a contingent, contextual, and selective accomplishment of practical and interested investors in a certain kind of cultural capital.

A similar story is told by the Empirical Program of Relativism (EPOR) developed by Harry Collins and his followers (H. Collins 1975, 1981a, 1985). EPOR is interested in the mechanisms through which contemporary scientific controversies are closed. The standard philosophical model suggests that controversies are closed through fairly unambiguous experimental replications. But Collins and his associates have repeatedly found that replications are very controversial themselves and, hence, cannot safely settle controversies on purely rational grounds. There is an infinite "experimenter's regress" built into replications: the criteria determining what counts as a proper replication, and the criteria for deciding who counts as a competent experimenter, are not mutually independent and unproblematic (H. Collins 1985). During controversies, the voices of Reason and Reality are many. EPOR concludes that "social factors"—such as power, rhetoric, and exclusion from "legitimate science"—determine closures regularly, not just during spectacular episodes of "politicized" science.

"Relativism," then, means that reality itself does not decide or determine fully what statements are accepted as true. Reality is the outcome of scientific construction, not its independent cause. Relativism views knowledge as a contingent and selective social construct rather than as a neutral mirror reflecting what reality really looks like. As a result, relativism denies that any discourse or worldview enjoys cognitive privileges or a special epistemic authority that would follow from its superior rationality and its close contact with reality.[4] The relativist worldview is thoroughly pluralistic and antihierarchical. It does not believe in safe foundations and transcendental securities.

At this juncture, the following question arises: If science's descriptions of reality are not objective representations of that reality but, rather, social constructs, what about the sociological descriptions of science as a social construct? This is the familiar *tu quoque* attack against the apparently paradoxical and self-refuting consequences of relativism, which leads right into the problem of reflexivity (see Ashmore 1989). If all knowledge is relative, so is the statement that this is the case, which restores realist objectivity for the moment, only to be destroyed again at the next metalevel, and so on. Ashmore (1989) demonstrates this for, amongst others, Kuhn (a Kuhnian reading of Kuhn relativizes Kuhnian historiography as one more self-contained historiographic paradigm) and ethnomethodology (an ethno-methodological reading of ethnomethodology deconstructs the foundational claims of this field as one more practical accomplishment of folk reasoning).

Steve Woolgar (1982) was among the first in SSK to notice the apparent discrepancy between sociologists' realist or relativist understanding of science, and the empiricist understanding of their own work. Woolgar notes that lab ethnographies typically emphasize the constructed and negotiated character of natural science, but forget about the constructive and selective operations shaping their own accounts. These ethnographies portray their findings as if they simply corresponded to the external reality of science, and at the same time point to the nature of science as a contingent social construction.

In SSK, there have been, at least, three reactions to this apparent inconsistency. Mulkay and Gilbert's discourse analysis (DA) drops the program to describe science "as it actually happens" altogether (Mulkay 1981; Mulkay and Gilbert 1982; Gilbert and Mulkay 1984). In their studies of oxidative phosphorylation, they find that scientists' own accounts of what happens in science vary with the contexts in which these accounts are presented. Scientists use the "empiricist" discourse of objectivity and rationality in formal settings and when accounting for statements they perceive as true or their own beliefs. Conversely, scientists use the "contingent" discourse of subjectivity and fallibility in informal settings and when accounting for statements perceived as false, or the statements of their opponents. For Mulkay and Gilbert, this contextual variability of scientists' discursive practices means that it is impossible for SSK to describe the actual reality of science. The sociologist can only reconstruct how scientists' accounts of science covary with the contexts in which these accounts are given.

But, as Halfpenny (1988) has observed, Mulkay and Gilbert simply replace the "actual reality of science" as SSK's referent by the "actual reality of scientists' discursive practices as they covary with contexts." Mulkay and Gilbert still claim empiricist status for their own accounts (of scientists' accounts), but deny such status for the accounts of nature given by science. They do not solve the problem of representation, but simply move it to the next metalevel of scientists' discourse and the sociological accounts of that discourse.

Equally unconvincing is Harry Collins's suggestion to "ban" reflexivity altogether. Collins claims relativist status for natural science, and empiricist status for SSK and EPOR ("special relativism"). While science is based on social negotiations, sociology describes science "as it actually happens":

> My prescription is to treat the social world as real, and as something about which we can have sound data, whereas we should treat the natural world as something problematic—a social construct rather than something real. This seems to me to be an entirely natural view for a social scientist. (Collins 1981b, pp. 216-217, note 2)

It is these apparent paradoxes and inconsistencies that reflexivistism, the third reaction toward the problem of representation, take as their starting point.

THE PROBLEM OF REFLEXIVITY

Reflexivists examine what happens when SSK inspects its own epistemic and textual practices in the same way as it analyzes the practices of natural science. SSK is seen to be an excellent case for demonstrating the essential reflexivity of social scientific discourse, for SSK constructs knowledge claims about how natural science constructs knowledge claims (Woolgar 1988a). Unlike EPOR and DA, reflexivism does not grant SSK any special status or cognitive privileges. SSK's knowledge is itself approached as a contingent social and textual construct. Reflexivism's central relativist message is that science has no cognitive privileges, that SSK has no cognitive privileges in pointing out that science has no cognitive privileges, and that reflexivism has no cognitive privileges in pointing out that SSK has no cognitive privileges in pointing out that science has no cognitive privileges.

Malcolm Ashmore (1989) has explored the "strange loops" of self-referential or reflexive discourse most thoroughly. A prime target for his reflexive critiques is Harry Collins's and EPOR's aforementioned replication studies. Collins shows that replications in natural science are never unproblematic and straightforward, as suggested by the standard model of testing and falsification in the orthodox philosophy of science. Rather, the outcomes of replications depend on complex social negotiations and flexible interpretations. Collins's main conclusion is that there is no such thing as independent and unproblematic replication in science, so that controversies are usually closed through "social factors," such as power, rhetoric, and professional politics.

Yet Collins (1981b) also claims that this major finding has now been independently replicated by his own further studies and those of his associates.[5] That is, Collins claims for his own studies what he denies to natural science: that replication is unproblematic and leads to secure knowledge about how the world really looks like. But this claim for special status has paradoxical consequences. If Collins's original claim ("there is no such thing as independent replication in science") is correct, then his own and EPOR's replication studies cannot plausibly count as independent replications either, and then his original finding is not a solid fact but highly problematic (which was, of course, Collins's original claim). If his original claim is wrong (i.e., "there is independent replication in science"), then his and his associates' studies may well also count as replications, but then his claim about the problematic character of replication in natural science becomes itself very problematic (which should be, of course, Collins's secondary claim about sociological replications, were he to be consistent).

Replicating Collins's replication claim, Ashmore shows that Collins's replications are as problematic and, possibly, controversial as replication claims in natural science. They cannot really claim special status and do not provide any absolute epistemic securities. In another sense, however, the problematic status of Collins's and EPOR's replication studies only confirms and exemplifies his original claim: that, indeed, all replications are problematic. In short, reflexive self-reference oscillates between self-exemplification and self-contradiction, or between tautology and paradox.

The general outcome of Ashmore's and other reflexive studies (see Woolgar 1988b; Mulkay 1985) appears to be the relativist proposition that no discourse, including reflexivism, can claim special cognitive status or epistemic privileges. When applied to itself, SSK does not portray the reality of science as it actually happens, but instead exemplifies the constructed, negotiated, and contingent nature of its own and all discourse. In Mulkay's (1984) words,

> Maybe there is no single coherent story. . . . Why not relax and accept that none of us is engaged in describing *the* social world? We are creators of meanings appropriate to the occasion, like dramatists, novelists and ordinary speakers. (p. 278)

At this point, reflexive SSK turns into a special version of deconstructionist literary criticism.[6] The critical target is representational realism and the illusions of facticity and objectivity sustained by its rhetorical conventions. Because, according to relativism, no discourse may claim cognitive privileges in the sense of describing what reality really looks like, the attention shifts reflexively to the textual practices writers employ to make us believe that their stories are more than just stories.[7] The old philosophical distinctions between the word and the world, between rhetoric and logic, or between fact and fiction are deconstructed. An account that pretends to be more than an account manages to do so only by concealing its constructive work and by glossing over its interpretive contingencies. A reflexivist discursive practice restores the essential interpretive flexibility and hermeneutic uncertainty of all accounts. It does so by deconstructing the empiricist and realist fictions of "corresponding to reality" and "following the rules of method." There are only stories about the world, not the world itself, or true versus false stories.

To avoid the traps of the *tu quoque*, reflexivists must themselves resist all realist temptations in their own metadiscourse. This is the role played by the "New Literary Forms" (NLF) in SSK. NLF, such as play, drama, irony, dialogue, recursive textual loops, and self-referencing footnotes abandon the conventions of the empiricist monologue. Because relativism and reflexivity deny cognitive privileges to any discourse, including their own, NLF practice nonprivileged and self-critical writing. The intention is not so much to "solve" the "problems" of relativism, reflexivity, and the *tu quoque*, but to "celebrate the monster" (Ashmore 1989). NLF liberate the suppressed "other" by giving voice to alternative interpretations and conflicting readings. Reflexive texts are essentially multivocal, for only multivocal discourse can reveal the problematic and controversial nature of all accounts. NLF exemplify the accomplished status of representation by revealing the literary secrets of their own fabrications.

The problem of reflexivism (and deconstructionism generally), I believe, has not so much to do with its skeptical and relativist epistemology, but with its practical consequences for SSK and social scientific discourse generally.[8] If SSK were to follow reflexivism, SSK would move away from the world (of science), and become immersed in its own words or textual practices and their ongoing deconstruction. Ironically, from there it is not too far to the obsession with linguistic purity that haunted the logical positivists. By turning into literary criticism, reflexivism strengthens the philosophical inclination of SSK and its preoccupation with the problem of representation. I believe this is unfortunate, for the important cognitive gains in the field have come from detailed empirical case studies conducted in the realist mode, not from epistemological critique or textual deconstruction.

In a radical sense, nonrealist discourse can have no empirical referent. But not being about anything is neither a desirable nor possible goal for any discourse. A discourse that intends not to be about anything has a hard time being taken seriously and defending itself against the charming alternatives of silence and music. And a discourse that is about something, even if it is about itself, has some minimal realist ambitions, such as the ambition to be trustworthy and reliable. This does not mean that we need to reinstall the grandiose philosophical notions of truth and correspondence. But why be more fictional than fiction? The linguistic conventions of realism are just that: conventions. And as conventions, they will survive the deconstruction of their foundations, just like the conventions of positive legislation survived the decline of the natural law doctrine. Realist discourse is just a good way of making points and arguments. As long as we still want to do that, there is no need to abandon the conventions of realism.

There is a strong antirealist temptation in reflexive discourse to "go beyond" a given level of discourse to its metalevel, and from there to the next metalevel, and so on. This is so because reflexivism, in talking about some object, must also talk about how it talks about, and constructs, this object. It must thematize and problematize everything at once to escape from the traps of the *tu quoque*. But, as Luhmann (1988) notes, the infinite regress in reflexivism that results from adding layer upon layer of deconstruction must be interrupted somewhere, and it is precisely at this point that discourse cannot help but regain some of its realist ambitions.

The deconstructionist antirealism in reflexive SSK targets the allegedly authoritarian omniscience of conventional empiricist discourse. But this critique is rather idealistic and sociologically naive. It is idealistic because, in most cases, "deconstruction" involves much more than textual and literary criticism. For example, one cannot deconstruct the practice of natural science by simply deconstructing its texts. One would also have to deconstruct labs, machines, funding agencies, and the state; a task that is clearly too big for literary criticism. Textual deconstruction works only for those fields who have nothing but texts and literary devices to back up their statements. Generally speaking, many social sciences (with some notable exceptions such as experimental small group research and massive quantitative survey projects) meet this criterion. But it is precisely these fields that do not really need deconstruction. As Latour (1988) says, the problem of these fields is that their claims are not believed enough, not that they are too strong and authoritative. Such "textual" fields are weak to begin with, and it just does not make much sense to accuse them of empiricist omniscience and cognitive authoritarianism. Especially barely established subfields such as SSK, whom no one except their practitioners notices much and takes too seriously, do not really have to worry that someone will (mis)understand their claims as "representing objective reality" and "describing science as it actually happens."

Reflexivism and deconstructionism are sociologically naive because they fail to realize that weak fields are highly reflexive and constantly deconstruct themselves anyway. In weak textual fields there is no need for a special activity of deconstruction. Weak fields already produce statements that are not strongly backed up by a large number of allies, and then those weak statements are further weakened by the deconstructive gaze of peer and gatekeeper critics. This means that others will deconstruct one's statements anyway, and so it is rather redundant to deconstruct one's own statements through self-referential critique and NLF. Others will surely give voice to conflicting readings and alternative interpretations, so why do their job for them? In fact, it strikes me that there is even more arrogant monological omniscience and cognitive authority claimed in reflexive studies than in conventional empiricist research reports. The latter at least give their critics a chance to speak for themselves, whereas the former try to silence them by anticipating their objections in an allegedly multivocal discourse that is, after all, constructed monologically.

AN ALTERNATIVE APPROACH
TO THE PROBLEM OF REPRESENTATION

I believe SSK has spent too much time and energy on philosophical problems and, of late, has become trapped in circular textual narcissism. My recommendation is to stop treating the problem of representation in a philosophical way for, as Bloor (1976) has remarked, asking philosophical questions often paralyzes the mind. This implies that I do not have to offer any philosophical "solution" to the problems of relativism and reflexivity. Neither do I perceive an urgent need, for the reasons specified above, to "celebrate the monster" through textual deconstruction and NLF. I want to propose that we no longer ask, "How can I defend my claims from a relativistic perspective?" or "How can I avoid any realist connotations by deconstructing my own discourse?" A more manageable and promising question, I believe, is why certain social groups and scientific fields have a more relativistic and reflexive self-understanding than others.[9] That is, I treat relativism and reflexivity, in a naively realist way, as "dependent variables," not as the foundational "problem of representation" in philosophical discourse. The explanatory framework for this approach is provided by the theory of scientific organizations (TSO) (Whitley 1984; Fuchs and Turner 1986; Fuchs 1992).

TSO's central concern is the relationship between the structures of social groups and their cognitive styles or discursive practices.[10] TSO is rooted in two sociological traditions: Durkheimian and neo-Durkheimian group sociology, and the technological paradigm in organizational research.[11] Two of the theory's main variables are the levels of task uncertainty (TU) and mutual dependence (MD).[12] TU refers to the ways in which groups perceive and solve their tasks and do their work. In science, TU is high when problems are innovative and complex, when a lot of exceptions and surprises occur during research, when methods are ambiguous, and when interpretations are controversial. Conversely, under conditions of low TU, problems are clearly defined, the research process is more routine, methods are straightforward, and interpretations widely accepted. MD indicates the extent to which scientific groups are closely coupled and socially coherent. MD is low when separate networks and individual practitioners enjoy a great deal of autonomy and discretion over their work. Such groups are rather fragmented, decentralized, and not highly stratified. MD is high when practitioners depend very closely on other practitioners and, especially, on elites in their work. Under these conditions, there are strong collective controls over knowledge production, leaving little room for multiparadigmatic dissent and deviance. The group is more firmly integrated, coherent, and stratified.

I want to propose that fields with high TU and low MD are more relativistic and reflexive than more routinized and closely coupled fields. Fields with highly uncertain and controversial work practices are structurally similar to literature or even poetry, for practitioners are comparatively independent from close collegiate inspection and control (Fuchs 1992). Good examples are SSK or social theory. In these fields, separate schools and reputational networks are independent enough to sustain distinct approaches and perspectives, none of which has sufficient resources to claim dominance in the entire field. In sociology, for example, there exists a large variety of fairly autonomous schools and worldviews that are organizationally based upon separate specialty and regional associations and journals (Mullins 1973). Due to pronounced organizational fragmentation, allies are very hard to enroll, and statements have a difficult time mobilizing the strong social support that is necessary to transform them into facts (Latour 1987).

As a result, such weak and fragmented fields produce "conversation,"[13] or informal exchanges between relatively independent specialty networks and their worldviews, rather than facts. Often, texts are the only supporting agents backing up statements in such fields, which is why they strongly resemble literature, frequently emphasize "good writing," and are led to believe that texts and their deconstruction are all there is.[14] Conversational fields are more hermeneutic than objectivist in that, for many, the word and its interpretation become more important than the world and its explanation. This is so because the high level of pluralism and competition in weak fields makes it highly implausible for any one of the many worldviews to claim having discovered what social reality actually looks like. In phenomenological terms, weak and fragmented intersubjectivity creates great skepticism toward the possibility of objective knowledge. Knowledge is not seen as representing reality but as giving expression to the limited and partial perspective of the particular social group that happens to believe in it.

Weak, fragmented, and highly controversial fields are very pluralistic and tolerate a great deal of alternative interpretations and deviant innovations. Weak fields are "multiparadigmatic" (Ritzer 1975). As a result, knowledge can more readily be seen as an active social construction, rather than a neutral mirror of reality. The role of active agency in manufacturing knowledge claims is stressed. There is not much confidence in the compelling force of the objective evidence or the universal rules of methodology. Statements are seen as contingent selections from other possibilities, for different schools and approaches make different, often even incompatible, selections and develop different rationales for those selections. In this situation, informal conversational exchanges and mutual deconstruction are more likely than fact production or normal science, and a skeptical and self-critical ideology is more likely than realist confidence in truth and cumulation.

In other words, weak conversational fields with high TU and fragmented control structures are rather relativistic (Fuhrman and Snizek 1990).[15] No interpretation, approach, or worldview can successfully and without strong opposition claim "special status" or "cognitive privileges." But this is not primarily so because all knowledge lacks secure epistemic foundations, but because the social support for any one interpretation or worldview is not strong enough to back up such claims. *Relativism expresses the absence of strong social support, not of secure cognitive foundations.* It is the ideology of fields whose fragmented social structures are more conducive to conversation and hermeneutics than to fact production and science.

A similar argument can be made, I believe, for reflexivity. Reflexivity expresses the self-critical sentiment that our words can never capture the objective world, and so the attention turns back on the words and their literary production and textual organization. In social theory, for example, a great deal of work is performed on metatheoretical issues, such as the presuppositions of sociological theorizing, the reading and rereading of the classics, the relationship between fact and values, or the convergence of history and systematics (see Ritzer 1990; Alexander 1982-83). This reflexive self-inspection follows from the pessimistic feeling in weak conversational fields that the "reality" of "the" social world can never be accurately represented. There is not a great deal of confidence in objective representation and accurate correspondence, and so "postpositivist" discourse modestly favors interpretive openness and hermeneutic pluralism over realist rigor and scientistic authority. Discourse becomes very philosophical and concerned with foundational issues, rather than solving concrete empirical puzzles and gradually improving knowledge about reality (Weinstein and Weinstein, Chapter 8, in this book). Because reality itself is seen as a social construct, there is not much hope of ever being able to represent its actual structure, and so the attention shifts reflexively toward the metalevel of how discourse constructs that reality through presuppositional decisions, normative commitments, textual devices, or transcendental "interests" in reproducing the species through work and interaction (Habermas 1970).

This situation changes in fields with low TU and high MD. Such fields are more "normal" and routinized, less controversial, and there is a higher level of social and paradigmatic integration. Practitioners depend very closely on each other, and especially on elites and gatekeepers who regulate access to the material means of scientific production (Traweek 1988). Collegiate control over individual scientists is closer, and the group as a whole has a more clearly defined and dogmatic *conscience collective*.[16] There is less room for individual initiative and discretion, and a stronger emphasis on conformity with the group's research standards.[17] The group forcefully believes in the "right ways" of doing science. There is competition, but it leads to cumulation and piecemeal advances in knowledge rather than to cognitive fragmentation and paradigmatic pluralism (Price 1970). The field as a whole is more cognitively unified, and there are fewer organizational opportunities to establish separate and autonomous specialties and reputational networks.

In this situation, fact production and science are more likely than conversation and hermeneutics. Knowledge is more likely to be seen as following from reality itself, not from social construction and negotiation. There is a fairly strong belief in the superior rationality of science that privileges its discourse over other worldviews and common sense. Change occurs as cumulation, not fragmentation. Because the field as a whole is more closely coupled and firmly integrated, practitioners are more likely to transform statements into facts through social support. Such fields are "strong" because they command more supporting agents, and they can more easily enroll the allies that are, according to Latour (1987), essential for fact production. Weak and disorganized fields produce conversation and hermeneutics, whereas strong and more closely coupled fields produce facts and science.[18] That is, strong fields will be more positivistic than relativist, and more objectivist than reflexive. They will be more confident in the representational nature of their discourse, and they will have to be *told* (for example, by SSK) that their knowledge is also based on contingent social constructions and informal negotiations. By themselves, practitioners will be more likely to turn to the world instead of the word.

NOTES

1. As opposed to Mertonian sociology of science and the broader term "social studies of science," SSK addresses the very core of scientific activity, usually from a "constructivist" perspective. Some central works are Mulkay (1979), Barnes (1974), Bloor (1976) and Woolgar (1988c). For a review of the various approaches in current sociology of science see Zuckerman (1988).

2. I am using here Halfpenny's (1988) terminology.

3. This process of conversion and transformation is one of the core areas of SSK: the study of scientific rhetoric and persuasion; see, for many others, Gusfield (1976), Myers (1985), Latour and Woolgar (1986), and Bazerman (1988).

4. The relativism controversy in SSK has greatly been influenced by the rationality debate in cultural anthropology (see Hollis and Lukes 1982). In both cases, the central problem is whether there are any cultural universals that would permit a neutral and impartial assessment of a worldview's or culture's truth and rationality value. Relativists deny that such universals exist.

5. See the special issue on "Knowledge and Controversy" of *Social Studies of Science* 11(1), 1981.

6. For a useful introduction to the "postmodern problematic" see Featherstone (1988).

7. A similar "rhetorical turn" can be observed in many other social sciences, such as philosophy (Rorty 1989), economics (McCloskey 1985), sociology (Brown 1987, 1990), or anthropology (Stocking 1983).

8. From a philosophical perspective, I believe relativism is indeed the only defensible epistemology. But to say that no discourse enjoys any epistemic privileges is not saying that there are no social privileges for certain discourses, such as science. Relativism, it seems to me, is a correct epistemology, but a very naive sociology. It has no eye for power, only for validity, and as such remains a philosophical position (cf. below).

9. In Ritzer's (1990) words, the following is an exercise in the "external-social" variant of the type of metatheory aiming at a "deeper understanding of theory" (p. 4).

10. One of the strengths of this theory is that it explains variations in cognitive styles for both ordinary and scientific groups; see Fuchs (1992).

11. For the Durkheimian and neo-Durkheimian traditions see R. Collins (1975), Douglas (1970), and, with special reference to science, Bloor (1983). For the technological school see Woodward (1965/80), Perrow (1967, 1984), Thompson (1967), and Lawrence and Lorsch (1967).

12. What follows is a skeleton view of TSO. Obviously, TU and MD are not extraneous variables, but seem to follow from variables such as resource concentration, reputational autonomy, and size; see Whitley (1984) and Fuchs (1992).

13. A term borrowed from Rorty (1979).

14. This is not equally true in all sociological specialties, though. There is not only variation between fields, but also between the various specialties in a field. In sociology, for example, mathematical sociology, survey research, and experimental small group research are "stronger" fields than, say, social theory or SSK, and this is why the former are the bastions of scientism and positivism.

15. This assessment actually corresponds to the findings of neo-Durkheimian group sociology and organizational research. Groups and organizations with weak internal structures and high complexity are more informal than bureaucratic, rely more on mutual negotiations than on administrative fiats to coordinate and control action, and have a more pluralistic symbolic culture; for groups see R. Collins (1975), Fuchs and Case (1989); for organizations see March and Olsen (1979). One could say that high TU/low MD organizations are hermeneutic, and low TU/high MD organizations are positivistic.

16. These are, in Douglas's (1970) terms, the "high group" societies. According to Douglas, such closely coupled groups have strongly reified worldviews, value cognitive consistency and internal purity, and are terrified of anomalies and strangers. In other words, the worldviews of such groups are rather "positivistic." This corroborates the more specific point I am making about science.

17. This conformity, however, will be tempered by a fairly high amount of discretion workers must be granted when dealing with highly uncertain tasks.

18. This, however, is a matter of degree, not of principle.

REFERENCES

Alexander, Jeffrey. 1982-83. *Theoretical Logic in Sociology*, 4 vols. Berkeley: University of California Press.

Ashmore, Malcolm. 1989. *The Reflexive Thesis: Wrighting Sociology of Scientific Knowledge.* Chicago: University of Chicago Press.

Barnes, Barry. 1974. *Scientific Knowledge and Sociological Theory.* London: Routledge & Kegan Paul.

Bazerman, Charles. 1988. *Shaping Written Knowledge. The Genre and Activity of the Experimental Article in Science.* Madison: University of Wisconsin Press.

Bloor, David. 1976. *Knowledge and Social Imagery.* London: Routledge & Kegan Paul.

———. 1983. *Wittgenstein: A Social Theory of Knowledge.* New York: Columbia University Press.

Brown, Richard H. 1987. *Society as Text.* Chicago: University of Chicago Press.

———. 1990. "Social Science and the Poetics of Public Truth." *Sociological Forum* 5:55-74.

Collins, Harry. 1975. "The Seven Sexes: A Study in the Sociology of a Phenomenon." *Sociology* 9:205-24.

———. 1981a. "Son of Seven Sexes: The Social Destruction of a Physical Phenomenon." *Social Studies of Science* 11:33-62.

———. 1981b. "Stages in the Empirical Program of Relativism." *Social Studies of Science* 11:3-10.

———. 1985. *Changing Order: Replication and Induction in Scientific Practice.* London: Sage.

Collins, Harry and Trevor J. Pinch. 1982. *Frames of Meaning: The Social Construction of Extraordinary Science.* London: Routledge & Kegan Paul.

Collins, Randall. 1975. *Conflict Sociology: Toward an Explanatory Science.* New York: Academic Press.

Douglas, Mary. 1970. *Natural Symbols.* New York: Pantheon.

Featherstone, Mike (ed). 1988. *Postmodernism.* London: Sage.

Feyerabend, Paul K. 1975. *Against Method.* London: New Left Books.

Fuchs, Stephan. 1992. *The Professional Quest for Truth: A Social Theory of Science and Knowledge.* Albany: State University of New York Press.

Fuchs, Stephan and Charles E. Case. 1989. "Prejudice as Lifeform." *Sociological Inquiry* 59:301-17.

Fuchs, Stephan and Jonathan H. Turner. 1986. "What Makes a Science Mature?" *Sociological Theory* 4:143-50.

Fuhrman, Ellsworth and William Snizek. 1990. "Neither Proscience nor Antiscience: Metasociology as Dialogue." *Sociological Forum* 5:17-36.

Gilbert, G. Nigel and Michael Mulkay. 1984. *Opening Pandora's Box: A Sociological Analysis of Scientists' Discourse.* Cambridge, England: Cambridge University Press.

Gusfield, Joseph. 1976. "The Literary Rhetoric of Science: Comedy and Pathos in Drinking Driver Research." *American Sociological Review* 41:16-34.

Habermas, Juergen. 1970. *Knowledge and Human Interests.* London: Heinemann.

Halfpenny, Peter. 1988. "Talking of Talking, Writing of Writing: Some Reflections on Gilbert and Mulkay's Discourse Analysis." *Social Studies of Science* 18:169-82.

Hollis, Martin and Steven Lukes (eds). 1982. *Rationalism and Relativism.* Cambridge, MA: MIT Press.

Knorr-Cetina, Karin D. 1981. *The Manufacture of Knowledge.* Oxford, England: Pergamon.

Kuhn, Thomas S. 1962/70. *The Structure of Scientific Revolutions.* Chicago: University of Chicago Press.

Latour, Bruno. 1987. *Science in Action: How to Follow Scientists and Engineers Through Society.* Milton Keynes: Open University Press.

———. 1988. "The Politics of Explanation: An Alternative." Pp. 155-76 in *Knowledge and Reflexivity*, edited by Steve Woolgar. London: Sage.

Latour, Bruno and Steve Woolgar. 1986. *Laboratory Life: The Construction of Scientific Facts*, 2nd ed., Princeton, NJ: Princeton University Press.

Lawrence, Paul R. and Jay W. Lorsch. 1967. *Organizations and Environment.* Cambridge, MA: Harvard University Press.

Luhmann, Niklas. 1988. "Tautology and Paradox in the Self-Descriptions of Modern Society." *Sociological Theory* 6:21-37.

Lynch, Michael. 1985. *Art and Artifact in Laboratory Science.* London: Routledge & Kegan Paul.

March, James G. and Johan B. Olsen (eds). 1979. *Ambiguity and Choice in Organizations.* Bergen, Norway: Universitetsforlaget.

McCloskey, Donald N. 1985. *The Rhetoric of Economics.* Madison: University of Wisconsin Press.

Mulkay, Michael. 1979. *Science and the Sociology of Knowledge.* London: Allen & Unwin.

———. 1981. "Action and Belief or Scientific Discourse?" *Philosophy of the Social Sciences* 11:163-71.

———. 1984. "The Scientist Talks Back." *Social Studies of Science* 14:265-82.

———. 1985. *The Word and the World.* London: Allen & Unwin.

Mulkay, Michael and G. Nigel Gilbert. 1982. "Joking Apart: Some Recommendations Concerning the Analysis of Scientific Culture." *Social Studies of Science* 12:585-613.

Mullins, N. 1973. *Theories and Theory Groups in Contemporary American Sociology*. New York: Harper & Row.

Myers, Greg. 1985. "Texts as Knowledge Claims." *Social Studies of Science* 15:593-630.

Perrow, Charles. 1967. "A Framework for the Comparative Analysis of Organizations." *American Sociological Review* 32:194-208.

———. 1984. *Normal Accidents: Living with High-Risk Technologies*. New York: Basic Books.

Price, Derek de Solla. 1970. "Differences Between Scientific and Technological and Non-Scientific Scholarly Communities." Paper presented at the 7th World Congress of Sociology, Varna, Bulgaria.

Ritzer, George. 1975. *Sociology: A Multiple Paradigm Science*. Boston: Allyn & Bacon.

———. 1990. "Metatheorizing in Sociology." *Sociological Forum* 5:3-15.

Rorty, Richard. 1979. *Philosophy and the Mirror of Nature*. Princeton, NJ: Princeton University Press.

———. 1989. *Contingency, Irony, and Solidarity*. Cambridge, England: Cambridge University Press.

Shapin, Steve and Simon Schaffer. 1985. *Leviathan and the Air-Pump*. Princeton, NJ: Princeton University Press.

Stocking, G.W. (ed). 1983. *Observers Observed: Essays on Ethnographic Fieldwork*. Madison: University of Wisconsin Press.

Thompson, James. 1967. *Organizations in Action*. New York: McGraw-Hill.

Traweek, Sharon. 1988. *Beamtimes and Lifetimes. The World of High Energy Physicists*. Cambridge, MA: Harvard University Press.

Whitley, Richard. 1984. *The Intellectual and Social Organization of the Sciences*. Oxford, England: Clarendon.

Woodward, Joan. 1965/80. *Industrial Organization: Theory and Practice*. Oxford, England: Oxford University Press.

Woolgar, Steve. 1982. "Laboratory Studies: A Comment on the State of the Art." *Social Studies of Science* 12:481-98.

———, (ed) 1988a. *Knowledge and Reflexivity: New Frontiers in the Sociology of Knowledge*. London: Sage.

———. 1988b. "Reflexivity Is the Ethnographer of the Text." Pp. 14-36 in *Knowledge and Reflexivity*, edited by Steve Woolgar. London: Sage.

———. 1988c. *Science: The Very Idea*. Chichester, England: Ellis Hotwood.

Zuckerman, Harriet. 1988. "The Sociology of Science." Pp. 511-74 in *Handbook of Sociology*, edited by Neil Smelser. Newbury Park, CA: Sage.

NAME INDEX

Alexander, J.C., 8, 11-12, 15, 18-19, 23, 27-47, 54, 56, 65-66, 72, 85, 162, 165
Anderson, P., 43, 47
Antonio, R. J., 11, 19, 20, 23, 41-43, 48, 88-106
Archer, M., 8, 15, 23
Aronson, R., 43, 48
Ashmore, M., 154, 156-157, 165

Balkwell, J. W., 112, 121
Barnes, B., 164-165
Barnes, H. E., 30, 48
Bazerman, C., 164-165
Bealer, R., 14, 23
Becker, H., 30, 48
Bellah, R. N., 33, 49
Berger, J., 8, 20, 23, 36, 45, 47-48, 51, 107-123
Berger, P. L., 72, 85
Bergesen, A., 56, 68
Bernstein, R. J., 8, 23
Bevins, G. M., 28, 49
Bierhoff, H. W., 112, 121
Blalock, H., 31, 48, 60, 66
Blau, P. M., 56, 67
Bloor, D., 160, 164-165
Boli, J., 119, 122
Botstein, D., 66-67
Bottomore, T., 43, 48, 64, 67
Bourdieu, P., 134
Brewer, J., 17, 23
Brown, C. E., 112, 122
Brown, J. D., 40, 48
Brown, R., 10, 23, 164-165
Buban, S. L., 43, 48
Buck, E., 112, 121
Burcher, R., 46, 48
Burke, P., 16, 23
Buroway, M., 41, 48
Butcher, R., 119, 123

Camic, C., 73, 86

Cantor, C., 66-67
Carnap, R., 54, 67
Case, C. E., 165-166
Cashen, J., 112, 121
Clayman, S. E., 44, 50
Coenen-Huther, J., 85-86
Cohen, B. P., 112, 121-123
Cohen, E. G., 109, 112-113, 121-123
Cohen, J., 23, 25
Colclough, G., 41, 48
Coleman, J. S., 20, 56, 65, 67, 73, 86, 126-128, 130-134
Colomy, P., 11-12, 15, 18-19, 23, 27-48, 56, 65-66
Collins, H., 152-153, 155-156, 165-166
Collins, R., 8, 15-16, 23, 28, 31-32, 42, 46, 48, 57-58, 64, 67, 128, 134, 164-166
Cook, K., 11-12, 24
Cooley, C. H., 92-93, 96-97, 106
Coser, L. A., 41, 49
Crombie, A. C., 16, 24
Crosland, M. P., 64, 66-67
Curelaru, M., 30, 35, 38, 49, 64, 67

Denzin, N. K., 149-150
Derrida, J., 137, 146, 149-150
Dewey, J., 95-96, 98-102, 106
Dilthey, W., 32, 49
Dogan, M., 32, 49
Douglas, M., 164-166
Dovidio, J. F., 112, 122
Driskell, J. E., Jr., 112-113, 123
Durkheim, E., 29, 31, 49, 55, 58-63, 67, 71, 74, 85-86, 92, 94, 96-97, 99-102, 106, 125-126, 128-129

Effrat, A., 14, 24
Ehrlich, D., 119, 123
Eisenstadt, S. N., 15, 24, 30, 35, 38, 49, 64, 67
Ekeh, P. K., 35, 49

SUBJECT INDEX

ABOUT THE CONTRIBUTORS

JEFFREY C. ALEXANDER is Professor and Chair in the Department of Sociology at the University of California, Los Angeles. His most recent books are *Rethinking Progress: Movements, Forces, and Ideas at the End of the 20th Century* and *Postpositivist Sociology: Essays on Rationality, Relativism, and the Problem of Progress,* Cambridge University Press, forthcoming.

ROBERT J. ANTONIO is Professor of Sociology at the University of Kansas. He works in the areas of critical, classical, and American social theory and also has interests in historical sociology and political economy. He is presently working with Douglas Kellner on *Theorizing Modernity* (London: Sage) and on other essays that explore the origins of and tensions within modern social theory and its connections to the new forms of postmodern theory. He is also exploring the thought of John Dewey and his relevance for contemporary critical theory.

JOSEPH BERGER (Ph.D., Harvard University) is Professor of Sociology at Stanford University and Senior Fellow (by courtesy) at the Hoover Institution. He was chairman of the Department of Sociology at Stanford University from 1976 to 1983 and 1985 to 1989. He is recipient of the 1991 Cooley-Mead Award. His current research interests are status processes and expectation states, reward expectations and distributive justice, and problems in the development of cumulative theory in sociology. He has coauthored and coedited many publications, including *Expectation States Theory: A Theoretical Research Program; Status Characteristics and Social Interaction;* and *Status, Rewards, and Influence: How Expectations Organize Behavior.*

PAUL COLOMY is Associate Professor of Sociology at the University of Denver. He has published articles in the areas of sociological theory, social change, and social psychology. He is editor of *Functionalist*

Sociology (1990) and *Neofunctionalist Sociology* (1990) and coeditor, with Jeffrey C. Alexander, of *Differentiation Theory and Social Change: Comparative and Historical Perspectives* (1990). He is currently writing one book on neofunctionalism and another on postpositivism.

STEPHAN FUCHS received his M.A. in History from Bremen University, Germany, in 1984 and his Ph.D. in Sociology from the University of California, Riverside in 1989. He is currently Assistant Professor of Sociology at the University of Virginia. His areas of interest are social theory, formal organizations, and sociology of science. Recent publications include: *The Professional Quest for Truth: A Social Theory of Science and Knowledge* (1992), "On the Microfoundations of Macrosociology," *Sociological Perspectives* (1989), and "Prejudice as Lifeform," *Sociological Inquiry* (1989) (with Charles Case). He is currently working on a book on contemporary social theory.

DOUGLAS KELLNER is Professor of Philosophy at The University of Texas at Austin and is the author of many books on social theory, politics, history, and culture, including *Camera Politica: The Politics and Ideology of Contemporary Hollywood Film*, coauthored with Michael Ryan; *Critical Theory, Marxism, and Modernity; Jean Baudrillard: From Marxism to Postmodernism and Beyond; Television and the Crisis of Democracy*, and (with Steven Best) *Postmodern Theory*. Forthcoming books include (with Robert J. Antonio) *Theorizing Modernity*, and *The Persian Gulf TV War*.

CHARLES LEMERT is Professor of Sociology at Wesleyan University. He has written on various aspects of social theory and is author or editor of *French Sociology, Michel Foucault*, and *Intellectuals and Politics*.

GEORGE RITZER is Professor of Sociology at the University of Maryland. He has served as Chair of the American Sociological Association's sections on Theoretical Sociology (1989-1990) and Organizations and Occupations (1980-1981). He has been Distinguished Scholar-Teacher at the University of Maryland and has been awarded a teaching Excellence Award. Professor Ritzer has held a Fulbright-Hays Fellowship and has been Scholar-in-Residence at the Collegium for Advanced Study in the Social Sciences. His main theoretical interests lie in metatheory as well as in the theory of rationalization. In metatheory, his most recent book is *Metatheorizing in Sociology*

(1991). Earlier books on this topic include *Sociology: A Multiple Paradigm Science* (1975) and *Toward an Integrated Sociological Paradigm* (1981). He has written numerous essays on rationalization as well as the soon-to-be published *The McDonaldization of Society* (Pine Forge Press, forthcoming).

EDWARD A. TIRYAKIAN is Professor of Sociology at Duke University, where he has taught since 1965. He received his B.A. from Princeton and Ph.D. from Harvard, and he taught at both before going to Duke. He has conducted field research in the Philippines, sub-Sahara Africa, Quebec, and Western Europe. He has written extensively in the areas of sociological theory, history of sociological thought, the sociology of religion, the sociology of sociology and the sociology of modernity. He is currently President of the International Association of French-Speaking Sociologists (AISLF) and was twice elected Chair of the American Sociological Association Theory Section. At Duke, he has served as Chairman of the Department of Sociology and Anthropology and Director of International Studies. He has published numerous articles in leading journals of sociology in the United States and abroad and contributed various chapters in books. Among the books he has published or edited are *Sociologism and Existentialism; The Prestige Evaluation of Occupations in a Developing Country: The Philippines; Sociological Theory; Values and Sociocultural Change; The Phenomenon of Sociology; On the Margin of the Visible; The Global Crisis: Sociological Analysis and Responses; Theoretical Sociology: Perspectives and Developments* (with J.C. McKinney); and *New Nationalisms of the Developed West* (with R. Rogowski).

DAVID G. WAGNER (Ph.D., Stanford University) is Associate Professor of Sociology at the State University of New York at Albany. His primary research interests include issues of cumulative knowledge growth in sociology, reward expectations and distributive justice, and the social control of status deviance. In addition to journal articles, his publications include *The Growth of Sociological Theories* and *Postmodernism and Social Theory* (edited with Steven Seidman). He is currently working on another book, *Strategies, Theories, and Programs*, concerned with questions of theory generation (from what sources sociological ideas come) and theory analysis (how we determine the worth of sociological ideas), as well as those of theory growth (how we improve sociological ideas).

WALTER L. WALLACE is Professor of Sociology, Princeton University. In addition to numerous journal articles and book chapters, Wallace is author of *Student Culture* (1966), *The Logic of Science in Sociology* (1971), *Principles of Scientific Sociology* (1983), "Toward a Disciplinary Matrix in Sociology" (in Neil J. Smelser, editor, *Handbook of Sociology*, 1988), author-editor of *Sociological Theory: An Introduction*, (1969), coauthor of *Black Elected Officials* (1976), and author of *A Positivistic Weberian Theory of Society* (forthcoming).

DEENA WEINSTEIN is Professor of Sociology at DePaul University. She coauthored the introduction to Simmel's *Schopenhauer and Nietzsche* and is currently working on *Postmodern(ized) Simmel*. Her other publications include *Bureaucratic Opposition: Challenging Abuses in the Workplace*, "Television as Religion," and *Heavy Metal: A Cultural Sociology*.

MICHAEL A. WEINSTEIN is Professor of Political Science at Purdue University. Among his published works are *Finite Perfection: Reflections on Virtue*, *The Polarity of Mexican Thought*, *Culture Critique: Fernand Dumont and the New Quebec Sociology*, and *The Wilderness and the City: American Classical Philosophy as a Moral Quest*.

MORRIS ZELDITCH, JR. (Ph.D., Harvard University) is Professor of Sociology at Stanford University and Chairman of the Department of Sociology at Stanford from 1964 to 1968 and 1989 to the present. He was editor of the *American Sociological Review* from 1975 to 1978. He has coauthored and coedited many publications, including *Status, Rewards, and Influence: How Expectations Organize Behavior; Status Characteristics and Expectation States*; and *Types of Formalization in Small Groups Research*. He is currently writing a book with Henry A. Walker on the politics of redistributive agendas.